CLIL
Content and
Language Integrated Learning

To b

CLIL
Content and
Language Integrated Learning

Do Coyle
Philip Hood
David Marsh

CAMBRIDGE UNIVERSITY PRESS
Cambridge, New York, Melbourne, Madrid, Cape Town, Singapore,
São Paulo, Delhi, Dubai, Tokyo, Mexico City

Cambridge University Press
The Edinburgh Building, Cambridge CB2 8RU, UK

www.cambridge.org
Information on this title: www.cambridge.org/9780521130219

First published 2010
Reprinted 2010

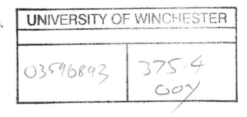

Printed in the United Kingdom at the University Press, Cambridge

A catalogue record for this publication is available from the British Library

Library of Congress Cataloguing in Publication data
Coyle, Do, 1952–
CLIL : content and language integrated learning / Do Coyle, Philip Hood, David Marsh
    p. cm.
ISBN 978-0-521-11298-7 (hardback) — ISBN 978-0-521-13021-9 (pbk.)
1. Language and languages—Study and teaching—Europe 2. Language arts—
Correlation with content subjects—Europe 3. Education, Bilingual—Europe.   I.
Hood, Philip, 1951– II. Marsh, David, 1956– III. Title. IV. Title: Content and
language integrated learning.

P57.E9C69   2010
418.0071904—dc22   2009048607

ISBN 978-0-521-11298-7 Hardback
ISBN 978-0-521-13021-9 paperback

Contents

Acknowledgements

The authors have been working in education for many years. Over this time, our paths have often crossed, and we have found ourselves working together in very different situations. In these situations we have encountered many people from different walks of life, from professionals in education through to children, young people and older learners in classrooms. Early on we came to realize that 'meetings of minds' brings about a very special form of synergy which is not only personally rewarding but also professionally enriching. The fact that this has involved people from across the globe living and working in different cultural contexts has also enabled us to work and embrace diversity as a source of creativity and innovation. This publication includes the voices of many of these people, because it is based on our long experience of collaboration and connection. 'Without bridges we would all be islands', and we are grateful for the opportunity to work with those many outstanding professionals who have helped us on our own learning curves in understanding the implications of this educational approach. There are far too many people to thank personally, so we wish to express our gratitude to all those that we have encountered for insight, advice, feedback and friendship.

There is now a professional community of CLIL practitioners, researchers and others which is growing in size and scope across the world. We wish to thank many of those people who have developed CLIL at the interface of practice in schools and classrooms, and through the reporting of research and forming of an evidence base for CLIL. The sharing of ideas and insights has been instrumental in forging this community and we are deeply grateful to be a part of the networks within it.

There are some field-based experts who have been particularly important in the development of our understanding of the potential and applications of CLIL. Many of the ideas incorporated in these pages have been discussed, applied and otherwise adapted as a direct result of close interaction, and we appreciate you all as individuals for influencing our thinking. In particular, we would like to thank teachers and trainers from Catalonia who have provided many examples in the book, and the trainee teachers 'BILDers', who were among the pioneer newly qualified CLIL teachers in Europe to be trained. For many years, CLIL has been an emergent process and because of our close and frequent professional contacts there is inevitably a natural interweaving of ideas, and we express our warmest thanks to all those who have contributed directly or indirectly to this publication.

Our sincerest thanks to the team at Cambridge University Press, who have given considerable support throughout the process, and often shown great patience, especially Anna Linthe, Alyson Maskell and Jane Walsh.

Finally, we would like to acknowledge the support of our families, who have so often been neglected whilst we have been working in different countries and juggling the complexities of our own working lives.

The authors and publishers acknowledge the following sources of copyright material and are grateful for the permissions granted. While every effort has been made, it has not always been possible to identify the sources of all the material used, or to trace all copyright holders. If any omissions are brought to our notice, we will be happy to include the appropriate acknowledgements on reprinting.

p31 the table from *A Taxonomy for Learning, Teaching, and Assessing: A Revision of Bloom's Taxonomy of Educational Objectives* by Lorin W. Anderson and David R. Krathwohl (eds), Longman, 2001; Text on p34 reproduced by permission of Bernard Mohan taken from *Language and Content: Second Language Professional Library*; Text on pp80–83 reproduced with permission by Florià Belinchón Majoral; Text on p91 taken from 'The art of playing a pinball machine: Characteristics of effective SLA-tasks', by Gerard Westhoff, published by *Babylonia*. Reproduced with permission; Text on p99 taken from *Teaching Mathematics and Science to English Language Learners* by Denise Jarrett, published by Northwest Regional Educational Laboratory; Text on pp102–3, 108–9, 122, 125, 127–8 and 130 was developed within the framework of the paid-study-leaves programme of the Department of Education of Catalonia; Text on p113 reproduced from 'Monitoring language skills in Austrian primary (elementary) schools: A case study', by Renate Zangl, published by *Language Testing*, Sage, 2000.

Preface

This book is intended for readers who not only want to widen their understanding of Content and Language Integrated Learning (CLIL), but also wish to engage with pedagogic issues, including strategies and techniques for introducing and developing the approach in classrooms and other learning environments. Subject and language teachers across sectors and age groups, teacher trainers, administrators and researchers will all find information on CLIL which supports both awareness raising and building on practice as well as providing access to very specific forms of knowledge and insight.

As authors, we have been involved with CLIL since its emergence as a concept in the early 1990s. From then on, each of us has been involved with different aspects of CLIL practice, including teaching, teacher training, transnational research, programme review, development of pedagogies and materials. After some 20 years of being at the cutting edge of this innovation in education, we have come together to produce *CLIL: Content and Language Integrated Learning*, the first publication which investigates the theories and practices of CLIL pedagogies in an in-depth way, whilst raising 'big' questions – and at times awkward and difficult ones – for key stakeholders.

Our aim has been to show *why* CLIL continues to establish itself as excellent educational practice, and *how* it can be introduced and developed across very different types of schools and classrooms. Innovation is often messy, because it involves complex processes. If a single blueprint for CLIL were feasible, then plenty of step-by-step guides would have been available years ago. However, the complexities of CLIL, and particularly the importance of the context in which it is situated, demand an understanding of the *why* and *how*. We know that CLIL must take account of local and regional needs as well as national and transnational exigencies which evolve from more generalizable rigorous principles. There has been a steep learning curve for those involved, including ourselves. However, we are now at a stage where it is possible to step back, look at the CLIL approaches which have taken root and flourished, and describe these for those readers who want to see the bigger picture and become part of it.

Innovation means changing the *status quo*. The chapters in this book confront the concerns and downsides which teachers and other decision makers and practitioners face when trying to bring about change in the curriculum. CLIL is not simply another step in language teaching, or a new development in content-subject methodology. We see CLIL as a fusion of subject didactics, leading to an innovation which has emerged as education for modern times. Yet, for CLIL to lead to high-quality learning, a sometimes major rethink of how we teach what we teach is often needed. This book offers a realistic picture of what is involved, along with proven tools for achieving success.

The book can be divided into three broad sections: the background to CLIL, classroom practice, and ways of sustaining and critically evaluating CLIL. In the first section, **Chapters 1** and **2** provide background to the CLIL 'movement' and explore different curricular models and variations of CLIL involving primary, secondary, tertiary and vocational contexts. Readers are provided with an overview of how CLIL currently operates across different sectors, in order to set the scene for the remainder of the book.

The next and largest section focuses on classroom practice. The chapters provide theories, principles, ideas, practical suggestions and arguments to inspire readers to reflect, debate and discuss their own practice and that of others and to continue pedagogic dialogue – as we say throughout the book, there are no 'easy' answers, but there are plenty of avenues to explore. **Chapter 3** lays the theoretical foundation for classroom pedagogies and introduces accessible perspectives on the planning and implementation of CLIL. **Chapter 4** provides practical examples for translating this theory into practice through the CLIL Teacher's Tool Kit. The Tool Kit grew out of work with groups of practitioners in the 1990s and has been evolving ever since, making it a tried and tested teacher resource for use at every stage of a school's CLIL development. Further materials are given in the appendix to this chapter. **Chapter 5** addresses the problem of the lack of available teaching materials by exploring principles for specific materials design and adaptation of existing resources. The complex issue of assessment is addressed in **Chapter 6**, in which arguments for a range of assessment approaches are illustrated with classroom examples, based on ideas and practice from teachers.

The final section returns to a broader view of CLIL which focuses on its sustainability and future development. **Chapter 7** suggests ways of reflecting on CLIL programmes and evaluating their impact systematically – a crucial stage in sustaining CLIL and ensuring high-quality experiences for learners. Finally, **Chapter 8** looks to the future in terms of social, cultural and economic developments, and positions CLIL as having the potential to play a major role within educational systems across the globe.

1 A window on CLIL

1.1 What is CLIL?

Content and Language Integrated Learning (CLIL) is a dual-focused educational approach in which an **additional language** is used for the learning and teaching of both content *and* language. That is, in the teaching and learning process, there is a focus not only on content, and not only on language. Each is interwoven, even if the emphasis is greater on one or the other at a given time. CLIL is not a new form of language education. It is not a new form of subject education. It is an innovative fusion of both. CLIL is closely related to and shares some elements of a range of educational practices. Some of these practices – such as bilingual education and immersion – have been in operation for decades in specific countries and contexts; others, such as content-based language teaching or English as an Additional Language (EAL), may share some basic theories and practice but are not synonymous with CLIL since there are some fundamental differences. CLIL is content-driven, and this is where it both extends the experience of learning a language, and where it becomes different to existing language-teaching approaches. Throughout this book, we will clarify the evolving CLIL phenomenon by exploring core principles which permeate different applications. Whilst CLIL is flexible and can be adapted to different contexts, nonetheless, for the approach to be justifiable and sustainable, its theoretical basis must be rigorous and transparent in practice. The term CLIL is inclusive in that it binds together the essence of good practice found in the different environments where its principles have been adopted. It involves a range of models which can be applied in a variety of ways with diverse types of learner. Good CLIL practice is realized through methods which provide a more holistic educational experience for the learner than may otherwise be commonly achievable.

> An **additional language** is often a learner's 'foreign language', but it may also be a second language or some form of heritage or community language. Throughout the book we will use an inclusive term 'CLIL vehicular language' to refer to the language(s) used in CLIL settings.

The operational success of CLIL has been in transferability, not only across countries and continents, but also across types of school. The educational success of CLIL is in the content- and language-learning outcomes realized in classrooms. CLIL provides pathways to learning which complement insights now emerging from interdisciplinary research within the neurosciences and education (see, for example, CERI, 2007). Because of its potential, CLIL is gaining momentum and extending as an educational approach across continents (see, for example, Eurydice, 2006, or Graddol, 2006). It is also one of the reasons why this book has been written for a broad readership including subject and language specialists, and those responsible for educational planning and implementation.

1.2   The development of CLIL

Links with the past and demands of the present

Education in a language which is not the first language of the learner is as old as education itself. As individuals from different language groups have lived together, some have been educated in an additional language. This is as true of Ancient Rome as it is of the increasingly multilingual societies being created through mobility and globalization in the 21st century.

Two thousand years ago, provision of an educational curriculum in an additional language happened as the Roman Empire expanded and absorbed Greek territory, language and culture. Families in Rome educated their children in Greek to ensure that they would have access to not only the language, but also the social and professional opportunities it would provide for them in their future lives, including living in Greek-speaking educational communities. This historical experience has been replicated across the world through the centuries, and is now particularly true of the global uptake of English language learning. What is significant here is the way in which language learning, particularly when integrated with content learning or knowledge construction, has now been opened up for a broad range of learners, not only those from privileged or otherwise elite backgrounds. In the distant past, learning content through an additional language was either limited to very specific social groups, or forced upon school populations for whom the language of instruction was a foreign language.

The recent growing interest in CLIL can be understood by examining best practice in education which suits the demands of the present day. Globalization and the forces of economic and social convergence have had a significant impact on who learns which language, at what stage in their development, and in which way. The driving forces for language learning differ according to country and region, but they share the objective of wanting to achieve the best possible results in the shortest time. This need has often dovetailed with the need to adapt content-teaching methodologies so as to raise overall levels of proficiency, particularly since the introduction of global comparative measures ranking individual countries through the Programme for International Student Assessment (PISA) of the Organisation for Economic Cooperation and Development (OECD).

This need to be more adaptable and effective has led to attention being given back to cognitive processing and how learning successfully occurs. Discussion started in earnest in the 1950s with the advent of what was termed the 'cognitive revolution' (Broadbent,

1958). Although this was largely a response to behaviourism, focus on cognition and communication became ever more significant as technologies required insight into the development of artificial intelligence. Currently, there is increasing recognition that the exploration of learning by cognitive neurosciences provides alternative insights by which to improve overall efficiency.

Correspondingly, landmark work by Bruner (b. 1915), Piaget (1896–1980), and Vygotsky (1896–1934) led to the development of socio-cultural, constructivist perspectives on learning. These perspectives have had an immense impact on educational theory and practice. Related areas such as multiple intelligences (Gardner, 1983), integration (Ackerman, 1996), learner autonomy (Holec, 1981; Gredler, 1997; Wertsch, 1997; Kukla, 2000), language awareness (Hawkins, 1984) and language-learning strategies (Oxford, 1990) all played a key role in examining ways to raise levels of curricular relevance, motivation and involvement of learners in their education. Moreover, the balance between the individual and the social learning environment has led to alternative means by which to teach and learn both content subjects and languages. Since CLIL straddles these two different but complementary aspects of learning, parallels between general learning theories and second language acquisition (SLA) theories have to be harmonized in practice if both content learning and language learning are to be successfully achieved. In addition, over the last few years, education has been reaching new thresholds as a result of the ability not only to study behaviour and performance, but also to see inside the 'learning brain' (CERI, 2007). As these different elements of learning come together, a new wave of knowledge is consolidating the position of CLIL as an educational approach in its own right (see, for example, Doidge, 2007; Tokuhama-Espinosa, 2008; Marsh, 2009).

Defining Content and Language Integrated Learning

The term 'Content and Language Integrated Learning' (CLIL) was adopted in 1994 (Marsh, Maljers and Hartiala, 2001) within the European context to describe and further design good practice as achieved in different types of school environment where teaching and learning take place in an additional language. Schools in very different contexts across the world had been finding their own ways to enrich learning, sometimes for many years. CLIL set out to capture and articulate that not only was there a high degree of similarity in educational methodologies, but also an equally high degree of educational success. Identifying this success was one major driver within the education professions; mainstreaming the experience for a wider general public was the other.

CLIL is an educational approach in which various language-supportive methodologies are used which lead to a dual-focused form of instruction where attention is given both to the language and the content:

> . . . [A]chieving this twofold aim calls for the development of a special approach to teaching in that the non-language subject is not taught *in* a foreign language but *with* and *through* a foreign language.

(Eurydice, 2006: 8)

This opens up doors on an educational experience which can be very hard to achieve in a language-learning classroom. There are various reasons for this which are explored in Chapter 3. CLIL is an approach which is neither language learning nor subject learning, but an amalgam of both and is linked to the processes of convergence. Convergence involves the fusion of elements which may have been previously fragmented, such as subjects in the curriculum. This is where CLIL breaks new ground.

CLIL as a form of convergence

To give a parallel example common in recent times, we can take studies on the environment. In the 1960s, Richard Buckminster Fuller (1895–1983) warned of climate change in the publication *Operating Manual for Spaceship Earth* (1963), and through his work on what was then called 'synergetics'. As a visionary and author, his articulated rationale and concerns only entered the public consciousness very much later.

Some 50 years on, world opinion on climate change remained divided, often because of socio-economic reasons. However, in some countries, recognition that human activity was leading to a degradation of the environment led to a need to educate young people in schools so as to both inform and, perhaps more crucially, influence behaviour. Topics relating to the environment could already be found in chemistry, economics, geography, physics, and even psychology. Yet, as climate change became increasingly worrying, education responded to the need to influence change.

This happened during the 1980s and 1990s through the introduction of a new subject, or set of modules, which focused on the environment. 'Environmental studies' is an example of a newly emerged 'integrated' subject which can be found in schools throughout the world. In order to structure this new subject, teachers of different disciplines would have needed to climb out of their respective mindsets grounded in physics, chemistry, geography, psychology and so on, to explore ways of building an integrated curriculum, and to develop alternative methodologies by which to implement it.

Such a process involves developing professional interconnectedness so as to activate forms of innovation. Pooling skills and knowledge to change existing practice can lead to alternative approaches. Climate change is a global and local phenomenon, so the increasing availability in some countries of information and communication technologies during the 1990s provided tools by which to make some of these methodologies operational.

If we return to languages and CLIL, we have a similar situation. The late 1990s meant that educational insight was firmly set on achieving a high degree of language awareness. Appropriate methodologies were to be used to attain the best possible results in a way which accommodated diverse learning styles. The impact of globalization, like climate change, was being increasingly felt in some parts of the world, especially in Europe during the period of rapid integration from 1990 to 2007. This impact highlighted the need for better language and communication educational outcomes.

In order to respond, it was necessary to examine how more appropriate language teaching and learning could be achieved, and which approach might be most suitable for respective age groups. For instance, the view that the hours allocated for language teaching within the curriculum were often insufficient to produce satisfactory outcomes was one issue under frequent discussion. Interest in looking at how some language teaching could be done whilst students were learning other subjects, thus providing more exposure to the language overall, was then considered. But this was only one of the issues. Others concerned the need for better linguistic and communicative competence, more relevant methodologies, and higher levels of authenticity to increase learner motivation. This attention given to the need for improved learning results was also found in other subject areas within the curriculum.

CLIL in the Knowledge Age

As with Fuller's vision and the development of environmental sciences, CLIL developed as an innovative form of education in response to the demands and expectations of the modern age. Input from different academic fields has contributed to the recognition of this approach to educational practice. In an age characterized by 'quick fix' solutions, however, which may or may not lead to any form of sustainable outcomes, it is important to contextualise CLIL historically. CLIL is not merely a convenient response to the challenges posed by rapid globalization; rather, it is a solution which is timely, which is in harmony with broader social perspectives, and which has proved effective.

Fragmentation was very much a characteristic of the Industrial Age. Power blocks such as countries, societies and even educational systems operated according to territory, borders and boundaries. The Industrial Age was marked by strategies of position and physically based resources. But globalization and the emergence of the new technologies have moved us into a new era, the Knowledge Age. This has resulted in sweeping changes in how societies, and the educational systems that serve them, operate. In the Knowledge Age, the two main strategies are of movement and unlimited resources, because of the significance of ideas, creativity and intelligence. It is hardly surprising that such a seismic change in global culture pressurizes change within educational systems. Integration, convergence and participative learning are three key characteristics of Knowledge Age organizations which are influencing decisions on what, and how, we teach young people.

The key performance drivers of the Knowledge Age society are commonly cited as the 'Knowledge Triangle' (EURAB, 2007). This triangle integrates education, research and innovation, which are the core features for managing successful change and adaptation. These are also core issues influencing how we can reshape the ways in which we teach languages. When Graddol (2006: 86) describes CLIL as the 'ultimate communicative methodology', he points to one of the major differences between the communicative language teaching movement in the 1980s and the emergence of CLIL in the 1990s. Communicative language teaching was one step towards providing a more holistic way of teaching and learning languages, but for various reasons, especially relating to authenticity, has been insufficient in realizing the high level of authenticity of purpose which can be achieved through CLIL. Much CLIL classroom practice involves the learners being active participants in developing their potential for acquiring knowledge and skills (education) through a process of inquiry (research) and by using complex cognitive processes and means for problem solving (innovation). When the teacher pulls back from being the donor of knowledge and becomes the facilitator, as is often found in CLIL practice, forces are unleashed which empower learners to acquire knowledge whilst actively engaging their own and peer-group powers of perception, communication and reasoning.

As CLIL practice often preceded research (although some fundamentally important research was available through the 1980s and 1990s, drawing on the experience of Canadian immersion) it was some time before scientific validation of the approach could be made. But as research results became available (see Chapter 7), those involved with forms of CLIL increasingly came to the view that variants of this approach could be seen as providing education which goes beyond language learning. So, whereas in one situation the language may be the dominant focus, in another it may be the content, but in each there is a fusion resulting from the methodologies which can lead to positive educational outcomes. What separates CLIL from some established approaches such as content-based language learning, or forms of bilingual education, is the planned pedagogic integration of contextualized content, cognition, communication and culture into teaching and learning practice (Coyle, 2002: 45). This is explored in detail in Chapters 3 and 4.

1.3   **What are the driving forces behind CLIL?**

There are two major reasons which underpin the interest in CLIL within a specific country or region. These involve reactive (responding to situations) and proactive (creating situations) responses to challenges or problems.

Reactive reasons

There are countries in the world where the language of instruction is foreign to the majority of the learners in schools and colleges. An official language may be adopted as the medium of instruction for some part of schooling, often at secondary level, which acts as a language of national unity.

This is typical in some countries in sub-Saharan Africa. For example, Mozambique, which has some 20 distinct first languages, has adopted Portuguese, as has Angola. Tanzania and Ethiopia, likewise having a mosaic of languages amongst their populations, have adopted English. In the past, both South Africa and Namibia adopted Afrikaans, before widely switching to English. Even though there are some 2,000 languages in Africa, three languages are commonplace as medium of instruction: English, French and Portuguese.

In Mozambique, about six per cent of citizens view Portuguese as their first language, and it is estimated that some 27 per cent can speak or otherwise understand the language (Benson, 2002). Figures like these invite the question of how children and young people manage in their school years when the language of instruction may be far removed from their life experience. An educational language policy, as found in Mozambique, may be one reason why school wastage is sometimes huge. In South Africa alone it is estimated that some 75 per cent of children fail school (Heugh, 2000), and part of the reason for this is widely attributed to language issues and not adapting classroom methodologies to the demands of learning through an additional language.

Considering that human competence-building is critical for the social and economic development of any country, such figures make alarming reading. In terms of language policy, the issue is whether the medium of instruction is instrumental in weakening educational development. Language policy needs to be implemented with language pragmatism and CLIL emerges as one solution for achieving this in different countries.

Language problems are by no means exclusive to some continents. The sub-Saharan cases here are extreme examples, but there are many challenges found elsewhere in relation to nurturing minority or threatened languages, or accommodating the needs of migrant children who have low fluency in the major language of instruction. Recent changes in European classroom demographics resulting from migration is one example.

If a country is to convert a language problem into language potential then solutions have to be identified which are workable in the classroom. Regardless of policy decisions, it is the social microcosm of the classroom, and learning practice, which reflect the successes or failures of the community as a whole.

CLIL plays a role in providing a pragmatic response towards overcoming linguistic shortcomings, and in promoting equal access to education for all school-aged students, including those with additional support needs. In the reactive scenario, the problem of medium of instruction is recognised, and followed by methodological and curricula adjustment. Methodologies, sometimes called language-supportive, or language-sensitive, can be introduced for the teaching of subjects across the curriculum. This means that all teachers need to take responsibility for language development through a dual focus when teaching other subjects. The type of approach may differ, but any language burden on children or students can be alleviated if CLIL methodologies are embedded in teaching and learning.

Proactive reasons

Proactively identifying solutions by which to enhance language learning, or some other aspect of educational, social or personal development, is the other major reason why attention is given to forms of CLIL.

For example, French immersion in Canada was developed to strengthen bilingualism in the country. Accounts differ as to why it became so popular so quickly, but it is reasonable to assume that this was due to a simultaneous grassroots and top-down pressure. At the grassroots, there was frustration at the failure of traditional French language teaching, which led parents to support the 1965 introduction of immersion in a school (St Lambert) in Quebec.

However, at a higher socio-political level, Canadian society was experiencing pressure for change. In July 1967, Charles de Gaulle made his infamous statement 'Vive le Québec libre', which resulted in heated political debate throughout the country. This was followed, in 1968, by the appointment of Pierre Trudeau as Prime Minister. He sought to preserve national unity, especially between French and English speakers. This led to the Official Languages Act which resulted in Canada having two official languages and the right for anyone to use either of these languages anywhere in the country. One single overarching reason that immersion received so much support and attention was a proactive need to strengthen national unity. Thus immersion in schools served as a pragmatic response to a linguistic and cultural problem. By 2006, the number of young people undertaking immersion education in Canada was in excess of 300,000.

Another example is Europe, where discussion on economic unity during the 1950s included focus on language policies, and the need for greater levels of multilingualism. In 1958, a European Economic Community regulation (EEC, 1958) determined which languages would be official within the newly forming union of separate countries. From this point it was clear that the new Europe would be a plurilingual entity, and that educational systems would need to make greater efforts to provide language education for more young people. In 1976, the European Education Council (EC, 1976) listed language-learning objectives and argued for the promotion of language teaching outside the traditional school systems. Then, in 1978, the European Commission made a proposal to the member states (EC, 1978) that encouraged teaching in schools through the medium of more than one language. This was a landmark point which acted as a catalyst for the development of CLIL across the continent.

In 1984, the European Parliament questioned weaknesses in languages education, and this was followed in the same year by the Education Council, which accepted that there was a need to give greater impetus to the teaching and learning of foreign languages (EP, 1984). From that year on, there were a range of declarations and statements made about the need to explore alternative paths in languages education. In addition, as with Canadian immersion, finance was invested in projects which led to the development of practical educational solutions such as CLIL. From 1990 onwards, CLIL became increasingly prioritised within the European Union as a major educational initiative (Eurydice, 2006), culminating in the 2005 European Council recommendations that CLIL should be adopted throughout the entire European Union (EC, 2005).

In 2006, the first statistical study on where and how CLIL was being implemented in Europe was published (Eurydice, 2006). It was now clear that, since the launch of the term in 1994, there had been exponential uptake of CLIL across countries. This was due to four simultaneous major proactive forces: families wanting their children to have some competence in at least one foreign language; governments wanting to improve languages education for socio-economic advantage; at the supranational level, the European Commission wanting to lay the foundation for greater inclusion and economic strength; and finally, at the educational level, language experts seeing the potential of further integrating languages education with that of other subjects.

Looking beyond Europe, changes in the world economy mean that several large countries (Brazil, Russia, India and China) have encountered rapid growth as their economies have become interconnected with others around the world. This is one aspect of globalization which results in a reconfiguration of territory so that enterprises become increasingly networked and dependent on others which may be physically distant. These major countries and their increasingly borderless economic global dependency means that communication and the ability to use a lingua franca is becoming a prerequisite for individual success. There are also other countries such as Malaysia, Singapore and Thailand, which are in the outer economic circles of substantial change, but which also wish to attract various forms of work which is outsourced and which often requires an English-language-proficient workforce.

Whilst it must be stressed that CLIL is not synonymous with English language learning and teaching, the potentially huge global demand for learning English means that it is a popular vehicular language in non-Anglophone areas. Projections are that some one-third of the world's population will be actively learning the language by 2010 (Graddol, 2006: 101). This correspondingly means considerable interest in 'learning content subjects through English' being shown in those countries where it is a vehicular language. It is likely, but not yet sufficiently documented, that such countries will explore which methodologies best suit education where children learn through English as a foreign or second language. Thus CLIL may be increasingly adopted as a proactive means by which to maximize the potential for success. However, whilst for many countries English is the targeted medium, there are other countries, including Anglophone countries, where the vehicular language is not English. Obvious examples include the Canadian immersion movement in French, Basque trilingual programmes involving a heritage language, and CLIL in the UK, where French, German and Spanish are promoted.

1.4 Why is CLIL relevant to contemporary education?

The forces of global change, converging technologies and adaptability to the subsequent Knowledge Age present challenges for education. And within education as a whole, they present challenges for the teaching and learning of additional languages. This is true for the learning of English globally, and for the learning of regional, minority and heritage languages in different parts of the world. As we have previously pointed out, CLIL is not exclusive to the promotion of English as a world language but is embedded in the socio-economic, political and cultural traditions of different nations. For example, some parts of the world such as Australia promote LOTE (Languages Other Than English), where CLIL vehicular languages include Asian, European and heritage languages. In border areas such as between France and Germany, the CLIL language might focus on mutual sharing of both languages. However, we believe that CLIL as a promoter of LOTE has yet to reach its potential in the global arena and may not do so until after the 'saturation' of English as the CLIL medium. Pioneering work using a wide range of languages is gaining momentum and making a crucial contribution to developing CLIL pedagogies – especially in Anglophone countries (Chapter 7 presents one such example).

One change brought about by the new technologies and lifestyle change concerns the learners' mindset. Generation Y (1980–1995) and Generation C (also known as Generation Z, 1995–2015) have been and are being increasingly exposed to advanced technology at a very young age in the form of game consoles, mobile communication and entertainment devices, personal computers, the Internet and so on. Such technology may be harder for older generations to adapt to, they having been brought up with different thinking conventions; but young people growing up with this technology are prone to developing a mindset to which educators need to respond. This has been described as a desire to 'learn as you use, use as you learn' and differs from the older experience of 'learn now for use later'.

Much education is still locked into the second of these adages, which may well continue to be necessary in certain respects. But educational practice always needs to adapt to the cultural demands of those involved – learners, teachers and communities. Integration has become a key concept in the modern age, alongside immediacy of purpose. Both of these reflect the experience of increasing numbers of young people, and are accommodated within the CLIL educational approach.

Socio-economic change is happening now at a faster pace overall than may have been experienced in the past. Although some countries have undergone very rapid change because of forms of specific pressure, new technologies are also bringing about transformations throughout the world. This means that educational systems also need to adapt even more swiftly than they have done in the past. Some would argue that education tends to adapt slowly, and that, for instance, to change educational practice in the classroom can take some 15–20 years to achieve. If we put this into the context of technological and subsequent lifestyle change, we can see how this is too long a period in a world undergoing rapid transition. It took 40 years for the radio to reach an audience of 50 million, 20 years for the fax machine to reach some ten million customers, under ten years for the mobile phone, and some five years for the Internet. The acceleration of new technologies is having an impact on the lives and aspirations of many people now on an unprecedented scale. 'Globalisation is not incidental to our lives today. It is a shift in our very life circumstances' (Giddens, 1999), and this means that better access to language learning, and learning methods for accelerating performance, are now crucial in many communities.

1.5 **Why is CLIL relevant to the teaching profession?**

Putting aside the often-cited advantages which a CLIL approach offers – such as enabling learners to access subject-specific vehicular language terminology, or otherwise preparing them for future studies and/or working life – there is the issue of advancing a learner's cognitive development. The ability to think in different languages, even if to a modest extent, can have a positive impact on content learning (Marsh, 2009). The need to regenerate content teaching so that it closely fits the requirements of the modern age has been closely linked to the 'learning brain' (CERI, 2007). To achieve this, the content teacher will need to adapt subject-specific methods so as to accommodate the additional language focus. This does not mean adopting the role of a language teacher. What it does is to open doors on alternative ways of using methodologies which can be rewarding for both the teacher and learners.

From this perspective, CLIL not only promotes linguistic competence, it also serves to stimulate cognitive flexibility. Different thinking horizons and pathways which result from CLIL, and the effective constructivist educational practice it promotes, can also have an impact on conceptualization (literally, how we think), enriching the understanding of concepts, and broadening conceptual mapping resources. This enables better association of different concepts and helps the learner advance towards a more sophisticated level of learning in general.

Motivation is also an issue. If a learner participates voluntarily in learning through the medium of an additional language, it can enhance overall motivation towards the subject itself. There are many reasons why this might occur in a specific context, but it is clear that there are benefits, both cognitive and motivational, which can enhance content learning, and the position of the content teacher.

We have already highlighted the importance of authenticity and relevance as key to successful learning. It is challenging for language teachers to achieve appropriate levels of authenticity in the classroom. For example, even if 'authentic' texts are used, and the subject matter is highly relevant to the lives of the learners, the predominant reason for these texts being in the lesson remains language learning. And when this is measured by tests which assess the learner often according to grammatical correctness, then the real focus of the lesson will be language itself. If this type of learning takes place alongside forms of CLIL, then the learner is exposed to two complementary experiences, one of which involves primarily language learning, and the other, language acquisition. Issues such as these are explored further in Chapters 5 and 6.

There is now greater understanding of the differences between 'acquiring' and 'learning' languages. Interest in early language learning has been influenced by the view that children adapt well to learning languages if it is integrated into other types of learning and carried out in a 'naturalistic' environment. This is typical of much good practice at primary level. But in our education systems, older children and adults are often taught languages in language-learning classrooms through the use of a textbook (although digital technology is increasingly being used to supplement this). The amount of time dedicated to language learning is often constrained because of pressure from other subjects within a curriculum. Successful language learning can be achieved when people have the opportunity to receive instruction, and at the same time experience real-life situations in which they can acquire the language more naturalistically. Learning, for example, a topic from geography through the vehicular language, in a cognitively supported way, can help achieve a comparable sense of greater authenticity. The idea of successfully learning content in an additional language may appear counter-intuitive to parents and young people themselves, and greater understanding depends on recognizing the subtle overlap between language learning (intentional) and language acquisition (incidental).

The language classroom is essential for the learner to understand the 'nuts and bolts' of language – the grammar, vocabulary and so on. But there is rarely enough time in the classroom for the language teacher to go beyond this essential part of the learning process. Learners need time to build things with these 'nuts and bolts' – to put into practice the things which they see in theory on paper.

CLIL can offer learners of any age a natural situation for language development which builds on other forms of learning. This natural use of language can boost a learner's motivation towards, and hunger for, learning languages: 'It is this naturalness which appears to be one of the major platforms for CLIL's importance and success in relation to both language and other subject learning' (Marsh 2000: 5).

A new age has dawned in additional language teaching methodology which directly reflects wider changes in the world. In the corresponding sea-change in educational philosophy, CLIL presents an opportunity and a threat to accepted language teaching practice. As with immersion, formal language instruction remains integral to most CLIL models. But for this to be synchronous to subject teaching through an additional language, curricular and methodological adjustment is often required. The extra exposure to the language, methods used, and attitudes of learners towards the language, can enhance language teaching and learning for the benefit of all. This offers an opportunity for language teachers to regenerate their profession.

This chapter has explored the broader landscapes which have led to the development of CLIL. We have seen that there are many factors which led to its introduction, and also that, because it involves the integration of content and language, it is not solely a form of language learning. It is an educational approach which is content-driven, and this is a fundamental reason why it has emerged as an educational phenomenon which complements both content and language learning, and is within the domain of each. CLIL is not simply education *in* an additional language; it is education *through* an additional language based on connected pedagogies and using contextual methodologies which we will explore further throughout this book.

References

Ackerman, E. (1996) 'Perspective-taking and object construction: Two keys to learning', in Kafai, Y. and Resnick, M. (eds.) (1996) *Constructionism in Practice: Designing Thinking and Learning in a Digital World*, Mahwah, NJ: Lawrence Erlbaum Associates, pp25–32.

Benson, C. (2002) *PASE, Assessment in the Primary School in Mozambique: Looking Back, Looking Forward*, Maputo: INDE.

Broadbent, D. E. (1958) *Perception and Communication*, Oxford: Pergamon.

Buckminster Fuller, R. (1963) *Operating Manual for Spaceship Earth*, Santa Barbara: Buckminster Fuller Institute.

CERI (2007) *Understanding the Brain: The Birth of a Learning Science*, Paris: OECD.

Coyle, D. (2002) 'Against all odds: Lessons from Content and Language Integrated Learning in English secondary schools', in Daniel, W. C. and Jones, G. M. (eds.) (2002) *Education and Society in Plurilingual Contexts*, Brussels: Brussels University Press, pp37–55.

Doidge, N. (2007) *The Brain that Changes Itself*, London: Penguin.

EC (1976) *Education Council Resolution 9 February*, Brussels: EC.

EC (1978) *European Commission Proposal June*, Brussels: EC.

EC (2005) *European Council of the European Union, EDUC 69 Resolution*, Brussels: EC.

EEC (1958) *European Economic Community Regulation 1 June*, Brussels: EC.

EP (1984) *Resolution April*, Brussels: EP.

EURAB (2007) *Energising Europe's Knowledge Triangle of Research, Education and Innovation through the Structural Funds. EURAB 07.010*, Brussels: EC.

Eurydice (2006) *Content and Language Integrated Learning (CLIL) at School in Europe*, Brussels: Eurydice.

Gardner, H. (1983) *Frames of Mind: The Theory of Multiple Intelligences*, New York: Basic Books.

Giddens, A. (1999) *Globalisation. Reith Lecture 1*, London: BBC.

Graddol, D. (2006) *English Next*, London: British Council.

Gredler, M. E. (1997) *Learning and Instruction: Theory into Practice*, Upper Saddle River, NJ: Prentice Hall.

Hawkins, E. (1984) *Awareness of Language: An Introduction*, Cambridge: Cambridge University Press.

Heugh, K. (2000) *The Case against Bilingual Education and Multilingual Education in South Africa*, Cape Town: PRAESA.

Holec, H. (1981) *Autonomy and Foreign Language Learning*, Oxford: Pergamon.

Kukla, A. (2000) *Social Constructivism and the Philosophy of Science*, London: Routledge.

Marsh, D. (2000) 'An introduction to CLIL for parents and young people', in Marsh, D. and Langé, G. (eds.) (2000) *Using Languages to Learn and Learning to Use Languages*, Jyväskylä: University of Jyväskylä.

Marsh, D. (ed.) (2009) Report by the Core Scientific Research Team, *Study on the Contribution of Multilingualism to Creativity*, EACEA/2007/3995/2, Brussels: European Commission.

Marsh, D., Maljers, A. and Hartiala, A-K. (2001) *Profiling European CLIL Classrooms*, Jyväskylä: University of Jyväskylä.

Oxford, R. L. (1990) *Language Learning Strategies: What Every Teacher Should Know*, New York: Harper and Row / Newbury House.

PISA, OECD, [Online]. Available at: www.pisa.oecd.org [Accessed 18 March 2009].

Tokuhama-Espinosa, T. (2008) *Living Languages: Multilingualism Across the Lifespan*, Westport: Praeger.

Wertsch, J. V. (1997) *Sociocultural Studies of Mind*, Cambridge: Cambridge University Press.

2 Curricular variation in CLIL

In Chapter 1 we looked at why and how CLIL has emerged, and the diverse reasons why it is implemented. In Chapter 2 we examine a range of curricular models which have been developed in different contexts. These models have been used to achieve one or more of CLIL's main educational objectives embedded in and responding to contextual variables. We would wish to point out that, whilst there are lessons to be learned, ideas to be borrowed and developed based on existing CLIL models, one size does not fit all – there is no one model for CLIL. We have seen a range of types which depend largely on the reasons for wishing to introduce the approach and the capacity to implement CLIL which is available within an educational setting. These are now explored. It may be useful to start by summarizing two of the key issues which schools need to consider before developing any particular model: the operating factors – such as teacher availability and learner assessment – and the scale of the CLIL programme.

2.1 Operating factors

- **Teacher availability** is crucial because it is usually the starting point for designing a model. How the teachers work together – whether individually or through teamwork – influences both planning and implementation.
- The levels of teacher and student target **CLIL-language fluency** determine the teacher's input and role in the classroom.
- The amount of **time** available is fundamental in setting objectives. Issues such as when the CLIL teaching is to be scheduled within the curriculum, and over what period of time, influence the choice of a CLIL model.
- The ways in which **content and language** are integrated influence decision-making on how each is handled within the model. For example, this may be through language-learning preparation before the CLIL course, language learning embedded in the CLIL course, or language learning parallel to the CLIL course.
- Linking the CLIL course to an out-of-school or **extra-curricular** dimension, enabling **task-based communication** with learners in other schools/countries and **networking** with teachers/visitors from outside the school/country, all impact on the scale and scope of the model.

- Finally, there are issues relating to **assessment processes** – formative or summative, focused on content only, content and language, or language only – which influence model design (see Chapter 6 for a discussion of assessment in CLIL).

2.2 Scale

Extensive instruction through the vehicular language

In this model, the vehicular language is used almost exclusively to introduce, summarize and revise topics, with very limited switches into the first language to explain specific language aspects of the subject or vocabulary items. There is a clear triple focus on content, language and cognition. Content is taught using methods which support language learning and understanding to a greater or lesser extent in lessons. This supported – or scaffolded – approach is used to introduce new vocabulary and concepts, grammatical usage and so on, in conjunction with the content. This may be done by a single content teacher, through cooperation with a language teacher – especially where certain linguistic structures are pre-taught – or language may be taught parallel to the content learning in separate language classes. Content-relevant language may also be taught by a language teacher who takes responsibility for teaching the content area.

Extensive instruction in the vehicular language requires that the curriculum be purpose-designed with objectives that not only lead to high levels of content mastery but also linguistic proficiency. In some cases, 50 per cent or more of the curriculum may be taught in this way. The content taught through CLIL may be drawn from any set of subjects, depending on the school's individual context. Teachers work together so that generic study skills, and the language to successfully implement these, are given shared significance in the different lessons. For context-based reasons (for example, an international stream within the school which may include learners who have little proficiency in the school's first language) it may be the case that the CLIL language is used very extensively so as to create an even playing field for all students.

Partial instruction through the vehicular language

In models which involve partial instruction through the vehicular language, specific content, drawn from one or more subjects, is taught through CLIL according to limited implementation periods – possibly less than five per cent of the whole curriculum will be taught through CLIL. In this case a project-based modular approach is often used and the responsibility for teaching may rest with the content or language teachers, or both. As with models where the instruction through the CLIL language is extensive, there is again a clear triple focus on content, language and cognition.

Quite often partial instruction through the vehicular language is manifested in bilingual blended instruction involving code-switching between languages. Here the lessons involve systematic use of both the CLIL language and the first language. For example, sometimes one language might be used for outlining and summarizing the main points, and the other for the remaining lesson functions. Alternatively, the two different languages may be used for specific types of activity. This is a type of code-switching which has been termed **translanguaging** and which leads to a dynamic form of bilingualism in the classroom. The systematic switch between languages is based on a planned development of content, language and cognition – for example, some learners may use a textbook in the first language when doing homework in order to build confidence and check comprehension; other learners may ask for explanations from the teacher in a particular language; beginner CLIL learners may use their L1 to speak to the teacher when problem solving, but the CLIL teacher will answer questions and support learners in the vehicular language.

> **Translanguaging** refers to a systematic shift from one language to another for specific reasons.

One concern of some teachers has been whether learning through an additional language can result in learners not understanding key terms in the first language. Translanguaging may be used to overcome this concern; for example, by using first-language materials (vocabulary and concept checklists and so on) to support teaching in the CLIL vehicular language.

2.3 Examples of curricular models

We now go on to examine models of CLIL at pre-school level and in primary, secondary and tertiary education, including examples of models at the school-level stages. These models have developed from a variety of contextual variables which are summarized in Table 1 under the headings of *Context, Content, Language* (communication), *Learning* (cognition) and *Culture.*

Pre-school 3–6 years

The most typical models found with pre-school children often involve games and other play-based activities – a ludic approach, where the vehicular language is used to a greater or lesser extent. These models are often called 'immersion' and involve introducing sounds, words and structures where the main focus is on stimulating, fun activities.

It is often hard to distinguish CLIL from standard forms of good practice in early language learning. This is because the learning topic is often highly authentic for the children. Whilst they are aware that they are learning to listen to and use sounds and words from another language, their main focus is on the doing – be it playing, singing, drawing, building models, or other activities. Often realised as forms of 'language clubs', pre-school CLIL is generally found in the private sector (as is much pre-school provision globally)

Table 1: Common reasons for introducing CLIL

Context	• Preparing for globalization, e.g. developing the whole school curriculum through the medium of other languages. • Accessing international certification, e.g. outside a national examination system such as International Baccalaureate. • Enhancing school profiles, e.g. offering CLIL gives strong messages about plurilingual education.
Content	• Multiple perspectives for study, e.g. modules in history where authentic texts are used in different languages. • Preparing for future studies, e.g. modules which focus on ICT which incorporate international lexis. • Skills for working life, e.g. courses which deal with academic study skills equipping learners for further study. • Accessing subject-specific knowledge in another language.
Language	• Improving overall target-language competence, e.g. through extended quality exposure to the CLIL language. • Developing oral communication skills, e.g. through offering a wider range of authentic communication routes. • Deepening awareness of both first language and CLIL language, e.g. those schools which offer 50% of the curriculum in other languages in order to develop a deeper knowledge and linguistic base for their learners. • Developing self-confidence as a language learner and communicator, e.g. practical and authentic language scenarios such as vocational settings. • Introducing the learning and using of another language, e.g. lessons which are activity-oriented are combined with language-learning goals, such as in play-oriented 'language showers' for younger learners.
Learning	• Increasing learner motivation, e.g. CLIL vocational courses which explicitly target confidence-building through the use of the CLIL language where learners feel they have failed in traditional language-learning classes. • Diversifying methods and approaches to classroom practice, e.g. courses integrating learners who are hearing impaired, where the sign language is the CLIL language. • Developing individual learning strategies, e.g. upper-secondary courses in science which attract learners who are confident in the CLIL language, but much less confident in science, who might not otherwise have opted for further study in the first language.
Culture	• Building intercultural knowledge, understanding and tolerance, e.g. module of psychology on causes of ethnic prejudice. • Developing intercultural communication skills, e.g. student collaboration on joint projects across nations. • Learning about specific neighbouring countries/regions and/or minority groups, e.g. 'school hopping', which engages students and teachers in border regions in sharing resources and curricular objectives. • Introducing a wider cultural context, e.g. comparative studies involving video links or internet communications.

(Adapted from Marsh, Maljers and Hartiala, 2001: 16)

with much attention given to use of kindergarten teachers and others who have a high degree of fluency in the vehicular language. This is because the teacher as a role-model speaker of the language is especially important when working with children of this age group, particularly in relation to phonology (Garcia, 2009: 348).

Primary 5–12 years

CLIL may be used as a form of pre-language-teaching 'primer' at this level. A range of models are commonplace, from task-based learning, involving simple use of the vehicular language, through to whole content topics taught in the CLIL language. Increasing motivation towards language learning and building learner self-confidence are seen as particularly important where the vehicular language is distant from the lives of the learners and has the status of a foreign language. In other cases, where migrant children may have limited access to the majority language of the environment, CLIL can be used as a 'leveller' to make both the CLIL language and content accessible to all learners, regardless of first language. This has been the case in North America for many years, and is increasingly found in European contexts where the demographics of classroom participation have moved towards greater cultural and linguistic diversity.

Whilst there is no finite agreement with regard to the age factor in language learning, nonetheless, as interest in the significance of early language learning continues to grow, so too does interest in primary-level CLIL. Views which hold that 'earlier is better' and that the introduction of an additional language should be as 'naturalistic as possible' following the framework of 'incidental learning' support the introduction of CLIL at an early age (see García Mayo and García Lecumberri, 2003, and Johnstone, 2002, for further discussion).

Model A1

Confidence-building and introduction to key concepts
Theme-based module on climate change. Fifteen hours of learning time involving class-based communication with learners in another country. Class teacher approaches the module using CLIL-designed materials and networking system.

→ Instructions and set-up in first language with language support provided for key concepts in CLIL language.
→ Communication and outcomes through CLIL language.

Model A2

Development of key concepts and learner autonomy
Subject-based learning on home economics. Forty hours of learning time involving translanguaging, where activities are

developed through the CLIL language using bilingual materials. Subject and language teachers work together.

→ Key concepts provided in first and CLIL language. Key thinking skills for inquiry-based tasks on aspects of home life and behaviour.

→ Assessment of key principles in first language; portfolio assessment in the CLIL language.

Model A3

Preparation for a long-term CLIL programme

Interdisciplinary approach involving a set of subjects from the natural sciences where the learners are prepared for in-depth education through the CLIL language. Subject and language teachers work together following an integrated curriculum.

→ CLIL language teaching complements content teaching with major focus on words and structures which enable learners to access thinking skills.

→ Assessment of key principles in CLIL language, with parallel first-language assessment of major concepts.

These three examples differ principally in terms of objectives and implementation time. But there are other subtle differences which influence how CLIL may be implemented at this level.

Model A1 may be carried out by a class teacher with more limited fluency in the CLIL language, and without the support of a language teacher. Such a model is useful in countries where there is a lack of availability of language teachers or multilingual content teachers. Using purpose-designed materials, the class teacher embarks on a limited exposure to CLIL even if constraints exist. This example is particularly effective in introducing the wider world of the vehicular language to the learners. Use of this model can be important for most educational contexts, but particularly those in which learners have little authentic access to languages and cultures beyond their own. It can also be managed in contexts where funding and resources are limited, because low technology can be used for classroom communication across schools and often countries – for instance, through artefacts, pictures, letters and videos sent through postal services. This has taken place, for example, between two classes in Rwanda and the UK: the schools worked on a joint eco-project using French as the vehicular language and exchanging project data via letters and video.

But is it worth the effort? Can any learner be expected to benefit from such a short exposure to the CLIL language? Can learners really be expected to succeed in producing outcomes in that language when their own command of the language may be very limited?

These are questions which arise in the minds of educators when they examine such a model. In order to answer these, it is necessary to recognise that the confidence-building objective is often difficult to evaluate, other than anecdotally, because it relates to the affective dimension of learning. The anecdotal evidence, however, is widely reported (see, for example, Genesee, 2004).

Model A2 suits situations where a language teacher is available in the school alongside a subject teacher who has sufficient proficiency in the CLIL language, and where teamwork is possible given the constraints of the curriculum and teaching schedules. It is possible that both teachers would be in the classroom for some time, but with most classroom interaction involving one teacher (if only because it is usually too cost-heavy to have two teachers working simultaneously in a classroom). Example A2 is an attempt to cover the ground found in Example A1, and go further, by deepening understanding of content concepts and developing metalinguistic awareness. In addition, it can act as a catalyst to introduce what may be alternative methodologies, such as formative assessment and enhanced learner autonomy.

Model A3 depends on a purpose-designed support framework if it is to be implemented in a way which ensures that the full potential of learners is realized. It is not feasible to expect such an approach to work unless the teachers in the classroom have the full support of the surrounding educational structures. These include school management, national/regional administrative structures, and even gate-keeping agencies such as examination boards.

Secondary 12–19 years

Secondary-level CLIL allows for more sophisticated models to be implemented. This is often because the learners have already learnt some of the CLIL language, and have developed more advanced learning skills than at primary level. However, CLIL can also be used to introduce a second additional language at this level, leading to yet another implementation type. Secondary-level students are increasingly motivated to use new technologies for communicating across languages and often borders. This is a potential learning resource which can be exploited by using class time to encourage learners to use the new technologies in a way which actively supports not only their education overall, but also their skills in using these media to engage in authentic communication in the CLIL language.

Much of the drive for introducing CLIL with this age group relates to parental and school-based attitudes towards globalization, and this is where English, in particular, has a dominant position as a CLIL language in many countries. When thinking of future education and working life, there is a view that experience of academic and vocationally based study can help prepare students for opportunities which may require use of the CLIL language in later life. Therefore, some of the models found at secondary level place fairly high demands on cognition, and need to be designed with carefully integrated principles. This is also true of vocational education where knowledge building and skills development require accuracy which cannot be impeded through problems in using the CLIL language.

Model B1

Dual-school education

Schools in different countries share the teaching of a specific course or module using VoIP (Voice over Internet Protocol, e.g. Skype™) technologies where the CLIL language is an additional language in both contexts.

→ Learners work with input from both language and content teachers, engage in collaborative problem-solving tasks using new media, and work predominantly in the CLIL language.

→ Sometimes linked to forms of international certification, which provides added value in terms of learner access to formalized assessment systems.

Model B2

Bilingual education

Learners study a significant part of the curriculum through the CLIL language for a number of years with the intention of developing required content-learning goals and advanced language skills.

→ Learners participate in 'international streams' and develop advanced CLIL language skills for these specific subjects. This is complemented by language learning which focuses on interpersonal skills and cognitive language proficiency.

→ Often linked to international certification, and national/regional special status assessment and recognition.

Model B3

Interdisciplinary module approach

A specific module, for example environmental science or citizenship, is taught through CLIL involving teachers of different disciplines (e.g. mathematics, biology, physics, chemistry and language).

→ Learners engage in an across-the-curriculum module which is taught in the CLIL language because of the international dimension of the content learning (e.g. the environmental responsibilities of individuals worldwide).

→ Used in international network partnerships between schools, and often focuses on formative portfolio-type assessment. Both of these aspects are seen as complementing language teaching by providing an extra platform for authentic language use.

Model B4

Language-based projects

This type differs from Examples B1–B3 in that it is the language teacher who takes primary responsibility for the CLIL module. This may be done through international partnerships and is an extension of both content-based and communicative language teaching. The module involves authentic content learning and communication through the CLIL language, and is scaffolded through language-teacher input.

→ Learners view this as part of language teaching but see it as an authentic way in which to use the language to learn non-language content.
→ Content assessment is usually formative and complementary to existing language assessment.

Model B5

Specific-domain vocational CLIL

Learners develop competence in the CLIL language so that they are able to carry out specific task-based functions which might range from customer service through to accessing and processing information in different languages. Where applicable, this is carried out by content and language teachers working in tandem. It marks a shift away from existing practice such as teaching language for specific purposes towards practice which seeks to achieve the same objectives through a closer tie to content teaching and learning.

→ Learners learn through the CLIL language and the first language, so that they can carry out specific tasks in diverse contexts.
→ Assessment is often bilingual and competence-based.

The lower-secondary curriculum often provides a particularly suitable environment for the introduction of CLIL. Pressures of examinations tend to complicate higher-level curricula in secondary education. This can occur where the educational system fails to recognise experience of CLIL in compulsory national examination systems, such as in the Netherlands.

Vocational curricula are particularly interesting because even if some of the students may not have achieved well in earlier language learning, the opportunity to learn content through CLIL can provide a second chance to access the CLIL language. Vocational fields long accustomed to including language learning, such as business studies, are now being joined by a wide range of others because of globalization and the changing nature of working life. The added value of being able to use more than one language now permeates vocational sectors in different countries.

Model B1 requires institutional cooperation and sufficient school-based recognition and support. Although technology is continuously evolving and becoming increasingly accessible, this example is fairly sophisticated and needs to be sufficiently resourced. But the benefits may be considerable and different ways of using the vehicular language can be found – for example, when students training to be chefs can engage in interactive work-based learning with a Master Chef and her or his employees via video conferencing in a restaurant kitchen where two other languages are used. There needs to be curricular alignment so that each school is fulfilling context-specific objectives, and the cognitive demands that learners in each school will need to respond to are balanced.

Model B2 also requires highly developed curricular and institutional support. For a long time this type has been used with the more privileged sections of certain societies where experience of learning through a specific language has been seen as a mark of status. However, there are cases (depending on the degree of egalitarianism within a specific educational system) where it is used in a non-elite way to provide this specific type of educational experience for a broad cohort of learners.

Model B3 represents what may be considered a knowledge-based-society form of education – one which is marked by both convergence (of knowledge and application) and competences (to know and be able to apply specific types of learning). It only really suits more widely used languages (either globally or regionally), and when implemented can act as a major tool for re-developing existing educational practice across subjects.

Language teachers have been involved with **Model B4** for some years, leading to content-based projects which complement more formal forms of language instruction. These often involve content teachers, and work effectively when the purpose of the exercise is embedded into the curriculum, as opposed to some form of additional (practising language) task.

Model B5 takes us into the vocational and professional education sectors. These have traditionally had differing status in specific countries, and in some cases the curricula have not included language teaching at all. CLIL can act as a means by which to both introduce languages into the curriculum, and to enhance existing practice. Geared as they often are to preparation for working life, these can be very successful in achieving higher levels of motivation towards language learning, and recognition of domain-specific and partial competences.

Tertiary (higher education)

The emergence of English as a global lingua franca has had a significant impact on higher education throughout the world. English has become the most dominant adopted vehicular language in Europe (Wächter and Maiworm, 2008), and beyond, as a direct result of international competitiveness linked to the General Agreement on Trade in Services

(GATS). There are strong indications that this will continue to be the case for some years to come (Graddol, 2006).

The shift towards adoption of English as a vehicular language does not automatically correlate with the introduction of CLIL. This may be due to the assumption that students studying through the medium of English as an additional language do not require an integrated approach where both content and language objectives are included. But the cognitive demands of tertiary programmes are often high, and there are examples of CLIL being introduced to both further develop additional language skills and to accommodate the learning needs of migrant students who do not have a high level of proficiency in the medium of instruction adopted.

CLIL can act as a professional development catalyst within faculties of a higher education institution. In some countries, higher education teaching and research staff have not been explicitly trained in educational methodologies. In these cases, higher education has been viewed as characterized by transactional modes of educational delivery (largely imparting information), rather than the interactional modes (largely process-oriented) characteristic of CLIL. At the same time, staff have come under pressure to become increasingly multi-skilled. This is not only in respect of teaching and report-writing, but also professional representation and the resourcing of external funding. Therefore interactional skills in widely used languages have become increasingly relevant in modernizing the workforces found in certain types of higher education. Training programmes in CLIL can therefore have a knock-on effect in developing staff in other ways beyond teaching skills.

The introduction of CLIL in this sector has been influenced by discussion over whether the ability to know and use a specific language is a basic competence, or an additional competence. This, in turn, has opened discussion on whether language teaching is a part of the core of academic life, or a secondary auxiliary science. If language teaching and language specialists have been viewed as 'auxiliaries' in some countries, then teachers may have a lower position within hierarchies. And yet the rising importance of a global language such as English has led to some re-positioning of this specific profession. This is similar to the way in which certain levels of ICT expertise have achieved a high status within organisations which have become dependent on ICT as a basic operating competence.

Finally, the adoption of an additional language such as English in higher education has put pressure on secondary-level providers to prepare students through CLIL for future studies.

> ### Model C1
>
> **Plurilingual education**
> More than one language is used through CLIL during different years in related content programmes.
>
> → Students are expected to master content and the ability to be sufficiently skilled in more than one language prior to entering working life or further studies.

→ Closely linked to prestigious forms of higher education where internationalization is viewed as a key part of institutional strategy so as to attract and retain high-performing students from different countries.

Model C2

Adjunct CLIL

Language teaching runs parallel to content teaching with specific focus on developing the knowledge and skills to use the language so as to achieve higher-order thinking.

→ Language teaching is field-specific (e.g. mechanical engineering or physics) with language teachers embedded in departments and not seen as external providers, and courses complement stage-by-stage higher-education programmes.

→ Students successfully learn content and gain the ability to use the CLIL language for specific purposes.

Model C3

Language-embedded content courses

Content programmes are designed from the outset with language development objectives. Teaching is carried out by content and language specialists.

→ Students, even those with less than optimal proficiency in the CLIL language, have support throughout the educational process so that dual learning takes place.

→ Particularly suitable where higher education attracts students from diverse linguistic and cultural backgrounds, so that they can both cope with and benefit from learning in the additional language.

Whereas **Model C1** can only be implemented in very specific types of higher-education institution (for example, business and management faculties where students attend courses with a reasonable level of proficiency in the target languages), **Models C2** and **C3** are more commonplace. The position of CLIL is clearly at an exploratory stage in higher education in many countries and although there are situational and structural variables which work against its introduction, there are also forces which give it considerable potential (cultural and linguistic diversity, and competence-based learning).

The risks involved with inappropriate adoption of an additional language as medium of instruction are considerable at any educational level. The increasing need for higher-education institutions to strengthen international profiles so as to achieve competitive advantage entails increasing pressure to ensure a suitably high quality of performance. Global competition often means teaching certain degree courses through the medium of English. This may involve simply expecting students and teaching staff on those courses to have sufficient command of the language to cope without extra support. In those cases where support is recognised as necessary, there are moves towards the adoption of CLIL.

We have now seen examples of curricular models across the educational spectrum. There are other types, for instance in adult education and workplace training, and these often replicate the examples found in more formal educational contexts. In Chapter 3 we will look at theoretical implications for integrating content and language learning, before examining in Chapter 4 how this can be applied to the diverse contexts which we have begun to explore in this chapter.

References

Garcia, O. (2009) *Bilingual Education in the 21ˢᵗ Century: A Global Perspective*, Oxford: Wiley-Blackwell.

García Mayo, M. P. and García Lecumberri, M. L. (eds.) (2003) *Age and the Acquisition of English as a Foreign Language*, Clevedon: Multilingual Matters.

Genesee, F. (2004) 'What do we know about bilingual education for majority language students?', in Bhatia, T. K. and Ritchie, W. (eds.) (2003) *The Handbook of Bilingualism and Multiculturalism*, London: Blackwell.

Graddol, D. (2006) *English Next*, London: British Council.

Johnstone, R. (2002) *Addressing "The Age Factor": Some Implications for Languages Policy*, Strasbourg: Council of Europe.

Marsh, D., Maljers, A. and Hartiala, A-K. (2001) *Profiling European CLIL Classrooms*, Jyväskylä: University of Jyväskylä.

Wächter, B. and Maiworm, F. (2008) *English-Taught Programmes in European Higher Education. The Picture in 2007*, Bonn: Lemmens.

3 CLIL as a theoretical concept

Whilst Chapters 1 and 2 have laid the foundations for exploring the development of CLIL, Chapter 3 explores the theoretical implications of integrating content learning and language learning. CLIL is not about 'translating' first-language teaching and learning into another language in the hope that learners will be immersed in a *bains linguistique* and seamlessly learn *in* another language. Neither is CLIL an attempt to 'disguise' traditional language learning by embedding systematic grammatical progression of the target language in a different type of subject content such as deforestation, photosynthesis or medieval history:

> Teachers have found that content and language integrated learning is about far more than simply teaching non-language subject matter in an additional language in the same way as the mother tongue . . . [It] is not a matter of simply changing the language of instruction.

> (Marsh, Enner and Sygmund, 1999: 17)

All learning is complex, and understanding the potential of integrating content and language demands an exploration of emergent synergies. The word *synergy* comes from the Greek *synergos* which implies working together 'in a dynamic state' where the whole is greater than the sum of the parts. Yet CLIL will not *automatically* lead to realising this potential. Instead, careful analysis of what can be achieved by integrative learning *through* a second or additional language is needed, based on a conceptual theoretical framework. This chapter introduces the framework for integration and the theoretical issues surrounding it.

3.1 Connecting content learning and language learning

> In every kind of knowledge-based, progressive organization, new knowledge and new directions are forged through dialogue . . . The dialogue in Knowledge Age organizations is not principally concerned with narrative, exposition, argument, and persuasion (the stand-bys of traditional rhetoric) but with solving problems and developing new ideas.

> (Bereiter and Scardamalia, 2005)

The content of learning

A useful starting point is to consider the content of learning. The concept of what constitutes content in a CLIL context is much more flexible than selecting a discipline from a traditional school curriculum such as geography, music, biology or physics. Whilst curricular subjects such as these might be appropriate for some CLIL programmes, contextual variables such as teacher availability, language support, age of learners and the social demands of the learning environment may mean that a different choice of content is more appropriate. In other words: what exactly is meant by 'content' in CLIL will depend on the context of the learning institution – an issue already raised in previous chapters. Content can range from the delivery of elements taken directly from a statutory national curriculum to a project based on topical issues drawing together different aspects of the curriculum (for example, the Olympic Games, global warming, ecosystems). Content in a CLIL setting could also be thematic, cross-curricular, interdisciplinary or have a focus on citizenship, for example. Themes might include issues-led investigations into climate change, carbon footprint or the Internet; cross-curricular studies might involve inquiry into health in the community, water or genocide; interdisciplinary work which encourages collaboration on a common theme whilst maintaining the integrity of each subject could, for example, lead to designing an eco-friendly house; and citizenship might focus on global issues such as race, global communication or learning across continents. CLIL, therefore, offers opportunities both within and beyond the regular curriculum to initiate and enrich learning, skill acquisition and development. The exact nature of these opportunities will depend on the extent to which the CLIL context demands an approach which is more content-led, more language-led, or both. However, the crucial point here is that, no matter whether issues concerning the content or the language are more dominant at a given point, neither must be subsumed or the interrelationship between the two ignored.

The learning of content: Synergies, scaffolding and social interaction

Identifying the type of content involved does not, however, automatically address a fundamental question: what is meant by content learning? It might be useful to start by considering some issues to do with content learning in general, before identifying specific challenges presented through using a second or additional language as the medium for that learning.

Syllabuses and programmes all have their aims and objectives, often with articulated goals and outcomes for teaching and learning. But these alone do not address the *how* of content learning – only the *what* of content teaching. The impact of general learning theory and how individuals learn, based on work from eminent theorists such as Bruner, Vygotsky and Wood (see Bigge and Shermis, 1998, for an overview) does not always directly influence classroom practice. But if CLIL is to build on potential *synergos,* then considerations of how effective learning is realized must be brought into the equation. In other words, CLIL demands an analysis of what is meant by effective pedagogies in different contexts.

Different pedagogic approaches have been debated across continents in recent times (see Chapter 1). The dominant model in many Western societies has emphasized a transmission of knowledge where the expert (the teacher) deposits information and skills into the memory bank of the novice (the learner). This has been called a 'banking model' (Freire, 1972) and tends to be teacher-controlled and teacher-led. Alternative, social-constructivist approaches to learning emphasize 'the centrality of student experience and the importance of encouraging active student learning rather than a passive reception of knowledge' (Cummins, 2005: 108). Social-constructivist learning in essence focuses on interactive, mediated and student-led learning. This kind of scenario requires social interaction between learners and teachers and scaffolded (that is, supported) learning by someone or something more 'expert' – that might be the teacher, other learners or resources. When learners are able to accommodate cognitive challenge – that is, to deal with new knowledge – they are likely to be engaged in interacting with 'expert' others and peers to develop their individual thinking. Vygotsky (1978) introduced the term 'zone of proximal development' (ZPD) to describe the kind of learning which is always challenging yet potentially within reach of individual learners on condition that appropriate support, scaffolding and guidance are provided. In settings shaped by social-constructivist approaches, the teacher's role involves facilitating cognitive challenge within an individual's ZPD. This involves the teacher in maintaining a balance between cognitive challenge for learners and appropriate and decreasing support as learners progress.

The learning of content: Cognitive engagement, problem solving and higher-order thinking

Developing the arguments above leads us to summarize that, for content learning to be effective learning, students must be cognitively engaged. CLIL teachers will have to consider how to actively involve learners to enable them to think through and articulate their own learning. This in turn implies that learners need to be made aware of their own learning through developing metacognitive skills such as 'learning to learn'. Interactive classrooms are typified by group work, student questioning and problem solving. If in a CLIL classroom students are required to cooperate with each other in order to make use of each other's areas of strength and compensate for weaknesses, then they must learn how to operate collaboratively and work effectively in groups. Leaving these skills to develop by chance is not an option. Instead, we need to support students in developing life skills such as dealing with the unexpected, observational skills, and constructing knowledge which is built on their interaction with the world, yet purposefully guided by values and convictions (van Lier, 1996).

Therefore, for CLIL teaching to support effective learning, it has to take into account not only the knowledge and skills base, but also cognitive engagement by the students. For example, the Queensland School Reform Longitudinal Study (1998–2000) reported on the need to 'shift teachers' attention and focus beyond basic skills to key aspects of higher-order thinking . . . towards more productive pedagogies' (Department of Education, Queensland, 2002: 1). Evidence showed that, to raise achievement levels, learners had to be intellectually challenged in order to transform information and ideas, to solve problems, to gain understanding and to discover new meaning. Effective content learning has to take account not only of the defined knowledge and skills within the curriculum or thematic plan, but also how to apply these through creative thinking, problem solving and cognitive challenge. Young people not only need a knowledge base which is continually growing and changing, they also need to know how to use it throughout life. They need to know how to think, to reason, to make informed choices and to respond creatively to challenges and opportunities. They need to be skilled in problem solving and higher-order, creative thinking, in order to construct a framework through which to interpret meaning and understanding:

> If learning is to be retained and to be readily available for use, then learners must make their own construction of knowledge – make it their own – and must learn to take responsibility for the management of their own learning.

(Nisbet, 1991: 27)

Towards a thinking curriculum: Dimensions and processes

So what is a thinking curriculum for CLIL? If the previous arguments about the importance of cognitive engagement are central to the CLIL classroom, it is not enough to consider content learning without integrating the development of a range of thinking and problem-solving skills. Since the publication of Bloom's **taxonomy** outlining six different thinking processes in 1956, the categorisation of different types of thinking has been the subject of great debate (McGuinness, 1999). In 2001, Anderson and Krathwohl published an updated version of Bloom's taxonomy by adding a 'knowledge' dimension to Bloom's 'cognitive process' dimension (see Table 2). This transparent connecting of thinking processes to knowledge construction resonates with conceptualizing content learning in the CLIL setting. The cognitive process dimension consists of lower-order thinking (remembering, understanding and applying) and higher-order thinking (analysing, evaluating and creating), both of which are integral to effective learning. The knowledge dimension provides a framework for exploring the demands of different types of knowledge: conceptual, procedural and metacognitive.

> A **taxonomy** (from Greek *taxis* meaning 'arrangement' or 'division' and *nomos* meaning 'law') is a system of classification which provides a conceptual framework for discussion, analysis, or information retrieval. A useful taxonomy should be simple, easy to remember, and easy to apply. Bloom's taxonomy (1956) is a good example because it classifies different types of thinking in a straightforward manner which we are able to apply to content. A more complex but logical framework is provided by Anderson and Krathwohl (2001). This classifies different types of thinking associated with different types of knowledge construction.

Other theorists have subsequently continued to develop the idea of taxonomies for different types of thinking (Marzano, 2000). However, the important point is not the choice of taxonomy, but rather the transparent identification of the cognitive and knowledge processes associated with the CLIL content. This is essential not only to ensure that all learners have access to developing these processes, but crucially that they also have the language needed to do so. We discuss how to put this into practice in Chapter 4.

Table 2: Bloom's taxonomy, revised by Anderson and Krathwohl

The Cognitive Process Dimension	
Lower-order processing:	
Remembering	Such as producing appropriate information from memory, e.g. • Recognizing • Recalling
Understanding	Meaning-making from experiences and resources, e.g. • Interpreting • Exemplifying • Classifying • Summarizing • Inferring • Comparing • Explaining
Applying	Such as using a procedure, e.g. • Executing • Implementing
Higher-order processing:	
Analysing	Breaking down a concept into its parts and explaining how the parts relate to the whole, e.g. • Differentiating • Organizing • Attributing
Evaluating	Making critical judgements, e.g. • Checking • Critiquing
Creating	Putting together pieces to construct something new or recognizing components of a new structure, e.g. • Generating • Planning • Producing
The Knowledge Dimension	
Factual knowledge	Basic information, e.g. • Terminology • Specific details and elements
Conceptual knowledge	Relationships amongst pieces of a larger structure that make them part of the whole, e.g. • Knowledge of classifications and categories • Knowledge of principles and generalizations • Knowledge of theories, models and structures
Procedural knowledge	How to do something, e.g. • Knowledge of subject-specific skills and algorithms • Knowledge of subject techniques and methods • Knowledge of criteria for determining when to use appropriate procedures
Metacognitive knowledge	Knowledge of thinking in general and individual thinking in particular, e.g. • Strategic knowledge • Knowledge about cognitive tasks • Self-knowledge

(Adapted from Anderson and Krathwohl, 2001: 67–8)

The implications of promoting cognitive engagement in learning settings where the medium of instruction is not the learner's first language will be considered in section 3.4 on page 41.

3.2 Language learning and language using

[W]e should not let ourselves be trapped inside a dichotomy between focus on form and focus on meaning but rather use the term focus on language . . . [I]n practice it becomes impossible to separate form and function neatly in the interactional work that is being carried out.

(van Lier, 1996: 203)

Form versus meaning or form as well as meaning?

Having considered theoretical aspects of content learning, we will now investigate what is meant by language learning in CLIL contexts. Within a traditional foreign language learning context, language teaching has its roots in the learning of grammar and the reading of texts. However, as noted in Chapter 1, in the latter part of the 20th century, second language acquisition theories influenced a range of approaches used for learning foreign languages (Richards and Rodgers, 2001). These theories have led to teaching methods such as grammar–translation, audio-lingual, input–output and communicative approaches. More recent explorations into general learning theories have also started to impact on reconceptualizing how languages can be *learned* as well as *taught* effectively. These include socio-cultural theory, interactionism and connectionism (de Graaff, Koopman, Anikina and Westhoff, 2007; Ellis, 1997; Lantolf, 2000; Mitchell and Myles, 2004; VanPatten and Williams, 2006).

Probably the most well-known approach to language learning in recent history promotes communication. Communicative approaches are based on theories of language learning requiring a focus on meaning as well as on form (grammar):

Approaches to foreign language learning have also moved from orientations almost exclusively directed to grammar and translation to more eclectic approaches geared to learning how to communicate in a second or foreign language.

(van Esch and St John, 2003: 23)

But a focus on communication has brought with it notions of communicative competence resulting in tension between focusing on form (grammar) and/or focusing on meaning. Savignon (2004) highlights principles for communicative language learning which are all relevant for CLIL since language learning is conceptualized within authentic contexts for use. These can be summarized as follows:

- Language is a tool for communication.
- Diversity is recognized and accepted as part of language development.
- Learner competence is relative in terms of genre, style and correctness.
- Multiple varieties of language are recognized.
- Culture is instrumental.

- There is no single methodology for language learning and teaching, or set of prescribed techniques.
- The goal is language using as well as language learning.

These principles are fundamental to language learning in a CLIL context. Yet in terms of classroom learning there appears to be a gulf between theory and practice, where so often 'communication' in formal language learning settings is reduced to language practice based on grammatical progression rather than meaning-making. Whilst practice is an important part of language learning – and language learning involves understanding grammatical progression – unless learners are also supported in using language for content learning, then CLIL cannot succeed. This brings to the fore the tensions in language learning between focus on meaning and focus on form.

Savignon's final point, suggesting that the goal of language learning encompasses language using, emphasizes the importance of using language in authentic interactive settings in order to develop communicative skills, rather than focusing almost exclusively on grammar. Students have to be able to use the vehicular language to learn content *other* than grammatical form otherwise this would not be CLIL. But the question remains: how can learners use a second or additional language for this purpose if they do not know *how* to use it? In other words, ignoring progressive language learning in a CLIL setting is ignoring the fundamental role played by language in the learning process. It reduces the learning context to teaching *in* another language:

> It is obvious that teaching a subject in a foreign language is not the same as an integration of language and content . . . Language teachers and subject teachers need to work together . . . [to] formulate the new didactics needed for a real integration of form and function in language teaching.
>
> (de Bot, 2002: 32)

Clegg suggests there are two alternative approaches to CLIL – one which is language-led and which 'imports parts of subjects [and] highlights language development' (2003: 89) and another which is subject-led and 'may well exclude language teachers and explicit language teaching' (ibid.). Perhaps it is more helpful to see the integration of content and language positioned along a continuum which relates to the contexts in which the learning and teaching take place:

> The social situation in each country in general and decisions in educational policy in particular always have an effect, so there is no single blueprint of content and language integration that could be applied in the same way in different countries – no model is for export.
>
> (Baetens Beardsmore, 1993: 39)

We would argue that in order to adopt a CLIL approach – where language and content are integrated in some clearly identified way – certain pedagogical principles must be addressed. For example, task-based language learning, whilst sharing some CLIL features, is not synonymous with CLIL, neither is subject-matter teaching, which traditionally pays little attention to language: 'Content must be manipulated pedagogically if its potential for language learning is to be realised' (Klapper, 1996: 70).

In the 1980s, Mohan, researching Canadian immersion (bilingual) programmes, critiqued well-known approaches to second language acquisition and learning (such as that of Krashen, 1985). He argued that they did not take into account content learning. In such instances content is seen:

> . . . only as a source of examples of the language code. However, if code is divorced from message, content is excluded; if form is divorced from function, there is no functional grammar; if language is divorced from discourse, there is no account of larger units of discourse . . . there is no attempt to account for language as a medium of learning, or for content learning.
>
> (Mohan, 1986: 65)

In an article published in 1997, Mohan and van Naerssen proposed that a different set of assumptions was needed to form the basis of pedagogical thinking relating to contexts where language is used as a *medium* of learning as opposed to the *object* of learning. The authors outline more appropriate assumptions for content-based learning and language learning as follows:

> 1 Language is a matter of meaning as well as of form.
> 2 Discourse does not just express meaning. Discourse creates meaning.
> 3 Language development continues throughout our lives, particularly our educational lives.
> 4 As we acquire new areas of knowledge, we acquire new areas of language and meaning.
>
> (Mohan and van Naerssen, 1997: 2)

We must emphasize that, whilst Mohan and van Naerssen's first point reinforces the view that language is as much about meaning as form, too little attention paid to form will have negative consequences. Lyster's (1987) work in French immersion programmes in Canada showed that whilst students could communicate effectively, they were not able to demonstrate first-language fluency nor consistent grammatical accuracy. As immersion teachers did not wish to discourage student language use by overcorrection, a type of 'immersion interlanguage' evolved (Lyster, 1987: 14). Swain (2000), also drawing on her research in Canadian immersion programmes, makes a strong case for there to be a clearer emphasis on form in content-driven learning contexts. She proposes that learners need to be exposed to tasks which require them to focus on problematic grammatical forms which can then be used in meaningful situations. Whilst language-learning theory may be a deficient model for content learning, Swain has also warned that:

> . . . content teaching needs to guide students' progressive use of the full functional range of language, and to support their understanding of how language form is related to meaning in subject area material. The integration of language, subject area knowledge, and thinking skills requires systematic monitoring and planning.
>
> (Swain, 1988: 68)

These arguments seem to suggest that in CLIL contexts it is not a question of whether to focus on meaning *or* form but rather that it is fundamental to address *both*, the balance of which will be determined by different variables in specific CLIL settings.

An alternative approach for using language to learn

Assuming that in CLIL settings it is necessary for learners to progress systematically in both their content learning and their language learning *and* using, as argued previously, then using language to learn is as important as learning to use language – both are requirements. Yet in many CLIL settings there is likely to be a difference in levels between cognitive functioning and linguistic competence – a situation which resonates with immigrant learners and the English as an Additional Language (EAL) agenda, for example. In other words, many CLIL learners have a cognitive level which is likely to be in advance of the linguistic level of the vehicular CLIL language. This assumption becomes more complex when we examine how language using connects with cognitive processing.

According to Freire, 'without dialogue there is no communication and without communication there can be no true education' (1972: 81). This puts classroom communication – interaction between peers and teachers – at the core of learning. There is also growing recognition that 'dialogic' forms of pedagogy – that is, where learners are encouraged to articulate their learning – are potent tools for securing learner engagement, learning and understanding. Focusing teaching and learning on quality discourse between learners, and between learners and teachers – where learners have different opportunities to discuss their own learning with others as it progresses, where feedback is integrated into classroom discourse and where learners are encouraged to ask as well as answer questions – promotes meaningful interaction fundamental to any learning scenario. This is what Wells (1999) terms 'dialogic learning'. The importance of interaction and teacher–learner and learner–learner dialogue is reflected in seminal work by theoreticians such as Bakhtin, Bruner, Mercer and Wood. The challenge, of course, in the CLIL setting is that learners will need to engage in dialogic learning using the vehicular language – a language in which they are probably unable to express themselves as well as in their first language.

This presents a pedagogic dilemma. If dialogic learning takes place in a context where learners are encouraged to construct their own meanings from activities requiring interaction with peers and the teacher in the vehicular language, then learners will need to be able to access language relating to the learning context. For example, if a younger learner needs to use the past tense in the CLIL language to describe an experiment in science, and if the past tense has not been learned in a formal grammar class, then the CLIL class will need to provide access to the appropriate use of the tense in that context. In other words, the language needed in CLIL settings does not necessarily follow the same grammatical progression one would find in a language-learning setting. Therefore, in addition to making choices about the grammatical forms needed to support language learning in context, an alternative approach to support language using in CLIL classrooms is required.

Still drawing on Canadian immersion experiences, Lyster advocated a new linguistic system for immersion to 'combine the program's communicative agents with a more systematic and graded language component aimed at second language learners' (1987: 715).

Moreover, Snow, Met and Genesee (1989: 205) usefully suggested identifying *content-obligatory* language (essential for learning the content) and *content-compatible* language (which 'supports the content of a lesson, as well as the linguistic cultural objectives of the curriculum' (ibid.)) to enable teachers to strategically sequence their language and content objectives. For strategic planning such as this to take place, teachers need to make explicit the interrelationship between content objectives and language objectives. A conceptual representation – the Language Triptych – makes these connections. It has been constructed to take account of the need to integrate cognitively demanding content with language learning and using (Coyle, 2000, 2002 and see Figure 1). It provides the means to analyse language needs across different CLIL contexts and transparently differentiates between types of linguistic demand which impact on CLIL. It also provides a means to conceptualize language using as language 'for knowledge construction' (Dalton-Puffer, 2007: 65). The Triptych does not replace grammatical progression but rather enhances it. It supports learners in language using through the analysis of the CLIL vehicular language from three interrelated perspectives: language *of* learning, language *for* learning and language *through* learning.

Figure 1: The Language Triptych

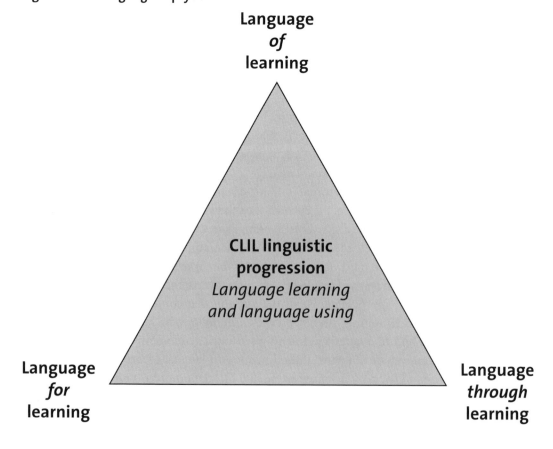

Language *of* learning is an analysis of language needed for learners to access basic concepts and skills relating to the subject theme or topic. There is a growing research interest in the role of genre analysis as it reveals the need to acquire language specific to subject and thematic content; for example, the language of science, or curriculum discourse. Drawing on systemic functional linguistics (Halliday, 2004), genre is seen as 'a social activity in a particular culture, the linguistic realisations of which make up a register' (Llinares and Whittaker, 2006: 28). For the language teacher this means shifting linguistic progression from a dependency on grammatical levels of difficulty towards functional and notional levels of difficulty demanded by the content. For example, returning to the learner needing to use the past tense in a science lesson, in the CLIL setting the learner needs to be supported in understanding the concept of 'pastness' and past 'markers'. This can be achieved through using certain phrases rather than having to learn paradigms of verbs conjugated in the past tense. Moreover, the selection of verbs used will depend on the content. Using the past tense for authentic purposes in a CLIL class arguably enables the learners to use language appropriate to the content in a meaningful way, which can then be further explored for grammatical cohesion in the language class. However, this does not imply that second or additional language lessons should be reduced to grammar lessons, but that a more varied menu can be created to provide a richer diet. For the subject teacher it requires greater explicit awareness of the linguistic demands of the subject or content to take account of literacy and oracy in the vehicular language.

Language *for* learning focuses on the kind of language needed to operate in a foreign language environment. Learning to use the language is challenging for both the teacher and the learner – each has a role to play. Learners need strategies to enable them to use the foreign language effectively. For many researchers (Mohan, 1986; Nunan, 1990; Snow, Met and Genesee, 1989; van Lier, 1996) planning is a prerequisite for effective scaffolding, and in CLIL settings this means that the learner will need to be supported in developing skills such as those required for pair work, cooperative group work, asking questions, debating, chatting, enquiring, thinking, memorizing and so on. Unless learners are able to understand and use language which enables them to learn, to support each other and to be supported, quality learning will not take place. Developing a repertoire of speech acts which relate to the content, such as describing, evaluating and drawing conclusions, is essential for tasks to be carried out effectively. Strategies for enabling learners to discuss, debate, get into groups and use the CLIL language independently will have to be transparent in both the planning (teaching) and the learning process.

Language *through* learning is based on the principle that effective learning cannot take place without active involvement of language and thinking. When learners are encouraged to articulate their understanding, then a deeper level of learning takes place. The CLIL classroom demands a level of talk, of interaction and dialogic activity which is different to that of the traditional language or content classroom. To return to Mohan and van Naerssen's point: 'Discourse creates meaning . . . As we acquire new areas of knowledge, we acquire new areas of . . . meaning' (1997: 2). In CLIL settings, new meanings are likely to require new language. This emerging language needs to be captured, recycled and developed strategically by teachers and learners. In other words, learners need language to support and advance their thinking processes whilst acquiring new knowledge, as well as to progress their language learning. Met sums this up as follows:

> Students need to communicate with the teacher, one another, or texts, in order to access or apply content. In so doing, the cognitive demand of tasks requires students to call upon their existing knowledge, concepts, skills and strategies . . . [R]esearch indicates that strengthening and making connections amongst concepts and knowledge increases learning and retention.

> (Met, 1998: 38)

In more practical terms, language ***through*** learning is to do with capturing language as it is needed by individual learners during the learning process – and this by definition cannot always be predicted in advance. It encourages the teacher to find ways of grasping emerging language *in situ*. It also addresses the need to define how linguistic development (language learning) will be systematically achieved through continuous recycling for further development of language, based on an upward spiral for progression rather than step-by-step grammatical chronology (Figure 2).

Figure 2: The spiral of language progression

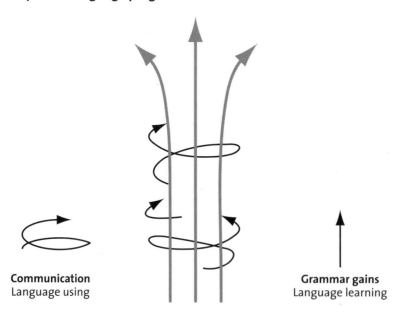

Communication
Language using

Grammar gains
Language learning

3.3 **From cultural awareness to intercultural understanding**

For CLIL to promote effective learning there is another consideration which should not be overlooked. Interconnectedness between the different elements of CLIL strengthens when links between language, cognitive processing and culture are explored. So what is meant by culture and what role does it play in CLIL?

How we define culture is highly contested and open to debate (Eagleton, 2000). Brown provides a useful explanation which links culture with thinking and language:

> Cultural patterns, customs, and ways of life are expressed in language: culture specific world views are reflected in language . . . [L]anguage and culture interact so that world views among cultures differ, and that language used to express that world view may be relative and specific to that view.
>
> (Brown, 1980: 138)

In the 1970s, Halliday defined language development as a 'sociological event, a semiotic encounter through which meanings that constitute the social system are exchanged' (1978: 139). If this social interactivity is transferred to learning settings where a foreign language is used, then language, cultural understanding, cognitive engagement and thinking are all connected to the content and context of CLIL. If we follow the idea that culture determines the way we interpret the world, and that we use language to express this interpretation, then CLIL opens an intercultural door, where learners can have experiences which they could not have had in a monolingual setting – meaning, for example, that it provides a rich catalyst for 'living' intercultural experiences which are fundamental to a deeper understanding of global citizenship. However, this puts responsibility on CLIL teachers to be proactive in developing whole-school partnerships and in using a range of technologies to make these connections. Chapter 4 provides some ideas for doing this.

Developing the discussion begun in the previous section and in line with sociocultural theorists such as Vygotsky and Bakhtin, language, thinking and culture are constructed through interaction. In first-language settings, meanings and values are learned *in situ* alongside language development; that is, social interaction is integral to **deep learning**. This means that language is not only part of how we define culture, it also reflects culture. Culture associated with a language cannot be 'learned' in a few lessons about celebrations, folk songs, or costumes of the area in which the language is spoken. Cultural awareness may focus on *knowledge about* different cultures, but the move towards intercultural understanding involves different experiences.

> **Deep learning** involves the critical analysis of new ideas, connecting them to already-known concepts, and leads to understanding and long-term retention of those concepts so that they can be used for problem solving in unfamiliar contexts. Surface learning is the acceptance of information as isolated and unlinked facts. It leads to superficial retention only.

At a micro level in CLIL contexts, cultural understanding demands meaningful inter-activity in the classroom with peers, teachers and resources in and through the vehicular language. At a macro level, extending social interaction beyond the classroom is also essen-tial if intercultural learning is to consist of collaborative meaning-making (Byram, 1989; Donato, 1994). In essence, intercultural skills and understanding need to be developed through interaction with a range of people in a range of contexts, so that new situations enable learners to adjust meaningfully in order to expand their own understanding. The European Commission's policy *European Agenda for Culture in a Globalising World* outlines ways in which the European Union supports the promotion of cultural diversity and inter-cultural dialogue:

> Culture and creativity touch the daily life of citizens. They are important drivers for personal development, social cohesion and economic growth. But they mean much more: they are the core elements . . . which . . . recognize and respect diversity. Today's strategy promoting intercultural understanding confirms culture's place at the heart of our policies.
>
> (Barroso, 2007)

Intercultural dialogue involves using skills to mediate between one's own and other cultures. It starts with raising awareness about one's own cultures, including culturally learned attitudes and behaviours. It embraces the development of learners' cultural knowl-edge, skills and attitudes in interactive settings. It invests in the development of competence building for learners to critically apply and analyse social processes and outcomes. The argument we are making is that, from a holistic perspective, CLIL has an important contri-bution to make to learners' intercultural understanding by developing:

> . . . an ability to see and manage the relationship between themselves and their own cul-tural beliefs, behaviours and meanings, as expressed in a foreign language, and those of their interlocutors, expressed in the same language – or even a combination of languages.
>
> (Byram, 1997: 12)

But in order for CLIL to have a cultural impact, learners need to engage in interactive and dialogic learning within the classroom and beyond. CLIL potentially offers a wide range of opportunities for intercultural interaction and has a fundamental role to play. The extent to which CLIL is successful will depend on the intercultural ethos of the classroom.

3.4 Integrating content and language learning: A holistic view

Students cannot develop academic knowledge and skills without access to the language in which that knowledge is embedded, discussed, constructed, or evaluated. Nor can they acquire academic language skills in a context devoid of [academic] content.

(Crandall, 1994: 256)

Mapping integration: The 4Cs Framework

In the first part of this chapter, different components of CLIL and their interrelationships have been considered in order to form a conceptual map for understanding CLIL.

The 4Cs Framework (Figure 3) integrates four contextualized building blocks: **content** (subject matter), **communication** (language learning and using), **cognition** (learning and thinking processes) and **culture** (developing intercultural understanding and global citizenship). In so doing, it takes account of integrating content learning and language learning within specific **contexts** and acknowledges the symbiotic relationship that exists between these elements. It suggests that effective CLIL takes place as a result of this symbiosis, through:

- progression in knowledge, skills and understanding of the content;
- engagement in associated cognitive processing;
- interaction in the communicative context;
- development of appropriate language knowledge and skills;
- the acquisition of a deepening intercultural awareness, which is in turn brought about by the positioning of self and 'otherness'.

Figure 3: The 4Cs Framework

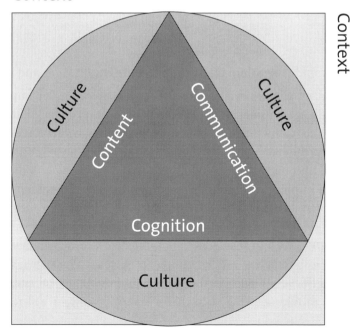

From this perspective, CLIL involves learning to use language appropriately whilst using language to learn effectively. It is built on the following principles:

1   Content matter is not only about acquiring knowledge and skills, it is about the learner *creating* their own knowledge and understanding and *developing* skills (personalized learning).

2   Content is related to learning and thinking (cognition). To enable the learner to create their own interpretation of content, it must be analysed for its linguistic demands.

3   Thinking processes (cognition) need to be analysed for their linguistic demands.

4   Language needs to be learned which is related to the learning context, to learning *through* that language, to reconstructing the content, and to related cognitive processes. This language needs to be transparent and accessible.

5   Interaction in the learning context is fundamental to learning. This has implications when the learning context operates through the medium of a foreign language.

6   The relationship between cultures and languages is complex. Intercultural awareness is fundamental to CLIL.

7   CLIL is embedded in the wider educational context in which it is developed and therefore must take account of contextual variables in order to be effectively realized.

In the 4Cs Framework, the terms 'language' and 'communication' are used interchangeably. This is not only a syntactical device for promoting the *C* concepts, but also a strategy for promoting genuine communication in the vehicular language if learning is to take place. It is an attempt to redress the criticism made by Donato that poorly conceived language experiences 'educate learners towards communicative incompetence rather than competence' (1996).

Implications for integration: Clarification, contextualization and inquiry

We will close this chapter by suggesting that there are three key implications for integration which need to be considered. The first focuses on the need for educators in each CLIL setting to identify and justify the means by which integrating content and language learning will be achieved, and the extent to which this is possible according to individual learning contexts and projected learning outcomes. Whilst this might seem obvious, the fact remains that integrating content learning and language learning is complex. It requires strategic planning as well as reflective evaluations. There are no quick-fix solutions or formulae for how this might be achieved. In this chapter we have constructed a conceptual map which provides a theoretical basis from which to start. However, building on principles developed in the previous chapter, it must be emphasized that this is a simple outline map which needs to be populated by rigorous discussion and clarification of purpose. Practical suggestions for doing this are contained in the following chapter. Inevitably, Chapter 4 will revisit fundamental issues to do with learning aims and outcomes. Unless these are clarified in the planning process, then CLIL is left to succeed or fail on an *ad hoc* basis.

The second implication, which is also one of the greatest challenges of CLIL, concerns the relationship between learners' language levels and their cognitive levels:

> Content specific methodology would have to focus on the learner, making language and content learning explicit and transparent, defining subject specific skills and thus enabling the learners to bridge the gap between the learners' conceptual and cognitive capacities and the learners' linguistic level.
>
> (Otten, 1993: 73)

In the CLIL classroom it is unlikely that the language level of the learners will be the same as their cognitive level. This might give rise to mismatches where either the language level is too difficult or too easy when set against the cognitive level. If the language level is too demanding, then arguably effective learning cannot take place. If the cognitive level is too low taking into account the language level, then learning is restricted. Whatever the capability of learners, effective learning demands cognitive engagement at the appropriate level for individuals:

> Research has shown that cognitively undemanding work, such as copying or repetition, especially when there is little or no context to support it, does not enhance language learning . . . [B]y actively involving pupils in intellectually demanding work, the teacher is creating a genuine need for learners to acquire the appropriate language.
>
> (Smith and Paterson, 1998: 1)

Ensuring that learners will be cognitively challenged yet linguistically supported to enable new dialogic learning to take place requires strategic and principled planning. As has already been discussed, it involves analysing in depth the type of language needed for effective learning. We suggest that an adapted version of Cummins' 1984 model – the CLIL Matrix – might be helpful in balancing linguistic and cognitive demands (see Figure 4).

Figure 4: The CLIL Matrix (adapted from Cummins, 1984)

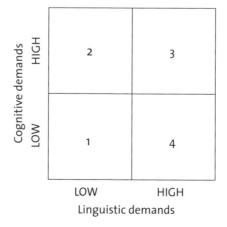

The CLIL teacher's own awareness of the vehicular language and the need to analyse the language carefully and systematically cannot be underestimated. The need to appreciate the learning demands in the vehicular language requires either an in-depth understanding of that language by the CLIL teacher or collaboration between the CLIL teacher and a language teacher. How the Matrix might help in strategic planning will be discussed further in Chapter 4. For the moment, it might be useful to take the CLIL Matrix and consider the implication of each of the four quadrants for effective learning. To ensure that the language of the learner does not impede learning, we need to focus on quadrant 2. Targeted progression in language learning whilst maintaining cognitive challenge will move the learner systematically over a period of time to quadrant 3. High linguistic demands in quadrant 4 are appropriate only during elements of CLIL where linguistic practice and focus on form is essential to progress learning.

In pedagogic terms, whilst quadrant 1 might build initial confidence in learners, in CLIL it is likely to be a transitory step on the way towards quadrant 2. However, the transition from quadrant 2 to quadrants 3 or 4 focuses on progression of individual learners and the realization of their potential over time. The Matrix provides a useful audit for CLIL teachers to track this progress in terms of planning and evaluating activities to extend student learning. Practical applications of the Matrix will be explored further in Chapter 4.

The third and final implication for integration is the need for those involved in CLIL to adopt an inquiry-based approach to classroom teaching and learning. Where CLIL is led by language practitioners, there are dangers that specific content demands are ignored or weakened. Where CLIL is led by content teachers, linguistic demands may be under threat. As Dalton-Puffer comments:

> At present, at least in Austria, a CLIL curriculum is defined entirely through the curricula of the content subjects, with the tacit assumption that there will be incidental language gains. But why should we be doing CLIL at all if there are no language goals present?
>
> (Dalton-Puffer, 2007: 295)

This reinforces the point yet again that there is no single model for CLIL and that its theoretical as well as practical basis has to take account of the context in which it is being developed. We suggest that this demands an inquiry-based approach to practice. Chapter 4 provides a model for involving both teachers and their learners so that, as the CLIL dynamic evolves, so too will our collective understanding. Professional learning in this sense is what van Lier (1996) calls articulating a **theory of practice**, where teachers construct their own theories of learning based on evidence from their own classrooms. According to Wong, when students are put at the centre of curriculum design and teaching:

> . . . the search for guiding principles to support their learning can be seen as a way of reclaiming methodology, from a series of narrow codified prescriptions, to an evaluation of which tools and resources will enable us to better understand how to support our students' language learning.
>
> (Wong, 2006: 205)

Working in professional learning communities (Wenger, 1998) means working towards the time when CLIL is no longer an 'either/or' in terms of content and language teachers, teaching and learning, but rather an integrated whole.

> A **theory of practice** emerges when the teacher begins to articulate his or her implicit knowledge and understanding about teaching and learning. The teacher's implicit knowledge becomes explicit through this process – that is, the teacher is aware of his or her own knowledge (theory of practice) and can begin to actively develop this. The starting point for a theory of practice is the teacher's own professional beliefs.

References

Anderson, L. W. and Krathwohl, D. R. (eds.) (2001) *A Taxonomy for Learning, Teaching, and Assessing: A Revision of Bloom's Taxonomy of Educational Objectives*, New York: Longman.

Baetens Beardsmore, H. (ed.) (1993) *European Models of Bilingual Education*, Clevedon: Multilingual Matters.

Barroso, J. M., President of the European Commission, on 10 May 2007 [Online press release]. Available at: http://europa.eu/rapid/pressReleasesAction.do?reference=IP/07/646 [Accessed 14 April 2009].

Bereiter, C. and Scardamalia, M. (2005) 'Technology and literacies: From print literacy to dialogic literacy', in Bascia, N., Cumming, A., Datnow, A., Leithwood, K. and Livingstone, D. (eds.) (2005) *International Handbook of Educational Policy*, Dordrecht, Netherlands: Springer, pp749–61.

Bigge, M. L. and Shermis, S. S. (1998) *Learning Theories for Teachers*, New York: Longman.

Bloom, B. S. (ed.) (1956) *Taxonomy of Educational Objectives, Handbook I: Cognitive Domain*, New York: Longman.

Brown, H. D. (1980) *Principles of Language Learning and Teaching*, Englewood Cliffs, NJ: Prentice Hall.

Byram, M. (1989) *Cultural Studies in Foreign Language Education*, Clevedon: Multilingual Matters.

Byram, M. (1997) *Teaching and Assessing Intercultural Communicative Competence*, Clevedon: Multilingual Matters.

Clegg, J. (2003) 'The Lingue E Scienze Project: Some Outcomes', in *Quaderni Publicati 6: L'uso veicolare della lingua straniera in apprendimenti non linguistici*, Torino: Ufficio Scolastico Regionale per il Piemonte.

Coyle, D. (2000) 'Meeting the challenge: Developing the 3Cs curriculum', in Green, S. (ed.) (2000) *New Perspectives on Teaching and Learning Modern Languages*, Clevedon: Multilingual Matters, pp158–82.

Coyle, D. (2002) 'From little acorns', in So, D. and Jones, G. M. (eds.) (2002) *Education and Society in Plurilingual Contexts*, Brussels: Brussels University Press, pp37–55.

Crandall, J. (1994) 'Strategic integration: Preparing language and content teachers for linguistically and culturally diverse classrooms', in Alatis, J. E. (ed.) (1994) *Georgetown University*

Roundtable on Languages and Linguistics. Strategic Interaction and Language Acquisition: Theory, Practice, and Research, Washington, DC: Georgetown University Press, pp255–74.

Cummins, J. (1984) *Bilingualism and Special Education: Issues in Assessment and Pedagogy*, Clevedon: Multilingual Matters.

Cummins, J. (2005) 'Using information technology to create a zone of proximal development for academic language learning: A critical perspective on trends and possibilities', in Davison, C. (ed.) (2005) *Information Technology and Innovation in Language Education*, Hong Kong: Hong Kong University Press, pp105–26.

Dalton-Puffer, C. (2007) *Discourse in Content and Language Integrated Learning (CLIL) Classrooms*, Amsterdam: John Benjamins.

de Bot, K. (2002) 'Relevance of CLIL to the European Commission's language learning objectives', in Marsh, D. (ed.) *CLIL/EMILE – The European Dimension: Actions, Trends and Foresight Potential*, Public Services Contract DG EAC: European Commission, Strasbourg, pp31–2.

de Graaff, R., Koopman, G. J., Anikina, Y. and Westhoff, G. (2007) 'An observation tool for effective L2 pedagogy in Content and Language Integrated Learning (CLIL)', *Bilingual Education and Bilingualism*, **10**, 5, 603–24.

Department of Education, Queensland (2002) *A Guide to Productive Pedagogies: Classroom Reflection Manual*, Education Queensland.

Donato, R. (1994) 'Collective scaffolding in second language learning', in Lantolf, J. and Appel, G. (eds.) (1994) *Vygotskian Approaches to Second Language Research*, Norwood, NJ: Ablex, pp33–56.

Donato, R. (1996) 'Sociocultural perspectives on foreign language learning, teaching practice and research', Paper delivered at the 11th World Congress of Applied Linguistics, AILA conference, Jyväskylä, Finland, August 1996.

Eagleton, T. (2000) *The Idea of Culture*, Oxford: Blackwell.

Ellis, R. (1997) *Second Language Acquisition*, Oxford: Oxford University Press.

Freire, P. (1972) *Pedagogy of the Oppressed*, New York: Herder and Herder.

Halliday, M. A. K. (1978) *Language as Social Semiotic: The Social Interpretation of Language and Meaning*, London: Arnold.

Halliday, M. A. K. (2004) *An Introduction to Functional Grammar*, London: Arnold.

Klapper, J. (1996) *Foreign-Language Learning through Immersion: Germany's Bilingual-Wing Schools*, The Edwin Mellen Press.

Krashen, S. D. (1985) *The Input Hypothesis*, London: Longman.

Lantolf, J. (ed.) (2000) *Sociocultural Theory and Second Language Learning*, Oxford: Oxford University Press.

Llinares, A. and Whittaker, R. (2006) 'Linguistic analysis of secondary school students' oral and written production in CLIL contexts: Studying Social Science in English', *View[z] Vienna English Working Papers*, **15**, 3, 28–32.

Lyster, R. (1987) 'Speaking immersion', *Canadian Modern Language Review*, **43**, 4, 701–17.

Marsh, D., Enner, C. and Sygmund, D. (1999) *Pursuing Plurilingualism*, Jyväskylä: University of Jyväskylä.

Marzano, R. J. (2000) *Designing a New Taxonomy of Educational Objectives*, Thousand Oaks, CA: Corwin Press.

McGuinness, C. (1999) *From Thinking Skills to Thinking Classrooms: A Review and Evaluation of Approaches for Developing Pupils' Thinking. Research Report 115*, London: Department for Education and Employment.

Met, M. (1998) 'Curriculum decision-making in content-based language teaching', in Cenoz, C. and Genesee, F. (eds.) (1998) *Beyond Bilingualism: Multilingualism and Multilingual Education*, Clevedon: Multilingual Matters.

Mitchell, R. and Myles, F. (2004) *Second Language Learning Theories*, London: Hodder Arnold.

Mohan, B. (1986) *Language and Content*, Reading, MA: Addison-Wesley.

Mohan, B. and van Naerssen, M. (1997) 'Understanding cause–effect: Learning through language', *Forum*, [Online] **35**, 4. Available at: http://eca.state.gov/forum/vols/vol35/no4/p22.htm [Accessed 15 April 2009].

Nisbet, J. (1991) 'Projects, theories and methods: The international scene', in Coles, M. and Robinson, W. D. (eds.) (1991) *Teaching Thinking* (Second edition), Bristol: Bristol Classical Press.

Nunan, D. (1990) 'Action research in the language classroom', in Richards, J. C. and Nunan, D. (ed.) (1990) *Second Language Teacher Education*, Cambridge: Cambridge University Press, pp62–81.

Otten, E. (1993) *Workshop 12A: Bilingual Education in Secondary Schools: Learning and Teaching Non-Language Subjects through a Foreign Language*, CDCC European Commission.

Richards, J. C. and Rodgers, T. S. (2001) *Approaches and Methods in Language Teaching* (Second edition), Cambridge: Cambridge University Press.

Savignon, S. (2004) 'Language, identity, and curriculum design: Communicative language teaching in the 21st century', in van Esch, C. and St John, O. (eds.) (2004) *New Insights in Foreign Language Learning and Teaching*, Frankfurt am Main: Peter Lang, pp71–88.

Smith, J. and Paterson, F. (1998) *Positively Bilingual: Classroom Strategies to Promote the Achievement of Bilingual Learners*, Nottingham: Nottingham Education Authority.

Snow, M., Met, M. and Genesee, F. (1989) 'A conceptual framework for the integration of language and content in second/foreign language instruction', *TESOL Quarterly*, **23**, 2, pp201–17.

Swain, M. (1988) 'Manipulating and complementing content teaching to maximize second language learning', *TESL Canada Journal*, **6**, 1, pp68–83.

Swain, M. (2000) 'The output hypothesis and beyond: Mediating acquisition through collaborative dialogue', in Lantolf, J. P. (ed.) *Sociocultural Theory and Second Language Learning*, Oxford: Oxford University Press, pp97–114.

van Esch, K. and St John, O. (2003) *A Framework for Freedom: Learner Autonomy in Foreign Language Teacher Education*, Frankfurt am Main: Peter Lang.

van Lier, L. (1996) *Interaction in the Language Curriculum: Awareness, Autonomy and Authenticity*, New York: Longman.

VanPatten, B. and Williams, J. (eds.) (2006) *Theories in Second Language Acquisition: An Introduction*, Mahwah, NJ: Lawrence Erlbaum Associates.

Vygotsky, L. S. (1978) *Mind in Society*, Cambridge, MA: Harvard University Press.

Wells, G. (1999) *Dialogic Inquiry: Towards a Sociocultural Practice and Theory of Education*, Cambridge: Cambridge University Press.

Wenger, E. (1998) *Communities of Practice: Learning, Meaning, and Identity*, Cambridge: Cambridge University Press.

Wong, S. (2006) *Dialogic Approaches to TESOL: Where the Ginkgo Tree Grows*, London: Routledge.

4 The CLIL Tool Kit: Transforming theory into practice

This chapter builds on the theoretical issues raised in the previous chapters. It provides a tool kit for teachers to map CLIL practice for their own context and learners. It is based on two core principles: that all learners have an entitlement to quality teaching and learning environments, and that CLIL has a contribution to make in achieving this.

Successful CLIL practice is likely to require teachers to engage in alternative ways of planning for effective learning. We recognize that, for busy professionals, this is a challenge. Connecting theoretical ideas to changing practice requires time, patience and professional support. This chapter suggests processes and tools which can be changed or adapted to suit any context without compromising the need to address fundamental issues of effective and appropriate integration of content and language learning. For those practitioners who are in the early stages of CLIL development, we suggest starting 'small' by piloting and experimenting with a few lessons as first steps. As confidence grows and as issues from specific contexts are addressed, then those involved become better prepared to explore tensions between visions or ideals and the realities of classroom contexts. As we discussed in Chapters 2 and 3, there is neither one preferred CLIL model, nor one CLIL methodology. The CLIL approach is flexible in order to take account of a wide range of contexts. Individual contexts have to define how integrated learning can be realized and to determine the combination and complementary value of the CLIL language (the medium for learning) and the non-language content. It is also the responsibility of key players in those contexts to interpret according to statutory or national/regional curricular requirements what is meant by quality content and language integrated teaching and learning. However, for CLIL to be effective, certain fundamental principles must be recognized as essential – it is not the case that any kind of teaching or learning *in* another language is CLIL. As CLIL is a flexible construct, it is all the more important that those involved with planning and delivering the CLIL curriculum should have the means to define and support a contextualized interpretation of CLIL, to make explicit the fundamental principles upon which it is based and to put in place rigorous monitoring and evaluation processes. In other words, there is both the need and the opportunity for teachers to develop professional confidence and to 'own' their practice. This chapter makes some suggestions about how 'owning' one's practice of CLIL might be approached.

The Tool Kit presented in this chapter is process-oriented. It describes six stages for creating a personalized Tool Kit. These stages are based on a class-based inquiry approach which stems from the widely used 'plan–do–review' cycle. At each stage, the Tool Kit provides a range of questions from which CLIL teachers can select and generate their own set of questions relevant to their own contexts. The questions are there to guide CLIL teachers in creating and developing their own classroom practices. They provide a starting point, a basis and a catalyst for further development, as well as a more holistic overview for CLIL planning. The complete set of questions can be found in the Appendix to this chapter. The Tool Kit does not include lesson planning templates, since these will grow from the tools selected in different contexts. However, there are some examples of how CLIL teachers have used the Tool Kit in the Appendix. Other conceptual tools described in Chapter 3 are also part of the Tool Kit, including the 4Cs Framework, the Language Triptych and the CLIL Matrix, to be used as appropriate.

The Tool Kit starts with the construction of a shared CLIL vision. Subsequent stages – analysing and personalizing the context, planning a unit, preparing a unit, monitoring and evaluating CLIL, and reflection and inquiry – lead towards the creation of or contribution to collaborative learning communities. In these professional communities, class-based inquiry further informs the development and transformation of CLIL according to context-specific agendas. The need for a continuing quality audit to monitor and evaluate the effectiveness of the CLIL programme is fundamental to successful classroom teaching and learning – flexibility is not to be mistaken for an 'anything goes' approach.

Finally, the stages are built on the principle that the questions are selective yet interactive triggers for discussion and reflection, which in turn contribute to professional learning at different levels.

Stage 1: A shared vision for CLIL

The first stage involves those interested in CLIL – language teachers, subject teachers, primary teachers and their colleagues, programme managers and so on, engaging in the construction of a shared vision for CLIL. If there is no tradition of CLIL in a school, the first challenge for pioneers is to bring together a group to share ideas and explore how CLIL might operate in their school. This 'starting small' approach may consist, for example, of one subject teacher and one language teacher or a class teacher working with a colleague as a critical friend. In some schools, where teachers are starting CLIL on their own, joining one of the CLIL virtual networks can provide a forum for sharing ideas. Creating a shared vision has benefits which go beyond CLIL.

> Vision allows us to look beyond the problems that beset us today, giving direction to our passage into the future. Even more important, vision energizes that passage by inspiring and guiding us into action.
>
> (Papert and Caperton, 1999)

The following ideas are suggestions for supporting professional dialogue using whichever language seems most appropriate. Two fundamental trigger questions invite some 'blue skies', creative thinking:

- What is our ideal CLIL classroom and what goes on there?
- In an ideal world, what do we want our CLIL learners and teachers to be able to achieve?

A range of brainstorming and discussion techniques for building an ideas bank provides the basis for vision sharing and prioritizing, so that relevant overarching goals can be constructed. These overarching goals will be referred to as 'global goals' to describe the longer-term vision for any CLIL programme, whatever the extent of that programme. Examples of global goals might be 'to increase learner engagement' or 'to develop confident learners who use the CLIL language spontaneously in a range of settings'. Global goals are not prescribed, although they may reflect wider educational values and beliefs. However, it is extremely important that global goals are 'owned' by the professionals involved. A 'Diamond 9' activity, for example, may provide a useful catalyst for identifying and sharing these goals in a reflective and supportive way. To start the activity, pairs or small groups of CLIL teachers require nine 'I want' statements. These statements can be created either from suggestions made by individual teachers, or by using the examples below. The statements need to be written on small squares of paper. Composing individual statements provides teachers with a chance to reflect on and articulate their own CLIL vision; for example:

I want my CLIL classroom to be a vibrant, interactive and motivating place.	I want learners to learn confidently in the target language – this means they will be willing to talk.	I want to ensure that learners achieve at least the equivalent academic standards in CLIL as they would in their first language.
I want to be part of a CLIL teaching and learning community where we can share ideas and resources.	I want to access a range of CLIL materials, including authentic materials at the appropriate level.	I want learners to benefit from CLIL by developing wider intercultural understanding through using language to learn.
I want to motivate learners to use the CLIL language in a range of different ways (e.g. for learning, for chatting, for organizing their learning, for conducting out-of-classroom work, for written project work).	I want to involve learners (and their parents or carers), colleagues and administrators in this innovation so that it will become part of the regular curriculum.	I want the theme of the CLIL unit to challenge learners and help them acquire new knowledge, skills and understanding.

In pairs or small groups, teachers discuss each square in turn and create a consensual diamond shape which prioritises individual statements in order to arrive at a shared vision – the most popular statement placed in position one, the next two in position two and so on. This kind of activity provides the working group with opportunities to agree on or challenge visionary statements:

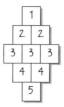

Priorities which emerge from the vision activities are the global goals – which by definition will be long term and overarching. Whilst global goals may change over time, nonetheless, it is the initial identification of these goals which provides a collective CLIL vision and which will steer the remaining stages. If, for example, one of the goals is to encourage learners to talk and use the CLIL vehicular language for learning, then this will not happen by osmosis. Instead, analysing what *enables* learners to talk is not only a theoretical consideration but a pragmatic one which permeates ethos-building, lesson planning, task types and assessment processes: What kind of language do learners need in this unit? What are the 'talk demands' of the tasks? What kind of tasks do we need in order to encourage 'talk progression'? If we ask learners to discuss or debate, do they have the necessary linguistic support to enable them to do this? If not, what kind of scaffolding will help them? Are 'talk demands' at an appropriate level for their age and cognitive level of ability? Do learners really have to interact to complete these tasks? and so on. Questions such as these will dominate subsequent stages and will act as a planning tool created by teachers for teachers.

> If you want to improve the quality of teaching, the most effective place to do so is the context of the classroom lesson . . . the challenge now becomes that of identifying the kinds of changes that will improve student learning . . . of sharing this knowledge with other teachers . . .
>
> (Stigler and Hiebert, 1999: 111)

Reflection points

- Who are the key players needed to form a CLIL teaching team?
- How can we communicate and share our ideas?
- Do we have a shared vision for CLIL? If so, what is it? If not, how shall we construct one?
- What is our ideal CLIL classroom and what goes on there?
- In an ideal setting, what do we want our CLIL learners and teachers to be able to achieve?
- Have we achieved a vision which is 'owned' by the group and which prioritizes different elements of our vision? (i.e. What are our global goals?)

As practice develops, visions can and do change over time. It is desirable that the CLIL vision is seen as a dynamic and iterative process which might change as the stages lead to reflection and review.

Stage 2: Analysing and personalizing the CLIL context

This stage requires those responsible for the CLIL programme to construct a model for CLIL which not only grows from the vision created in Stage 1, but which also reflects the local situation. In Chapter 2 we discussed the variables such as school type and size, environment, teacher supply, regional as well as national policies, which all have a role to play in determining the type of CLIL appropriate for different contexts. Different variants of CLIL are best seen on a continuum where the learning focus and outcomes differ according to the context in which a model is adopted. Again, Chapter 2 provided an overview of potential models. At this stage 'making the model our own' is not detailed, but identifies the fundamental principles or the building blocks. Here are some teacher examples:

> As geography teachers, we are interested in adapting some of our teaching units to explore the curriculum content from different perspectives. We thought a good starting point would be to choose a human geography unit on Senegal. If we teach the unit through French and use French resources, then this will give our students a very different experience.

> In our vocational college, there is an emphasis on foreign language skills for career enhancement. Instead of separate language courses, we want to focus on developing a catering course where foreign language skills are integrated. This means that we will teach the catering course through Italian.

> In our school, there is an emphasis on cross-curricular projects. As members of the senior management team, we want to involve both language teachers and subject teachers planning together. We had thought of three possibilities: a study of different aspects of eco-citizenship or the global village, fair trade or war and peace. We would also want to extend our international network through using new technologies and link with similar classes who could share the same language of communication.

> We want to bring language learning alive and make it more relevant for our young people. So we decided to work on a content-based type of approach to a theme. This might include taking a typical language topic such as *Where we live* and carrying out a comparative study between house and home in an African and European cultural context.

> In our primary school we want to extend our integrated approach across the curriculum. We thought that a study of 'water' through the medium of another language as well as in our own language could include science, geography, history, current catastrophes, water shortages, water for leisure, poetry, art, drama and music, linking language wherever possible to space and place.

> We want to think 'big' – do a global project similar to those organized by *Science Across the World*, where identical topics (e.g. global warming, renewable energy, what we eat) are studied by learners in different countries and in different languages and then the results compared.

There are many other variations. Whilst each CLIL model will have its own global goals, different models all share a common founding belief: that CLIL has a valid contribution to make to personal development and preparation for working in a plurilingual world through the integration, in some way, of content learning and language learning.

Reflection points

- How can we as teachers share our ideas and skills?
- Is there leadership support for CLIL? What are the implications of the support?
- Who is involved in the teaching and the learning? Subject teachers? Language teachers? General teachers? Assistants? All of these?
- What are the implications of the above for constructing our own CLIL model? (e.g. Which subjects, themes, topics and languages? Which learners, classes?)
- What are the implications of the above for less capable learners?
- Does our CLIL programme have a dominant language, subject or citizenship orientation or are these integrated? What are the implications?
- How do our global goals impact on our CLIL model?
- How do we involve the wider community, such as parents, carers and significant others?
- Have we agreed on contextual opportunities and constraints?

Stage 3: Planning a unit

Stage 3 provides a planning map for CLIL. It consists of four different planning steps using the 4Cs Framework and other conceptual tools which form part of the Tool Kit.

A conceptual framework

Before exploring the first step, it is useful to briefly revisit the 4Cs Framework. Its four major components can be summarized as follows:

Content

Summary	Progression in new knowledge, skills and understanding.

At the heart of the learning process lies successful content or thematic learning and the related acquisition of new knowledge, skills and understanding. Content is the subject or the CLIL theme. It does not have to be part of a discrete curriculum discipline such as maths or history, it can be drawn from alternative approaches to a curriculum involving cross-curricular and integrated studies. It is useful to think of content in terms of the knowledge, skills and understanding we wish our learners to access, rather than simply knowledge acquisition.

Communication

Summary   Interaction, progression in language using and learning.

Language is a conduit for communication and for learning which can be described as *learning to use language and using language to learn*. Communication in this sense goes beyond the grammar system, but at the same time does not reject the essential role of grammar and lexis in language learning. It involves learners in using language in a way which is often different from more traditional language lessons (of course, CLIL involves learners in learning language too, but in a different way). It is perhaps useful here to differentiate between language learning (often with an emphasis on grammatical progression) and language using (with an emphasis on the communication and learning demands of the moment). There are similarities with the kind of language approaches which influence CBI (content-based instruction), TBI (task-based instruction) and EAL (English as an Additional Language – that is, for those students who have to learn through the medium of another language, in this case English). All of these approaches explore to different degrees and with different emphases the relationship between language learning and the content within which it is situated. CLIL integrates content learning and language learning so that both are important.

Cognition

Summary   Engagement in higher-order thinking and understanding, problem solving, and accepting challenges and reflecting on them.

For CLIL to be effective, it must challenge learners to create new knowledge and develop new skills through reflection and engagement in higher-order as well as lower-order thinking. CLIL is not about the transfer of knowledge from an expert to a novice. CLIL is about allowing individuals to construct their own understandings and be challenged – whatever their age or ability. As we discussed in Chapter 3, a useful taxonomy to guide planning for cognitive challenge is that of Anderson and Krathwohl (2001), since it explores the relationship between cognitive processing (learning) and knowledge acquisition (of content) particularly relevant to CLIL. It is not suggested that taxonomies are rigidly followed, but rather that they serve as a stimulus and reference for planning, discussion and evaluating practice.

Culture

Summary   'Self' and 'other' awareness, identity, citizenship, and progression towards pluricultural understanding.

Culture is not a postscript. It is a thread which weaves its way throughout any topic or theme. Sometimes referred to as the 'forgotten *C*', it adds learning value to CLIL contexts, yet demands careful consideration. For our pluricultural and plurilingual world to be celebrated and its potential realized, this demands tolerance and understanding. Studying through a different language is fundamental to fostering international understanding. If learners understand the concept of 'otherness' then this is likely to lead to a deeper understanding of 'self' (Byram, 2008). It could be argued that in the CLIL classroom the use of appropriate authentic materials and intercultural curricular linking can contribute to a deeper understanding of difference and similarities between cultures, which in turn impacts on discovering 'self'. CLIL offers rich potential for developing notions of pluricultural citizenship and global understanding – but these need to be planned and transparent (Commission of the European Communities, 2008). Moreover, extending CLIL content to include intercultural understanding is not always obvious. It needs to be thought through to ensure meaningful connections rather than tokenistic reference. If there is a class-to-class link (or sister class) already connecting schools across different cultures, then including intercultural elements in project planning will be easier. In CLIL, culture can include extending the content – for example, 'the bicycle as a means of transport across the world' as a topic in a technology class; setting the context of the content in different cultures – for example, investigating patterns in Asian and European architecture in a mathematics or design class; discussing how learners in different cultures might approach the same content topic – for example, attitudes to recycling; or exploring and interpreting the curriculum as a global citizen.

Whilst the 4Cs can be outlined individually, they do not exist as separate elements. Connecting the 4Cs into an integrated whole is fundamental to planning. For example, exploring how cognitive elements interconnect with content will determine the type of tasks which will be planned. Similarly, relating cognition to communication will demand careful consideration of classroom activities to ensure that learners not only have access to the content language, but also to the classroom language needed to carry out the tasks.

However, it is content which initially guides the overall planning along the learning route. This is to avoid limiting or reducing the content to match the linguistic level of the learners. It is likely that learners will need to access some linguistic forms in CLIL lessons before they have met them 'formally', say, in a second or additional language grammar lesson. If we return to the example of the science experiment in Chapter 3, the context demands that learners use the past tense to give an explanation of what happens when chemicals react. Moreover, this explanation will have to follow the 'norms' of reporting a science experiment. In other words, the CLIL lessons will have to enable the learners to use the past tense appropriately and follow the discourse norms of the subject, thereby using the CLIL language in alternative ways. Instruction in the past tense may initially be in the form of using key phrases without studying tense formation at this stage. The emphasis is always on accessibility of language in order to learn. It is unlikely, however, that learners will have linguistic levels in the CLIL language which match their cognitive levels. It is not pedagogically acceptable for learners to be reduced either to using inappropriate tenses or to using language phrases which are cognitively undemanding – the 'I like it because I like it' syndrome – unless justified as confidence-building and using the familiar as a springboard at the start of a unit. Moreover, trying to progress the language too quickly without remedial work, practice and recycling linguistic functions and notions may result in confusion, error and demotivation.

CLIL integrates language learning and content learning at cognitive and cultural levels appropriate to the learners. It is this integration which results in new learning scenarios which are different from regular language or content lessons. CLIL demands careful planning for progression in all Cs, and the Cs may progress at different rates depending on the context. This enables teachers to adopt a more holistic and inclusive approach to classroom practice. Global goals may be a useful starting point (see Stage 1), but more detailed planning may be facilitated by using the 4Cs Framework.

Stage 3 is the most detailed stage in the planning process. It involves the careful analysis of different elements of CLIL as suggested in the 4Cs Framework. We recommend using a mind map or similar visual organizer to create a unit of work. A unit might consist of a series of lessons over a specific period of time or a theme. In the following section, we continue to provide suggestions for promoting team decision-making and collaborative planning. These suggestions are based on questions which are divided into four steps. By selecting questions relevant to individual contexts, each step will build up a picture so that, by the fourth step, planners will have an overview of a unit, consisting of key elements and prioritized aspects for teaching and learning. These components also relate directly to global goals identified in Stage 1. An illustration of a simple template which can be used as a starting point for each of the four steps is provided below.

Mind map template

 – Global Goal: ....
 – Unit Title: ....

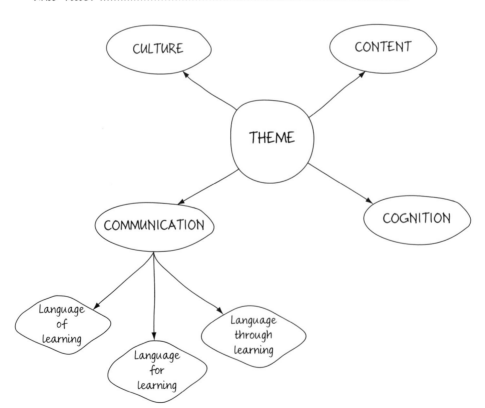

Throughout the four steps we construct a mind map using the template to build up an overview of an example unit, concluding with the complete mind map in Figure 5, page 66. This process does not go into the detail of individual lesson planning. Lesson plans require the completed map to provide the stimulus for task design and sequencing across different lessons of a unit. The mind map we construct in this chapter draws on a similar one created by a team of CLIL teachers in a planning workshop. The theme of their unit is *Habitats*. The teachers explored each step in depth, selecting questions, discussing them and adding points to their mind map. The teachers were working with learners at lower-secondary level. The global goal was to encourage more spontaneous talk between learners. Further examples from the teachers' workshop can be found in the Appendix.

- Global Goal: Encourage learners to talk more confidently

- Unit Title: Habitats

Four steps for unit planning

Step 1: Considering content

> **Reflection points**
>
> - Is there a choice of content? If so, which is the most appropriate for our CLIL setting?
> - Do we have to use an existing syllabus or curriculum?
> - How will we select new knowledge, skills and understanding of the theme to teach?
> - What will the students learn? (i.e. What are the learning outcomes?)
> - Is progression in learning taken into account?
> - Do we have to prioritize the content to be included?
> - How does the content develop our global goal(s)?

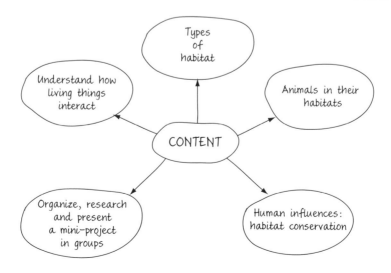

Step 2: Connecting content and cognition

Given an outline of the content, the next step is to analyse and select the thinking skills, problem solving and creativity which connect with the content. This process ensures that the cognitive level of the CLIL unit relates to the learners' own levels of development.

Reflection points

- Use a taxonomy of thinking skills such as Bloom's (1956) or Anderson and Krathwohl's (2001) for reference (refer to Chapter 3). Which cognitive skills seem to be most appropriate for development in terms of the content?
- Are we encouraging the use of higher-order thinking (HOTS) such as hypothesizing and problem solving as well as lower-order thinking (LOTS) such as remembering, understanding and applying new knowledge?
- Which activities or task types are likely to encourage the development of these skills?
- How do we deal with the linguistic demands of these tasks to ensure linguistic progression?
- What kind of questions must we ask in order to go beyond 'display' questions and present students with challenging problem-solving, hypothesizing, analysing and evaluation tasks?
- What kind of questions do we want our learners to ask?
- Have students been given opportunities to discuss their new knowledge and understanding?
- How do we know what the students have learned? How are our formative assessment tasks used to inform further learning?
- How does/do our global goal(s) fit with developing cognition?

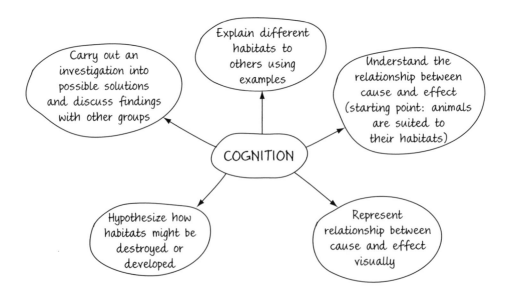

Step 3: Communication – Defining language learning and using

The next step links the content and cognitive demands with communication, using the Language Triptych described in Chapter 3 (language *of, for* and ***through*** learning). It is perhaps this step which is the most challenging – for subject teachers it demands an awareness of different types of language used for different purposes; for language teachers it requires an alternative approach to language learning and language using without rejecting successful classroom practice. It uses a pragmatic as well as a linguistic approach to developing language through use. It is not built on a grammatical model where progression focuses on a gradation of grammatical concepts, but incorporates grammatical progression from different perspectives. The Triptych starts with the language needed by content. It relates language learning to progression through the conceptual understanding of the content, rather than progression in grammatical awareness typified by learning present tense before past tense and so on. The Triptych does not reject grammar learning but instead approaches it initially through content demands. There may be times when specific grammar is needed and teachers will make decisions as to the range of options open; for example, teach the grammar point at the time when it is needed in the CLIL lesson to focus learner attention on the linguistic form; from a content perspective, liaise with the language teacher for its inclusion in a language-learning lesson; integrate the grammar point through different uses across CLIL lessons, adopting a more immersive approach; explore literacy practices across the school for a more integrated approach.

Identifying the language needed to learn in a CLIL classroom demands systematic analysis at the planning stage. The analysis reaches far beyond key words and phrases and other grammatical functions (content-obligatory language, which is necessary if the learner is to participate fully in learning the content). It addresses progression in form and function, process and outcomes, and encourages the creative use of spontaneous language by learners. It involves language practice and language use in the spiral of language progression – as introduced in Chapter 3 – where recycled language is developed further (content-compatible language, which allows the learner to operate more fully in the content subject). It requires an analysis of the linguistic genre – that is, the type of discourse and language which is embedded in different content subjects or themes. An example is the 'language of science', which goes far beyond key items of specialized vocabulary of the subject itself (content-obligatory language) and includes an understanding of language needed to operate successfully (report writing, carrying out laboratory experiments and so on – content-compatible language).

The Language Triptych

The term 'triptych' is used to identify an image consisting of three linked parts. Whilst each of the components of the Language Triptych have been explored in depth in Chapter 3 (and see Figure 1, repeated below), we recommend familiarizing the CLIL planning team with these elements before planning.

A preliminary activity useful for raising awareness of the linguistic genre associated with particular subjects or themes (in order to identify content-obligatory and content-compatible language) is to analyse a written or oral text drawn from the subject field. For example, science texts would typically contain 'cause and effect' constructions (*Explain what causes high blood pressure and how this affects an individual*) and use questions requiring evidence (*Justify the use of biofuels*). Reflect on how differently you might use the text in either a language lesson or a first-language content lesson. Another useful tool is to audio-record language used by teachers and students as they learn and interact in first-language classes to begin to build a **corpus** of the type of language used in classrooms for different purposes, to be transferred and developed in the CLIL language.

> A **corpus** is a collection of writing or speech which can be analysed to find out, for example, which words and grammatical structures writers or speakers typically use in particular texts or situations (see O'Keeffe, McCarthy and Carter, 2007, for information on the use and construction of corpora in the classroom).

Figure 1: The Language Triptych (repeated from page 36)

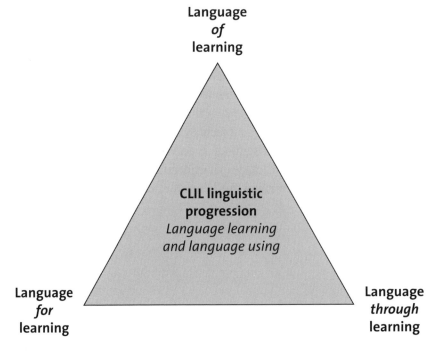

Language
of
learning

CLIL linguistic
progression
*Language learning
and language using*

Language
for
learning

Language
through
learning

Language *of* learning

The first aspect of the Triptych is the language *of* learning. This explores what language learners will need to access new knowledge and understanding when dealing with the content. In the case of the *Habitats* example, the language *of* learning consists of the key vocabulary and phrases related to habitats, deforestation, human influences, and so on. However, it goes beyond a list of key phrases. If the learners are required to define habitats, they will need to embed the lexis into 'defining' language. It is not enough to simply identify key words and phrases without considering *how* learners will need to use them in order to learn. The following reflection points will serve to identify key words and phrases and the language in which these will be embedded:

Reflection points

- What type of language (genre) does this subject or theme use? How shall we ensure learners have access to this?
- Define the content-obligatory language, such as key words, phrases and grammatical demands of the unit (e.g. the language of discussing, hypothesizing, analysing). How is this introduced and practised?
- What kind of talk do learners need to engage in and how do we build in progression over time? (e.g. the extension of the language of discussion over several lessons)
- What is the most effective way of teaching the language of learning? (e.g. specific tasks, content-embedded practice, grammar rules)
- Which of the identified language and skills shall we target for development in this particular unit?

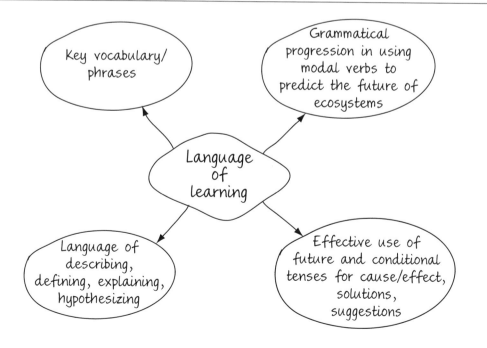

Language *for* learning

Arguably, the language *for* learning is the most crucial element for successful CLIL, as it makes transparent the language needed by learners to operate in a learning environment where the medium is not their first language. In the *Habitats* project, language *for* learning is linked to the language students will need during lessons to carry out the planned activities effectively. For example, if the students are required to organize, research and present a mini-project, then they will need language which will enable them to work successfully in groups, carry out their research and present their work without reading from a sheet.

Reflection points

- What kind of language do learners need to operate effectively in this CLIL unit?
- What are the possible language demands of typical tasks and classroom activities? (e.g. how to work in groups, organize research)
- How will these be taught?
- Which language skills will need to be developed? (e.g. discussion skills)
- How are we developing metacognitive strategies? (Learning how to learn – e.g. reading strategies, comprehension strategies)
- How can learning be scaffolded (supported) by the teaching and learning of specific language? (e.g. language used to seek additional information, assistance, explanation and access to other sources)
- How do students practise their new language and recycle familiar language?
- Have we prioritized the language for learning in this unit in relation to the content? (i.e. what students need to know at which stage of the content – e.g. focus on developing reasoning, making a case)
- Is the language which is used to assess the learning accessible to the learners?

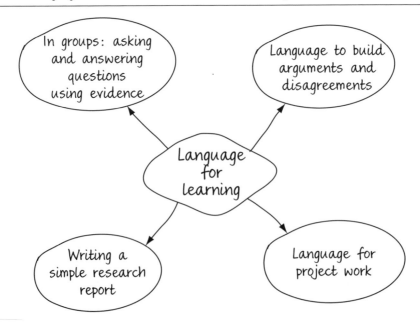

Language *through* learning

New language will emerge ***through*** learning. Not all the CLIL language needed can be planned for. As new knowledge, skills and understanding develop, then so too will new language. Moreover, as language is linked to cognitive processing, it is important to make use of opportunities (both spontaneous and planned) to advance learning – to encourage learners to articulate their understanding, which in turn advances new learning. The challenge for teachers is how to capitalize on, recycle and extend new language so that it becomes embedded in the learners' repertoire. Language progression in this sense can be defined as the systematic development of emerging language from specific contexts, supported by structured grammatical awareness, using known language in new ways, accessing unknown language and so on. Thinking of these processes as a spiral is helpful (see Chapter 3, Figure 2). It also provides an alternative approach to a transmission model where either much of the language input is pre-determined or translated from the first language. In the *Habitats* project, language ***through*** learning may emerge if, for example, during the mini-project preparation, students working in groups need language to express a new idea which they have constructed and which is not in their resources – this might involve dictionary work and teacher support.

Reflection points

- What necessary language functions and notions do the students know already? How can these be practised and extended?
- What strategies can our learners use to access new language for themselves?
- When new language emerges, how shall we capture and select language for further development?
- How can we define language progression in this unit?

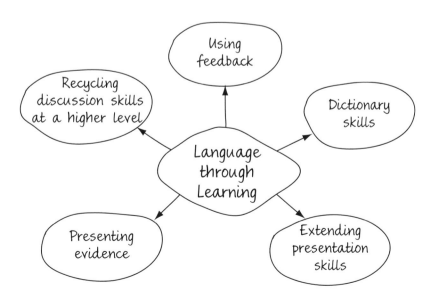

Step 4: Developing cultural awareness and opportunities

In previous chapters, reasons for embedding CLIL in a cultural agenda were discussed in depth. The point made was that, although raising cultural awareness is a starting point, often this resides in the 'foods and festivals' approach. The fourth *C* in effect permeates throughout the other *C*s, promoting CLIL as a key player in the plurilingual and pluricultural movement. It is therefore our responsibility to investigate the most accessible means through which our learners can work alongside other learners from different cultures and with different first languages. Shared learning experiences such as these go some way towards addressing fundamental issues of 'otherness' and 'self'. Integrating cultural opportunities into the CLIL classroom is not an option, it is a necessity. Intercultural experiences can be developed from different perspectives to make CLIL a 'lived-through' experience: for example, through the ethos of the classroom, through curriculum linking with other classes, through the content of the unit or through connections made with the wider world. As technology becomes more readily available and a feasible option for many schools, it is likely that such links may well involve a range of technologies.

Reflection points

- What different types of cultural implications are there for development in this topic?
- Can the content be adapted to make the cultural agenda more accessible?
- How do we actively involve the learners in developing their pluricultural understanding?
- What is the approach to CLIL culture in our school and beyond?
- What kind of curriculum links are available with other schools (regional, national, global)? How can these be best used?
- Where is the added value of studying this topic through the medium of another language? What opportunities arise?
- How does culture impact on the other Cs?

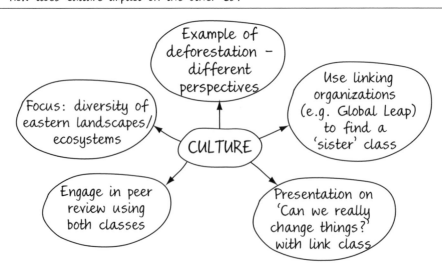

Stage 3 has focused on the construction of an overview of unit planning using a visual planning tool. It is unlikely that ready-made mind maps or published curriculum content lists will include the steps outlined in Stage 3. However, by constructing these maps, teachers 'own' the process. The time invested in such rigorous planning embeds CLIL pedagogies in classroom practice. The mapping process involves selecting appropriate questions – some easy and some difficult, some with answers and others without. The questions seek to move professional thinking forwards in a collaborative and supportive way. In other words, the mind-mapping process involves CLIL teachers in selecting and prioritizing *what* will be taught and *how* within the context of their own schools or institutions. Decisions sometimes result in potential opportunities being put aside to be reconsidered at another time. Other decisions are difficult to make. However, a sharp focus on which elements of the 4Cs most appropriately fit the global goals, the aims and objectives of the unit and the context in which it will be taught is crucial for overall effective planning and to ensure that learner progression over time is systemically reviewed. The 4Cs Framework can be adapted, changed and re-worked according to different contextual priorities. It is not a set formula. Readers may wish to refer to the complete set of questions in the Appendix to select items which best serve their contexts or add further questions of their own.

Stage 4: Preparing the unit

At the fourth stage, the mind map is transformed into materials, resources, tasks and activities. It involves bringing together good practice in non-CLIL settings with alternative approaches in order to match the demands of the teaching aims and outcomes determined by the unit. It involves the careful analysis of the map into a series of lessons based on the identified key elements. An example lesson plan is included in the Appendix. This stage is usually the most time-consuming. There are few ready-made materials which respond to the needs of context-specific units. Using materials designed for learning in non-CLIL contexts is potentially both linguistically and culturally problematic. In some countries, the textbook is the determinant of classroom practice. This is not so in CLIL (see Chapter 5 which deals with issues of materials and task design). Moreover, a *carte blanche* for materials can be overwhelming without appropriate support and time. Since innovation and change make demands on those involved, developing professional learning communities within and between institutions for sharing resources and ideas is a practical way forward. More CLIL digital networks are emerging and with them teacher support, materials banks and repositories.

It is also worth revisiting the role of what is arguably a teacher's most important resource: the use of questions. In CLIL environments, where cognition is integrated with learning and communication, teacher questioning, which encourages learner questioning, is fundamental to higher-order thinking skills, creativity and linguistic progression. We know that display questions are used in many classrooms: the teacher asks a question, the learner gives an answer and the teacher affirms or rejects the response, usually with a comment such as 'right', 'good', 'no'. We also know that this type of exchange limits communication. So, working with a range of question types for opening up communication in line

Figure 5: Habitats mind map

Global Goal: Encourage confident talk

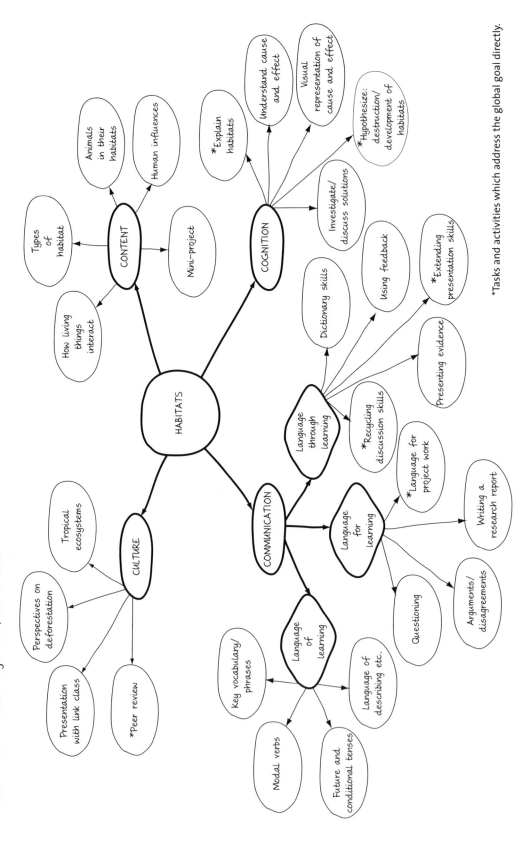

*Tasks and activities which address the global goal directly.

with the subject demands reminds us that CLIL is about effective classroom practice. However, the more demanding the questions, the more attention will be needed to ensure that learners can access the language needed to respond to and develop them. Perhaps the 'richest' tool for any CLIL teacher is asking learners the question 'why?', since a response activates a thread of simultaneous and integrated learning demands embedded in the 4Cs. More detailed discussion of issues relating to classroom discourse, tasks and activities are presented in the following chapter.

Reflection points

- Which materials/units are already available? How appropriate are they?
- Which resources need adapting and how?
- Which resources can be accessed via the Internet?
- Are there CLIL materials banks in our region? If not, how can we create them?
- How do we extend our repertoire of tasks and activities?
- Can we share lesson plan templates across institutions and contexts?
- What makes a good CLIL lesson?
- How can we ensure cohesion between our teaching aims and the learning outcomes?
- How can we plan for learner progression noting that, from a holistic view, students are not expected to develop across the 4Cs at the same rate (this will depend on the type of unit)?

Stage 5: Monitoring and evaluating CLIL in action

Monitoring the development of a unit and evaluating the processes and outcomes are integral to the teaching and learning process. This stage, however, is not about assessing student learning. Assessment is part of the learning cycle, but – due to its complex nature in CLIL – it will be explored in detail in Chapter 6. Stage 5, by contrast, focuses on understanding classroom processes as they evolve to gain insights which inform future planning. One of the greatest challenges for CLIL teachers is to develop a learning environment which is linguistically accessible whilst being cognitively demanding – one in which progression in both language and content learning develops systematically. The CLIL Matrix presented in Chapter 3 and based on Cummins' work (1984) is a tool which CLIL teachers find useful for 'measuring' and analysing the interconnectedness of cognitive and linguistic levels of tasks and materials used during a unit.

In the example at Figure 6, positioning tasks in appropriate quadrants illustrates how the CLIL Matrix can be used to monitor, sequence and scaffold learning. When tasks and activities are selected across a CLIL unit, a detailed picture emerges. The results provide CLIL teachers with a means to audit tasks and activities, to match these to their learners' needs and to monitor learning progression in terms of linguistic and cognitive development. Figure 6 audits four selected tasks over several lessons.

Figure 6: Auditing tasks using the CLIL Matrix (adapted from Cummins, 1984)

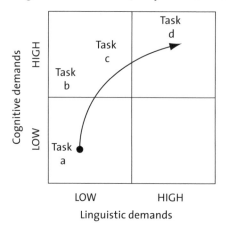

Linguistic demands

The tasks follow a route from low linguistic and cognitive demands to high linguistic and cognitive demands. Task (a) was aimed at instilling confidence in the learners by starting with familiar work as a point of reference. Task (b) used recycled language, but this task made cognitive demands on the learners by introducing abstract concepts whilst using visuals to scaffold the new knowledge. Task (c) continued to develop new knowledge, but this time the language demands involved extending familiar language into more complex structures required to carry out the activity. The final task (d) incorporated new language and new content where the learners were engaged in cooperative group work supported by technological and teacher mediation. The new language was practised in different ways.

The CLIL Matrix of course raises issues for discussion amongst teachers, such as what is meant by 'cognitively demanding' and 'linguistically accessible' in specific contexts. Other typical questions focus on how to make materials linguistically accessible, especially when concepts are challenging; which quadrants are desirable or acceptable and which are not; and how to progress from low to high linguistic demands whilst maintaining high levels of cognitive demand. Teachers have reported that the CLIL Matrix can reveal challenging information and unexpected gaps in support for learner progression.

Some teachers have also found it helpful to create their own unit checklists drawn from issues raised and prioritized in the unit mind map and CLIL Matrix task audit. An example of one such checklist is included in the Appendix. It was drawn up by a group of teachers from two schools working together on a CLIL unit. The teachers compiled the checklist by working through stages presented in this chapter. Whilst it could be argued that checklists have limitations, nonetheless, the processes involved in creating a unit checklist encourage reflection and discussion. Moreover, the checking process is part of monitoring learner progression in different ways (for example, through the 4Cs and the Matrix) and as such these tools provide essential understanding in a 'plan–do–review' reflective cycle. Examples of planning materials, including a lesson plan and teacher notes, are included in the Appendix.

> **Reflection points**
> - How can we monitor student progression in their learning?
> - What kind of formative and summative feedback tasks are built in?
> - Have we used the CLIL Matrix for a materials and task audit? Which quadrant and why?
> - Have we consulted learners about their progress and made it visible?
> - Have we built in times to revisit the unit mind map?

Stage 6: Next steps – Towards inquiry-based professional learning communities

To develop as CLIL professionals, to gain confidence, to explore the CLIL agenda, to take risks and move beyond the familiar, it is desirable that teachers belong to or build a professional learning community where everyone considers themselves as learners as well as teachers. Shulman (1999) goes further and suggests a model for pedagogical reasoning and action. This involves teachers sharing their own understanding of what is to be taught and learned, transforming ideas into 'teachable' and 'learnable' activities, connecting these with decisions about the optimal organization of the learning environment, followed by evaluation, reflection and new understandings for classroom teaching and learning. This mirrors the classroom learning cycle and supports teachers in asking questions about their own practice – isolated professionals rarely have these opportunities.

As the CLIL movement gains momentum, professional learning communities are also growing to meet emerging professional needs. The ease with which the Internet can connect CLIL professionals is rapidly increasing as more CLIL groups and individual teachers are networking for sharing ideas, materials and practice. However, for professional communities to be organic, they need to have a sense of purpose and involve a wide range of professionals in collaborative and innovative projects, as well as in supporting each other in a 'safe' environment:

> One of the most powerful resources that people in any organisation have for learning and improving is each other. Knowledge economies depend on collective intelligence and social capital – including ways of sharing and developing knowledge among fellow professionals. Sharing ideas and expertise, providing moral support when dealing with new and difficult challenges, discussing complex individual cases together – this is the essence of strong collegiality and the basis for professional communities.
>
> (Hargreaves, 2003: 84)

The following section gives an example of how one particular approach – LOCIT – has been successfully used by a range of teachers to provide a concrete way to share and discuss their classroom practice.

LOCIT: Lesson Observation and Critical Incident Technique

Sharing classroom practice in a forum which goes beyond materials preparation and learning outcomes involves CLIL teachers in constructing their own theories of practice. Over 30 years ago, Stenhouse noted: 'It is not enough that teachers' work should be studied: they need to study it themselves' (1975: 143). This still holds. The idea of teachers 'owning' their practice has permeated this chapter. It is particularly important in contexts where national curricula are prescriptive or the CLIL approach does not immediately fit with a government's pre-determined or traditional measures. Stage 6 is to do with sharing reflections on CLIL practice in order to move towards sharing inquiry-based practice. This reflects van Lier's belief that awareness-raising collaboration turns the classroom from 'a field of activity into a subject of enquiry [which] can promote deep and lasting changes in educational practice' (1996: 69).

In conjunction with the classroom research cycle – the 'plan–do–review' cycle referred to earlier in the chapter – a more recent contribution to the development of professional learning which involves inquiry-based practice is the Lesson Observation and Critical Incident Technique (LOCIT) process (Coyle, 2005). Used extensively with groups of CLIL teachers, LOCIT's overarching goal is to provide a framework for professional collaboration, confidence-building and theory development from a 'bottom-up' or practical perspective. The LOCIT process encourages teachers to work closely with each other to act as a supportive 'critical friend' – someone who is trusted to provide constructive feedback. LOCIT colleagues are 'buddies' – professionals who support and trust other professionals, who engage in supportive yet analytical dialogue.

So what is LOCIT?

LOCIT enables teachers to build up and share practice-based evidence of successful CLIL. The LOCIT process typically involves filming a whole lesson or series of lessons, editing the key 'learning moments' and comparing edited clips with learners and colleagues. The lesson selected for analysis is one chosen by the teachers or learners. When classroom learning is captured and discussed by teachers and learners together, it leads to shared understandings of learning which impact on practice. In other words, lessons are reviewed and analysed using the Critical Incident Technique (CIT) for reflection and in-depth, focused discussion. LOCIT involves listening to and working with learners and aims to give them a 'voice' to articulate their own learning. It defines and compares different 'learning moments' and above all it is positive and constructive. In the early stages of LOCIT, teachers often choose to record a lesson where they are confident that some good practice will be captured. In some cases a colleague observes the lesson, or the observation is carried out by a 'buddy' from a CLIL network school using video conferencing. It is also usual that the CLIL teacher will have an identified focus for developing CLIL learning in the classroom, such as exploring question techniques or encouraging learner talk.

Once a CLIL lesson has been recorded (LO), the next step is for participants to review, analyse and edit the film. The edited version of selected video clips must be no longer than 10–15 minutes. The objective of the analysis is to capture moments in a lesson when the teachers, colleagues and the learners consider that learning has taken place. The Critical Incident Technique (CIT) therefore guides the editing process of a particular lesson and first requires the editors (teacher, colleagues and/or students) to select small clips which in their view represent 'learning moments' in the lesson, often using agreed questions such as 'When did new learning occur in the lesson?', 'How did it happen?', 'Why did it happen?' Downloadable software can be used for editing purposes.

The CIT analysis demands reflection and discussion. For example, small groups of students can work on the lesson analysis in a technology lesson whilst improving their skills in using a digital editing tool. Alternatively, reviewing the lesson in small groups and describing the learning moments in a variety of ways, such as written descriptors, grids or oral reports, is also feasible. Whatever the medium, those involved in the LOCIT process need to select retrospective learning moments. In so doing, learners engage in shared reflections on what enables them to learn. Colleagues and researchers follow the same procedures.

The final stage is to compare the edited versions – either in class with students to encourage reflection and discussion about CLIL learning, or between colleagues/researchers, which tends to focus more on teaching. The edits act as a catalyst for deep discussions, comparisons and reflections on different aspects of CLIL practice. These discussions provide feedback which guides future planning and provides a forum for prioritizing classroom practice. In effect, these 'learning conversations' form the basis of an organic theory of practice – owned by teachers, learners and colleagues:

> Since all teachers have a theory of teaching, at least an implicit one, the first task of curricular renewal is to invite interested teachers to examine their own theory, making it explicit . . . and determine options for pedagogical action on its basis.
>
> (van Lier, 1996: 28)

Reflection points
- What methods can we use to evaluate what we have done and identify lessons learned?
- How can we feed into the next cycle what was successful and change what was not?
- Can we review progress with colleagues using LOCIT?
- How can we network and share materials with others?
- How can we network with other teachers and students outside our school?
- Where can we find more good ideas?
- How does this experience enable us to reflect on our own professional learning? What works well? What doesn't, and what must we do as a result?
- Are we constructing our own theory of practice? If so, can we talk it through?

In this chapter we have presented a series of tools which can be used and adapted for guiding CLIL practice: from the initial steps of sharing a vision to the planning, teaching and monitoring of learning and, to complete the cycle, a reflection of classroom events.

However, it is collaboration with other CLIL colleagues which feeds and supports our professional thinking and ideas. Professional learning communities where teachers can work together are fundamental to our work. The LOCIT process described above serves as a useful starting point for community building since sharing video clips is a tangible event. This sharing process starts well within an institution but begins to gain momentum when it connects teachers from a range of institutions, at different levels and from different subject orientations. CLIL science teachers have something to share with CLIL geography teachers or primary language teachers since the LOCIT clips do not focus on the subject itself, but at a deeper level on CLIL learning. Sharing ideas with evidence about how students of any age think they learn enables teachers to construct their own theories of practice – based on professional beliefs and practice-based evidence about how and why their students learn. Bringing CLIL teachers together in this way can lead to a deeper understanding of shared and individual practice – articulating what works and what doesn't in classrooms and why. Theories of practice are owned by the professionals who construct them and empower individuals as well as groups to take greater control of their own professional learning and to set realistic goals for the future. As one teacher who has experience of the LOCIT process explains:

> In my class, I think the pupils learn best by doing and experimenting, so I have to get them to use commentaries as they work. This means they have to talk about what they are doing and why and what they are learning. The thing is, they can only do that if I am there to support them by asking the right sort of questions. This is hard to organize but I think I am getting there. They are getting used to doing this in another language . . . [F]or CLIL to work, these pupils really need to talk about their learning, so that's what I'm working on.
>
> (quoted in Coyle, 2007)

As a postscript to this chapter we would like to reiterate that the ideas and suggestions are not meant to be interpreted as formulaic prescriptions for CLIL practice. Instead, they should stimulate debate and trigger ideas for individuals and groups to make sense of effective CLIL practice in their own settings, yet shared across CLIL communities and with other professionals – the focus is always on effective teaching and learning. As Wells concludes:

> By selecting which aspects of practice they [teachers] wish to problematise, and by critically examining recorded observational data, together with other evidence their students provide, they are taking charge of their own professional development.
>
> (Wells, 1999: 265)

References

Anderson, L. W. and Krathwohl, D. R. (eds.) (2001) *A Taxonomy for Learning, Teaching, and Assessing: A Revision of Bloom's Taxonomy of Educational Objectives*, New York: Longman.

Bloom, B. S. (ed.) (1956) *Taxonomy of Educational Objectives, Handbook I: Cognitive Domain*, New York: Longman.

Byram, M. (2008) *From Foreign Language Education to Education for Intercultural Citizenship. Essays and Reflections*, Clevedon: Multilingual Matters.

Commission of the European Communities (2008) *Multilingualism: An Asset for Europe and a Shared Commitment*, Brussels, [Online]. Available at: ec.europa.eu/education/languages/pdf/com/2008_0566_en.pdf [Accessed 16 February 2009].

Coyle, D. (2005) *Developing CLIL: Towards a Theory of Practice*, APAC Monograph 6, Barcelona: APAC.

Coyle, D. (2007) Unpublished data.

Cummins, J. (1984) *Bilingualism and Special Education: Issues in Assessment and Pedagogy*, Clevedon: Multilingual Matters.

Hargreaves, A. (2003) *Teaching in the Knowledge Society: Education in the Age of Insecurity*, Maidenhead: Open University Press.

O'Keeffe, A., McCarthy, M. and Carter R. (2007) *From Corpus to Classroom*, Cambridge: Cambridge University Press.

Papert, S. and Caperton, G. (1999) *Vision for Education: The Caperton Papert Platform*. Paper given at the 91st Annual National Governors' Association Meeting, [Online]. Available at: www.papert.org/articles/Vision_for_education.html [Accessed 13 March 2009].

Shulman, L. S. (1999) 'Knowledge and teaching: Foundations of the New Reform', in Leach, J. and Moon, R. E. (eds.) (1999) *Learners and Pedagogy*, London: Paul Chapman, pp61–77.

Stigler, J. W. and Hiebert, J. (1999) *The Teaching Gap*, New York: Free Press.

Stenhouse, L. (1975) *An Introduction to Curriculum Research and Development*, London: Heinemann.

van Lier, L. (1996) *Interaction in the Language Curriculum: Awareness, Autonomy and Authenticity*, New York: Longman.

Wells, G. (1999) *Dialogic Inquiry: Towards a Sociocultural Practice and Theory of Education*, Cambridge: Cambridge University Press.

Appendix
Creating a Tool Kit

The documents presented in this Appendix provide an illustration of the ways in which the Tool Kit is being used in practice by teachers. Chapter 4 provided a step-by-step guide which demonstrated how a series of questions (*reflection points*) can assist teachers in planning CLIL units of work. These questions can be selected from a pre-written battery of questions (such as that offered in this Appendix), or this battery of questions can be used to trigger new questions, all of which relate specifically to the opportunities and constraints that teachers work with in their own schools and institutions. The questions can then be used to create a more coherent overview of any unit of work built on the fundamental principles which underpin effective CLIL pedagogies. It is strongly recommended that the questions are used in conjunction with other tools suggested throughout the book, such as the 4Cs Framework, the Language Triptych, task-design principles and the CLIL Matrix. Used together, the tools can assist teachers and other planners in constructing their Tool Kit. Visual representations, such as mind maps for CLIL, can be used to guide CLIL implementation, ranging from curriculum design or evaluation to individual lesson planning and assessment.

Effective CLIL planning as conceptualized in this book is an iterative process. CLIL theories and practices are developing as the professional community evolves. It is for this reason that we do not see the tools as fixed and prescriptive, but recommend that groups of teachers use and adapt them for their own purposes. The ideas presented here have emerged from working with teachers as practitioners, as learners and as researchers.

The five items in this Appendix illustrate the CLIL planning process. Item **A: Six stages for reflection** presents the reader with the full battery of questions which were constructed in the *reflection points* in Chapter 4. It is from this list that teachers and planners are encouraged to select relevant questions for consideration which match their needs. Item **B: CLIL mind map** is based on a similar set of questions relating to planning a unit on *Ecosystems* for primary-level learners. This mind map was then used to plan a series of lessons with additional notes for teachers, exemplified in items **C: CLIL lesson plan** and **D: CLIL lesson plan – Teachers' notes** (these have been adapted from planning materials designed by Florià Belinchón Majoral, available at http://www.xtec.cat/cirel/pla_le/ nottingham/floria_belinchon/index.htm). The final item in the Appendix, **E: Unit checklist**, was compiled by a group of CLIL teachers to evaluate their classroom practice. The checklist is based on the group's plan for a specific unit, and it provides an example which other teachers may find useful.

A: Six stages for reflection

		SIX STAGES FOR REFLECTION Selecting key questions for generating our own Tool Kit	
PLAN	**Stage 1: VISION** Constructing and owning a CLIL vision: our global goals.	· Who are the key players needed to form a CLIL teaching team? · How can we communicate and share our ideas? · Do we have a shared vision for CLIL? If so, what is it? If not, how shall we construct one? · What is our ideal CLIL classroom and what goes on there? · In an ideal setting, what do we want our CLIL learners and teachers to be able to achieve? · Have we achieved a vision which is 'owned' by the group and which prioritizes different elements of our vision? (i.e. What are our global goals?)	
	Stage 2: CONTEXT Our school, our learners, our community. Situating the vision in our own context: our own model for CLIL.	· How can we as teachers share our ideas and skills? · Is there leadership support for CLIL? What are the implications of the support? · Who is involved in the teaching and the learning? Subject teachers? Language teachers? General teachers? Assistants? All of these? · What are the implications of the above for constructing our own CLIL model? (e.g. Which subjects, themes, topics and languages? Which learners, classes?) · What are the implications of the above for less capable learners? · Does our CLIL programme have a dominant language, subject or citizenship orientation or are these integrated? What are the implications? · How do our global goals impact on our CLIL model? · How do we involve the wider community, such as parents, carers and significant others? · Have we agreed on contextual opportunities and constraints?	
	Stage 3: UNIT PLANNING Using the 4Cs to guide planning a unit of work. Creating our mind map.	Step 1. Considering content · Is there a choice of content? If so, which is the most appropriate for our CLIL setting? · Do we have to use an existing syllabus or curriculum? · How will we select new knowledge, skills and understanding of the theme to teach? · What will the students learn? (i.e. What are the learning outcomes?) · Is progression in learning taken into account? · Do we have to prioritize the content to be included? · How does the content develop our global goal(s)?	

Step 2. Connecting content and cognition

- Use a taxonomy of thinking skills such as Bloom's (1956) or Anderson and Krathwohl's (2001) for reference (refer to Chapter 3). Which cognitive skills seem to be most appropriate for development in terms of content?
- Are we encouraging the use of higher-order thinking (HOTS) such as hypothesizing and problem solving as well as lower-order thinking (LOTS) such as remembering, understanding and applying new knowledge?
- Which activities or task types are likely to encourage the development of these skills?
- How do we deal with the linguistic demands of these tasks to ensure linguistic progression?
- What kind of questions must we ask in order to go beyond 'display' questions and present students with challenging problem-solving, hypothesizing, analysing and evaluation tasks?
- What kind of questions do we want our learners to ask?
- Have students been given opportunities to discuss their new knowledge and understanding?
- How do we know what students have learned? How are our formative assessment tasks used to inform further learning?
- How does/do our global goal(s) fit with developing cognition?

Step 3. Communication – Defining language learning and using

Language of learning

- What type of language (genre) does this subject or theme use? How shall we ensure learners have access to this?
- Define the content-obligatory language, such as key words, phrases and grammatical demands of the unit (e.g. the language of discussing, hypothesizing, analysing). How is this introduced and practised?
- What kind of talk do learners need to engage in and how do we build in progression over time? (e.g. The extension of the language of discussion over several lessons.)
- What is the most effective way of teaching the language of learning? (e.g. Specific tasks, content-embedded practice, grammar rules.)
- Which of the identified language and skills shall we target for development in this particular unit?

Language for learning
- What kind of language do learners need in order to operate effectively in this CLIL unit?
- What are the possible language demands of typical tasks and classroom activities? (e.g. How to work in groups, organize research.)
- How will these be taught?
- Which language skills will need to be developed?
- How are we developing metacognitive strategies? (Learning how to learn – e.g. reading strategies, comprehension strategies.)
- How can learning be scaffolded (supported) by the teaching and learning of specific language? (e.g. Language used to seek additional information, assistance, explanation and access to other sources.)
- How do students practise their new language and recycle familiar language?
- Have we prioritized the language for learning in this unit in relation to the content? (i.e. What students need to know at each stage of the content – e.g. focus on developing reasoning, making a case.)
- Is the language which is used to assess the learning accessible to the learners?

Language through learning
- What necessary language functions and notions do the students know already? How can these be practised and extended?
- What strategies can our learners use to access new language for themselves?
- When new language emerges, how shall we capture and select language for further development?
- How can we define language progression in this unit?

Step 4. Developing cultural awareness and opportunities
- What different types of cultural implications are there for development in this topic?
- Can the content be adapted to make the cultural agenda more accessible?
- How do we actively involve the learners in developing their pluricultural understanding?
- What is the approach to CLIL culture in our school and beyond?
- What kind of curriculum links are available with other schools (regional, national, global)? How can these be best used?

		· Where is the added value of studying this topic through the medium of another language? What opportunities arise? · How does culture impact on the other Cs?
	Stage 4: PREPARATION Questions to steer the design of appropriate materials and tasks.	· Which materials/units are already available? How appropriate are they? · Which resources need adapting and how? · Which resources can be accessed via the Internet? · Are there CLIL materials banks in our region? If not, how can we create them? · How do we extend our repertoire of tasks and activities? · Can we share lesson plan templates across institutions and contexts? · What makes a good CLIL lesson? · How can we ensure cohesion between our teaching aims and the learning outcomes? · How can we plan for learner progression noting that, from a holistic view, students are not expected to develop across the 4Cs at the same rate (this will depend on the type of unit)?
DO	**Stage 5: MONITORING AND EVALUATING** Questions which assist in monitoring learner progress and evaluating the effectiveness of classroom practice.	· How can we monitor student progression in their learning? · What kind of formative and summative feedback tasks are built in? · Have we used the CLIL Matrix for a materials and task audit? Which quadrant and why? · Have we consulted learners about their progress and made it visible? · Have we built in times to revisit the unit mind map?
REVIEW	**Stage 6: REFLECTION AND INQUIRY** Creating opportunities for classroom inquiry and reflection which promote ownership of a theory of CLIL practice.	· What methods can we use to evaluate what we have done and identify lessons learned? · How can we feed into the next cycle what was successful and change what was not? · Can we review progress with colleagues using LOCIT? · How can we network and share materials with others? · How can we network with other teachers and students outside our school? · Where can we find more good ideas? · How does this experience enable us to reflect on our own professional learning? What works well? What doesn't, and what must we do as a result? · Are we constructing our own theory of practice? If so, can we talk it through?

B: CLIL mind map

- Global Goal: Develop spontaneous classroom talk
- Unit Title: Ecosystems

ECOSYSTEMS

CONTENT
- What are ecosystems?
- Interaction between living things
- Types of ecosystem
- What ecosystems are made up of
- The food chain
- Recycling
- Human influence
- Global warming

COGNITION
- Understanding
  - Concept of global warming
  - How living things interact
  - Distinguishing habitats
  - Experiments/posters
- Doing
  - Classroom/online games
- Playing
- Identifying
  - Main habitats
  - Food interactions
- Assessing
  - Self-assessment
  - Group work
  - Project
- Learning
  - Preserving the planet is important
  - Recycling is important

CULTURE
- Pollution/deforestation
- Special ecosystems
- Landscapes from around the world

COMMUNICATION
- Language through learning
  - New expressions
  - New vocabulary
  - Questioning/answering
- Language for learning
  - Describing a chain/landscape
  - Giving advice
  - Comparing/contrasting
  - Superlative
- Language of learning
  - Key vocabulary
    - Ecosystems
    - Landscapes
    - Animals
    - Recycling
    - Types of food

C: CLIL lesson plan

GLOBAL GOAL: Develop spontaneous talk

UNIT 1   **WHAT ARE ECOSYSTEMS?**

LEVEL   4th grade   TIMING   2 lessons

Aims
• To present the content of the unit. • To introduce the concept of *Ecosystem* and its main features. • To make learners aware of and build on prior knowledge of ecosystems and living things. • To help learners understand that learning can be achieved in a second language. • To help learners understand that keeping a record of new words is important (their very own 'top ten word chart').

Criteria for assessment
Teacher, peer- and self-assessment processes will be used to assess how well learners: • understand ecosystems • distinguish between different types of ecosystems • recognize and classify living things • identify how animals adapt • construct and use a **KWL** chart (*what I know, what I want to know, what I learned*) • contribute to and use the classroom vocabulary chart.

TEACHING OBJECTIVES (*What I plan to teach*)	
Content	**Cognition**
• Introduction of the topic. • What ecosystems are. • Features of ecosystems. • Animal adaptation.	• Provide learners with opportunities to understand the key concepts and apply them in different contexts. • Enable learners to identify living things in specific ecosystems. • Encourage knowledge transfer about living things and predictions using visual images. • Vocabulary building, learning and using. • Arouse learner curiosity – creative use of language and learner questions.
Culture	
• Identify living and non-living things from the ecosystems of their own country and other countries. • Become aware of the importance of respecting the environment (especially the fact of wasting too much water). • Understand that they can learn, no matter which language they are using.	

Communication

Language *of* learning	Language *for* learning	Language *through* learning
• Key vocabulary: *plants, ecosystem, living things, non-living things, pond, savannah, grass, bushes, dry places, wet places, animal adaptation . . .*	• Asking each other questions: *What do you know about . . . ? Can you tell me something about . . . ?* • Classifying: *The different elements/animals in an ecosystem are . . .* • Comparing and contrasting: *The animals living in a savannah are bigger than the ones living in a pond.* • Other: *How do you spell . . . ?* *What does . . . mean?*	• Distinguish language needed to carry out activities. • Retain language revised by both the teacher and learners. • Make use of peer explanations. • Record, predict and learn new words which arise from activities.

LEARNING OUTCOMES
(What learners will be able to do by the end of the lessons)

By the end of the unit learners will be able to:
• demonstrate understanding of the concept of ecosystems and its related features
• distinguish between living things and non-living things
• demonstrate that ecosystems include the places and the living things that inhabit them
• describe how and why animals adapt
• classify information
• successfully engage in visual matching between concepts and images
• interpret visual information
• use language creatively
• ask and respond to *wh-* questions about their work
• use a class vocabulary record of new words.

D: CLIL lesson plan – Teachers' notes

UNIT 1   **WHAT ARE ECOSYSTEMS?**   Lessons 1 and 2

TEACHING/LEARNING ACTIVITIES

Lesson 1
- **Warm up:** Let's think (PowerPoint). General overview of the unit.
- **Previous knowledge:** Starting a KWL chart. Learners see and listen to different features of animals.
- **Game:** In order to check their comprehension, learners play a challenging game called 'I bet it's true!'.
- **Ending the lesson:** Learners think about animals that might live in dry/cool places.
- **Glossary:** Time to think about new words which learners don't know. One of the learners writes down (on a poster) which words they decided to choose.

Lesson 2
- **Starting routine:** What can you remember? Questions:
  Does an elephant live in the same place as a polar bear?
  Can a red rose live in a desert?
  Do all animals eat the same things?
- **Whole class:** Ecosystems.
- **Handout:** Classify living and non-living things. Handout (speaking and writing activity) + pair work.
- **Thinking activity:** Big and small ecosystems. Learners have to decide (with the help of a handout) where some animals live. They speak to a partner, and then they classify habitats and pictures. After that, the teacher checks their comprehension.
- **Thinking activity:** The teacher asks 'How do you think animals adapt to their ecosystems?' Learners play a matching game. Then the teacher writes down the correct matches. Learners copy them into their notebook.
- **Ending the lesson. Glossary:** Time to think about new words which learners don't know. One of the learners writes down (on a poster) which words they chose.
- **Self-assessment.**

INSTRUMENTS FOR ASSESSMENT

- Teacher monitors group and individual activities.
- Learners successfully play a matching game.
- Learners' interaction with a partner (speaking creatively).
- Learners' participation in all tasks and activities.
- Learners complete information gaps.
- Learners complete a self-assessment sheet.

SCAFFOLDING TIPS

The focus of the unit is on language:

Language for the teacher	**Language for the learner**
✓ Settle down quickly please, let's get started.	✓ I think they can live in the same ecosystem, because . . .
✓ Let's just recap on what we did the other day.	✓ I don't think so, because . . .
✓ What do you know about . . . ?	✓ I don't know . . .
✓ Can you tell me something about . . . ?	✓ Can you help us?
✓ Read out loud.	✓ In an ecosystem, there are living things like . . .
✓ Don't forget to write a note about the information your partner gives you.	
✓ Don't panic.	
✓ Find a partner to work with.	
✓ Is that clear?	
✓ You've worked well today. Good.	

RESOURCES

• Computer, projector and whiteboard.
• Worksheets.
• Pens and whiteboard.

NOTES

If this is the first time learners are experiencing the Ecosystems unit in English, teachers need to focus on learner confidence-building, enjoyment and a sense of achievement. Whilst individual outcomes will vary, providing a range of scaffolded learning tools will encourage learner participation and engagement. For example, take time to explain how the dictionary works.

E: Unit checklist

CLIL Unit Checklist

CLIL Theme ....   Date ....
Unit of Work ....   Class ....

Clarifying global goals, teaching aims and learning outcomes
- ☐   Are the global goals (vision) embedded in the unit planning?
- ☐   Are the teaching aims clear?
- ☐   Are the learning outcomes defined? Which ones can be measured? How?

Content
- ☐   Have I considered how to scaffold content learning?
- ☐   Are my presentations of new content clear?
- ☐   Is the content accessible?

Language/Communication
- ☐   Are the students involved in *using* language?
- ☐   Are students involved in *learning* language? Are there adequate opportunities for them to practise the new language structures?
- ☐   Are my instructions clear?
- ☐   Are the questions I ask at the appropriate level? Do the questions relate to the cognitive demands?
- ☐   Have the students got adequate vocabulary/language to answer my questions?
- ☐   Are my presentations of new concepts clear?
- ☐   Have I planned language *of* learning?
- ☐   Have I planned language *for* learning?

Cognition/Thinking
- ☐   Are the questions/problems to be solved at the appropriate cognitive level?
- ☐   Have I considered how I can ensure that the learners progress cognitively, and how I can measure this progress?
- ☐   Are there ways to assist learners in developing a range of strategies through the CLIL language?

Culture
- ☐   Have I thought about the contribution that this unit makes to changing classroom culture (e.g. from arguing or not taking account of others' views to listening and managing differences of opinions)?
- ☐   Have I considered how the theme of this unit can promote awareness of cultural difference/global citizenship?
- ☐   Have I identified opportunities that are now available for me to develop a pluricultural perspective on what I am teaching because I am using the medium of another language?
- ☐   Have I identified opportunities in this unit which encourage curriculum links? Can we communicate with and work alongside learners from other countries?

Activities
- ☐ Do the tasks designed relate to the global goals, aims and outcomes in terms of the 4Cs?
- ☐ Is progression built into language and content tasks?
- ☐ Do the activities help to develop talk for learning?
- ☐ Have I considered which language is needed to carry out each activity?
- ☐ Is this an initial/progress/summary/assessment activity?

Supporting learning
- ☐ Are there adequate opportunities for students to engage in practical activities to experience CLIL?
- ☐ Have I identified which type of teacher scaffolding is needed to support language and learning?
- ☐ Have I analysed the content and cognition for potential difficulties?
- ☐ Have I recycled new language from previous units to support learner progression?

Assessment
- ☐ Have I considered how the learners will know what they have learnt?
- ☐ Have I considered how I will know what they have learnt?
- ☐ Have I decided what to assess during the unit to ensure that feedback informs further learning?
- ☐ Do I know what my choices are in terms of what I will assess?
- ☐ Do I know what kind of formative and summative assessment tasks I will need?

Reflection
- ☐ Is there variety (groups, pairs)?
- ☐ Have I allocated enough time?
- ☐ Have I thought about what I might change in this unit?
- ☐ Have I thought about what I might add to or leave out from this unit?
- ☐ How can I collect students' views about this unit? And act on them?

5 Evaluating and creating materials and tasks for CLIL classrooms

Chapters 3 and 4 outlined the ways in which a teacher might visualize a unit of work and individual lessons, using a planning framework based around the 4Cs approach and considering language in three categories: the language *of* learning, the language *for* learning and the language *through* learning. This chapter explores the ways in which a teacher might assemble materials and tasks in an integrated way to create stimulating and effective CLIL lessons and units, and why such methods are likely to succeed.

It is important to remember that there is no single CLIL pedagogy. Accepted effective-practice pedagogies associated with individual subjects should offer the best approaches also for CLIL contexts, although, as the chapter will show, teachers will need to adapt their focus to meet the specific demands of the language dynamic. Nevertheless, the successful teaching strategies and devices which are proven to underpin learning in each content teacher's repertoire should still be the starting point for all CLIL course plans. Language-teaching pedagogy by itself tends not to be appropriate for CLIL courses, although language teachers' awareness of how learners learn is, of course, invaluable. When a good teacher begins to develop a unit on, for example, the lives of children in poverty, simultaneous equations or the use of tools in the technology workshop, that teacher will have a set of guiding principles about the nature of the learning experiences and the outcomes expected. This will include resources, activities and activity/task styles, teacher and student roles, classroom ethos, and means of assessment. When the teacher begins to plan units such as the above as part of a CLIL programme, these initial guiding principles should be the same.

This chapter will address the issues in the following way. Firstly, we will explore the factors which should be taken into account when materials are being evaluated or created. In contrast to the vast English language teaching coursebook and resource market, there are very few ready-made CLIL materials available, and so 'evaluation' is more appropriately linked to selecting and modifying texts (of all types) and tasks, largely from authentic internet sources, and this will feature in the next section of the chapter. We need, of course, to consider *text* separately from *task*, as both have individual crucial features, and this will be explored as part of this second section. Finally, we will examine issues around teacher creation of CLIL materials 'from scratch'.

5.1 Factors influencing materials and task evaluation and design

CLIL teachers in the early stage of course development often comment on a shortage of ready-made resources and a consequent need both to find and to create learning materials. It is important that, when teachers seek the materials which will shape their course, they have an underpinning curricular philosophy in mind. Some researchers, such as Shkedi (1998), maintain that curriculum design is not the same as materials design and can be seen as a remote, more theoretical activity which does not influence teachers. However, the 4Cs Framework and the CLIL Tool Kit outlined in Chapters 3 and 4 can be seen to act in this curriculum-forming role. Schwartz maintains that '[t]he focus of curriculum-writing should be shifted away from directing the students, and towards engaging, and even educating, teachers' (2006: 452). A CLIL curriculum is currently often created along with the materials which deliver it, and in such cases the divide mentioned by Shkedi (1998) does not exist. But where curriculum writers are shaping materials, it is vital that practice guidelines are also included which clearly address the learning intentions of the materials.

In the world of language teaching, especially in TESOL, materials design is a much discussed area (see for example, McGrath, 2002; Richards, 2001; Tomlinson, 2003). The danger for CLIL is that a conventional TESOL approach to materials development could focus attention only on linguistic, rather than on both content and linguistic, aspects of courses, modules and units. McGrath (2002) proposes that materials design should be subject to a continuous review process, as use will always determine how appropriate the materials are for different contexts and groups of learners. As CLIL contexts are often currently both new and specific, the need for such a process is clear. The focus in the McGrath book (ibid.) tends to be on the teacher's control of the process that follows the location of a potential resource. He suggests that this runs from evaluation – which constitutes both first-glance and close evaluation – through a series of broad steps, including adaptation for teaching, supplementation (with other materials), getting learners involved and, finally, evaluating effects.

In a CLIL classroom and in CLIL medium-term planning we need to focus equally on how the students *meet* the content subject (the input) and *what they do* while learning (how they *process* the input). The design process involving what is needed to meet content-subject concepts is especially skilled in CLIL lesson preparation, but so is the task design which steers how this material is processed and how understanding is expressed (the output). CLIL materials designers will naturally consider any constraints associated with aspects of the target content or with the language which accompanies it, but in this chapter we suggest that there should also be a focus on: student and teacher roles, affective factors (which relate to feelings and emotions, such as anxiety and motivation) and cognitive factors. These other perspectives also bring a deeper emphasis on good task and materials evaluation and design. The next section will briefly consider why these elements are important for learning and teaching generally and therefore also for task design.

Student and teacher roles

The respective roles of the teachers and students are central to CLIL, because its very nature tends to demand more student-centred approaches. Students regularly acknowledge that CLIL courses are difficult, especially at the beginning (see Chapter 7). Moreover, it is certain that engaging with and learning appropriately cognitively challenging content through another language requires a depth of processing which cannot be attained when the teacher is simply in transmission mode. Therefore, successful CLIL modules have often included a great amount of paired work, group work and cooperative learning techniques such as jigsaw tasks. Many move progressively through a unit to a group research/presentation task, perhaps centred on a **webquest**.

> **Webquests** are tasks designed to be undertaken by groups of learners. They involve working to a brief to collate material from the Internet and other sources and then to present findings to other learners. See http://webquest.org/index.php for more information.

Science units often focus on investigations, because they require students to talk, compare and contrast, discuss and draw conclusions – initially orally and then in written formats. The importance of designing multi-stage and multi-layered tasks which enhance the active role of the student seems clear.

The need to develop skills such as analysis, contextualization and metacognition are not, then, just items taken from a remote curriculum designer – they are integral to successful learning in a CLIL context, because of the increased demands made by that context. The fact that these demands exist means that it is all the more important to attend to both affective and cognitive issues when designing and evaluating tasks and materials. Although we want to challenge CLIL learners through the use of cognition objectives within the 4Cs structure, at the same time we must ensure that the challenge does not lead to anxiety and reduced motivation.

Affective factors: Motivation and anxiety

Motivation is a key theme for language learning. Dörnyei and co-authors alone have published over 20 articles, chapters and books on the subject since the millennium (for example, Dörnyei, 2001a; Dörnyei, 2001b; Dörnyei and Csizér, 2002). Why is it so important and how relevant is this for CLIL classrooms?

It is not contentious to state that considerable concentration, effort and willpower are needed to learn another language effectively. Both noticing and attention are key components of the required processes. As motivation sits on a higher affective and mental level than these components, it is a necessary prerequisite for them. Without it they will be absent. Motivation can stem from **integrative** or **instrumental** origins (Dörnyei, 2001b), or simply arise from an interest in the subject area or as a response to a challenge, as we see in this quotation from a CLIL learner:

When you do geography in French it's harder because you have to concentrate more, but then you learn it better.

(Hood, 2006)

> **Integrative motivation** is linked to a desire to have contact with the culture and speakers of a country which uses the target language. It is a more *intrinsic* form of motivation.
> **Instrumental motivation** is linked to a success framework – for example, passing an examination to please a parent, or gaining a better paid job. This is a more *extrinsic* form of motivation.

Dörnyei (2001a: 29) illustrates the importance of maintaining and protecting motivation through classroom practice in a complex diagram which notes how many features teachers need to keep in mind. One aspect of fostering motivation is the encouragement of positive retrospective self-evaluation as part of a focus on dynamic continual development, whereby goals are set, reviewed and progress noted. Creating tasks which support this process is essential. In a CLIL classroom, we may feel that learning goals (personalized to each learner and non-competitive) have a greater role than performance goals (measurement against a norm), as noted by Grant and Dweck (2003). This focus will lead to the design of more collaborative tasks and formative assessment (see Chapter 6 for more discussion). Fixed-entity and incremental views of intelligence (Blackwell, Trzesniewski and Dweck, 2007) divide learner attitudes towards personal potential into a 'fixed mode' (where learners believe they can do nothing to alter their capabilities) and a 'developmental mode' (where the belief is that they can work towards self-improvement). Clearly the former self-image could be an additional barrier in a CLIL context, where the work is probably 'harder' than usual and where this may be an 'across the board' judgment on personal capability. On the other hand, the 'double-subject' effect of CLIL may make this less influential. Some learners who have a more negative attitude towards either the content subject or the language may have greater motivation towards the other subject and through this may improve their attitude towards the less-liked element. Thus, having a combination of a content subject and a language may create a more flexible self-view.

Anxiety is another important feature often discussed in language learning, perhaps because of the performative aspect of language classrooms. Oxford's contention that '[o]nce language anxiety has evolved into a lasting trait it can have pervasive effects on language learning and language performance' (1999: 60) makes it clear that we are dealing with a construct as important as motivation. Horwitz (2001) points out that anxiety can be related to classroom climate and/or to the instructional conditions; for example, that speaking tasks may cause more anxiety than reading tasks. MacIntyre and Gardner (1994, reported in Onwuegbuzie, Bailey and Daley, 2000) propose that anxiety occurs at input, processing and output stages of language learning and so takes different forms – for example, worry about the speed of delivery of the target language, the presence of new vocabulary or the need to speak in front of others. Dörnyei (2001a) states that anxiety-reduction is something which should take place alongside the cultivation of a positive classroom climate and should therefore be considered at every step, including, by implication, task-level. He summarizes his advice with the following basic strategies:

- Avoid social comparison, even in its subtle forms.
- Promote cooperation instead of competition.
- Help learners to accept the fact that they will make mistakes as part of the learning process.
- Make test and assessment completely 'transparent' and involve students in the negotiation of the final mark.

(Dörnyei, 2001a: 94)

We will consider this final point as part of good practice in testing and assessment in Chapter 6.

Cognition

In McLaughlin's (1987) information processing model, controlled processing of new material requires much attentional control, and is limited by short-term memory. Through repeated activation sequences, processing then becomes automatic and thus restructuring of the linguistic system occurs, because learning has taken place. This could be seen in a narrow way to underpin audio-lingual, drill-based learning, but Hulstijn (1990) and McLaughlin, Rossman and McLeod (1983) suggest that *incidental* learning may occur when peripheral, rather than focal, attention is given to an aspect of a task – the way young children focus on communication but learn first-language grammar rules as a 'by-product' of this communication is an example of this. On the other hand, *intentional* learning requires focal attention.

Language learning as part of a CLIL curriculum results from a more peripheral attentional focus (that is, where the main focus is on the content of the unit and not on a language-learning objective *per se*). If this is so, we need to be very careful in our task design to create both the repeated activation sequences and the overriding and convincing purpose generated through the content-oriented tasks. This is something which has already been mentioned in Chapter 3 with reference to the spiral of language progression (Figure 2), and which we develop here to show the role of the content subject in this progression. Learning and neural networks is an area which is currently the focus of much research, and here again the notion of activation sequences comes to the surface:

... the information-processing abilities of biological neural systems must follow from highly parallel processes operating on representations that are distributed over many neurons.

(Mitchell, 1997: 82)

Westhoff also concurs, writing specifically about a CLIL context:

According to . . . connectionist theory, our brain keeps track of the regularities in the occurrence of combinations and of the frequency of these combinations. The frequency determines the 'weight' of the established connections between the features. This 'weight' accounts for the ease of activation . . .

(Westhoff, 2004: 60)

He makes the analogy with tasks which mirror authentic communicative situations and have a purpose, thereby involving multi-faceted processing. He concludes:

And finally, the richer in variety the features that are manipulated mentally, the more entrances to the emerging neural network will be created, which will make activation under different circumstances easier.

(Westhoff, 2004: 61)

Clearly, when we select or design materials, we need to visualize how – in terms of language – they present the essential content in a manageable way. As we lay out the tasks which accompany the stimulus materials, we need to consider whether they are formulated around real purposes, such as comparisons, decisions and conclusions. These processes should be organised so that the key language is repeated – but by using it for these real purposes and not just for the sake of repetition. The use of several parallel pathways should secure both conceptual and language learning.

We will end this section by considering the role of task design as it interacts with the language elements of the materials from the perspective of 'comprehensible input' (Krashen, 1981). Language specialists will already be familiar with this term and the debate around the relative importance for language development of input and output. We can summarize the implications for CLIL here.

Krashen (1981) considered comprehensible input to be crucial to language acquisition and so to the development of language competence. The purpose of more formal language learning was to act as a monitor during the output process to check that the language produced by the more natural acquisition process was accurate. His view of comprehensible input echoes the practice (typical of CLIL approaches) of using a whole range of linked stimuli, while also activating prior knowledge, so as to maximize comprehension of stimulus sources. The need for authentic messages to be involved is of course more than met by a CLIL context. He also believed that the input should be at a language level which he called 'i+1' (that is, just above the current language competence level). This echoes the need to review whether or not language is over-familiar and untaxing or whether it contains new linguistic items but still remains accessible. On the other hand, Swain (1996) considered that output was more important, as learners developed their language competence by being required to express their understanding. She found that in the Canadian immersion schools learners developed excellent comprehension, but lacked the grammatical knowledge to be fluent and accurate users of the language. So comprehensible input was not enough to develop language skills – the 'monitor effect' was also necessary, which was activated as understanding was expressed.

What we gain from a consideration of both of these standpoints is that we need to look not just at the content, accessibility and comprehensibility of the *input material*, but also at our *task design*. The nature of the task we set will determine how students make sense of the material and how they express that understanding.

5.2 Evaluating, assembling and modifying materials

At the beginning of this chapter, we discussed how CLIL teachers should stay true to their instincts as content teachers in terms of having a guiding methodology which is appropriate for that subject. History teachers, for example, naturally use a range of sources to expose students to the concepts both of the historical period under study and to the parameters and nature of history as a subject discipline; and science teachers use the experience gained through conducting experiments to raise questions and indicate methods of finding solutions. CLIL teachers must allow the subject to emerge in the same ways as it usually would despite the role of the other language. Pre-teaching of specific language in 'language teacher mode' is often not best practice. But what will be different is how the teacher sees the interaction of language with the content–cognition dynamic. The 4Cs Framework could be applied equally to first-language instruction as it reflects ways to plan effective teaching to enable effective learning and, as such, is not just a model for CLIL contexts. Following this logic, we can say that every good lesson requires learners to think while engaging with either previously learned or new content. Every good lesson uses language (although often this is the first language of a majority of the class) in a deliberate way to mediate that engagement. The learning process in classrooms is generally always structured in advance by the teacher through the choice and use of resources and can very often be divided into the sub-stages of meeting input, processing input (thinking) and producing a response. Each of these sub-stages needs to be considered in turn in relation to how this affects the choice or design of materials and tasks for learning and what the special implications are for a CLIL context.

Meeting input

In normally structured classrooms, learners meet the lesson content through hearing or seeing some kind of text (in the widest sense of that word – see Figure 8 on page 97 for examples of different text types) and they may be receptive or active whilst doing this. It is worth reflecting at this point about how we as teachers usually begin teaching a unit. Some examples of approaches might be:

- Start with visuals / real objects and brainstorm existing knowledge.
- Start with an activity which raises awareness and sets questions.
- Start with a presentation which introduces concepts and language (think also about the respective role and importance of the texts in the presentation, and of the teacher talk which accompanies these).
- Start with a linear text which introduces the ideas.
- Start with a set of questions.

When we find a text to use in a CLIL unit we need to consider it from different viewpoints, including:

- the focus of the 'message' (is it the content you want?)
- the clarity of the 'message' (is it expressed in an accessible way?)
- the mix of textual styles for presentation (does it have visuals, tables, diagrams, graphics as well as text which can be heard or read, including bulleted and continuous prose?)
- the level of subject-specific specialist vocabulary (is it the right amount and are they the right words?)
- the level of general vocabulary (are there complex words which are not necessary?)
- the level of grammatical/syntactical complexity (are the phrases and sentences too complicated and/or is the use of grammar more complex than is needed?)
- the clarity of the thread of thinking (is this overt? is inference or integration needed?).

The Internet is clearly a valuable source of material. Take, for example, the theme of photosynthesis, which can be studied at a lower or higher level. Sites such as Farabee's online *Biology Book*, and Watson's photosynthesis site (see list of references at the end of this chapter for links to both of these sites) both have a range of material, both textual and diagrammatic, with either objectives or in-built questions and further links. A teacher finding material such as this has to make choices about what to select, how to combine it, which order to use it in, and how to target different ability levels with different elements. She or he may still need to modify some sections of text which may be too advanced for learners, but there will be little need to create completely different material.

However, with other less commonly taught topics there may be difficulties in finding material, or it may be at a higher level and in more complex continuous text format. In such cases, the last four points of the checklist given above will take on a strong importance and there will almost certainly be a need to modify text, perhaps into bullet points or tabular form (see Figure 8). To give an example: a secondary-school history teacher who is planning a unit on Britain in Roman times for students who have been learning English for two to three years might look at an encyclopaedia such as *Encarta*. Here, she or he would find mainly continuous text which could be organized partly as a timeline to show major developments and partly as bullet points. But the teacher may want to use some continuous text as well, and the following extract is annotated to show how the original text could be modified for the CLIL lesson:

> Hadrian's **sojourn** in Britain **seems to have added considerable impetus** to urban life. During his reign a **vast** new basilica, perhaps modelled on the Basilica Ulpia in Rome, was constructed in London. Other towns **were similarly endowed**, notably Wroxeter, the capital of the Cornovii, where the dedicatory inscription dated AD 130 survives. The cities of the 2nd

> century had other public buildings such as baths (**best preserved** at Wroxeter and Leicester), amphitheatres (**such as that to be seen outside** Silchester), and theatres (**like that** at Verulamium). In addition private houses were built by **wealthy** citizens who **had them embellished** with wall paintings and mosaics (examples **of which are preserved** in Verulamium, Cirencester, and Leicester museums). By the end of the century, walls and gates **were being provided** as symbols of prestige as much as for defence.

(Encarta Online Encyclopaedia, 2009)

The emboldened words and phrases are examples of complex vocabulary or structures and are not strictly needed, as the vocabulary is not specialist core vocabulary for the topic (language *of*), nor is it needed for tasks (language *for*). If the content objectives are concerned with understanding how Britain's living spaces began to change, then clearly vocabulary such as *basilica, baths, amphitheatres, mosaics* and *theatres* (in their Roman manifestations), *prestige* and *defence* are necessary. Complex passive structures and abstract vocabulary such as *sojourn, impetus* and *endowed* are not vital to the topic. Some of the sentences may also be a little unclear for CLIL learners whose English is still developing. Of course, a teacher will always need to consider the possible links with the first language (if this is shared by the learners), and cognate vocabulary may be retained or adapted where appropriate. The changes made here are with Indo-European languages in mind.

A revised version might therefore read:

> Hadrian's **time** in Britain **brought changes** to urban life. During his reign a **gigantic** new basilica, perhaps modelled on the Basilica Ulpia in Rome, was constructed in London. Other towns **had similar buildings**, notably Wroxeter, the capital of the Cornovii, where the dedicatory inscription dated AD 130 survives. The cities of the 2nd century had other public buildings. **We can still see parts of the** baths (at Wroxeter and Leicester), **the** amphitheatre (outside Silchester), and **a** theatre (at Verulamium). In addition private houses were built by **rich** citizens who **decorated them** with wall paintings and mosaics (**see the** examples in Verulamium, Cirencester, and Leicester museums). By the end of the century, walls and gates **were used** as symbols of prestige as much as for defence.

(Adapted from Encarta Online Encyclopaedia, 2009)

In parallel with this process of text selection, all teachers need to consider how much new content material they can introduce at any one time, and in a CLIL context they need also to review how familiar the language is. The input sub-stage is not just an early feature of a topic scheme but occurs throughout a topic as new elements of content are introduced and the learners' understanding is extended in breadth, depth or both. Figure 7 offers a way

Figure 7: Content and language familiarity and novelty continuum

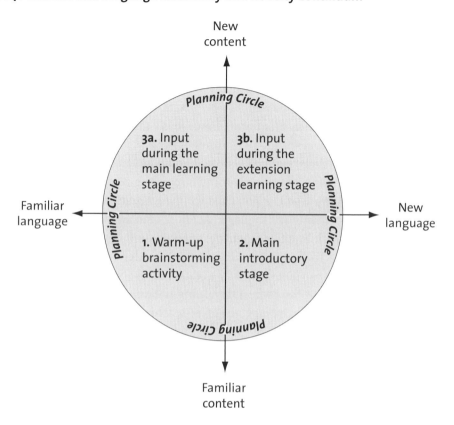

Content	Language	Inside the circle	Outside the circle
Familiar	Familiar	1. Settles and acclimatizes learners.	No cognitive challenge: danger that CLIL is seen as only re-learning old content in another language.
Familiar	New	2. Establishes departure point and introduces specialist language.	Danger that language becomes a barrier, although the content is already known. Objectives may become over-focused on language.
New	Familiar	3a. The language remains accessible as new concepts are introduced.	Danger that new content is 'dumbed down', as over-simple language cannot do justice to new material.
New	New	3b. The language becomes more complex as the new material is consolidated and subject confidence grows.	Cognitive challenge too high: danger that CLIL is seen as impossible. Objectives may become over-focused on language.

to consider the dynamic of familiarity and novelty of both the content of the lesson and the language needed for the input sub-stage. It demonstrates the need for the teacher to evaluate continuously how learners may initially comprehend new material and the role of language in this process. It also encourages teachers to make decisions about the scope of new concepts and the nature of the language chosen.

The diagram shows the different stages within a CLIL topic where we might stimulate activity through input, as well as how the teacher might monitor the role of familiarity and novelty in both content and language, so that learning is both accessible and challenging in the right ways at the right times. It suggests that we need to restrict any extremes in the level of familiarity of both content and language, and the table shows the various dangers of straying outside the 'planning circle'. The reason why 'familiarity' has a role here is of course because of the potential for the utilization of schemata, in terms of prior knowledge of content or language. A CLIL teacher has the opportunity to scaffold new content through familiar language, or to scaffold new language through the use of familiar content. But the latter is a danger area if it extends beyond the early stages of a unit, when the teacher's purpose is overtly to establish the baseline for new work: 'But we already know this' is one of the biggest devaluing statements that can be applied to a CLIL course. CLIL programmes are not about re-teaching already-learned material in another language. Starting off a CLIL unit which needs to build on prior learning not achieved through CLIL allows the teacher to be overt about the need to re-establish what is known: 'Let's summarize what we already know about this topic, so we can move on, but, to give a little more challenge about recalling what we know, we'll do it in our CLIL language'. This has a much more powerful motivating resonance and will deflect any complaints.

The main objective of the CLIL lesson remains the teaching of the concepts which are being introduced, explored or refined. Our three sub-stages of *meeting input, processing input* and *producing a response* are contained within the task we set and make use of some type of input – that is, a text that we have chosen. We now need to consider the nature of 'text' and the different qualities of different formats for the presentation of new concepts or information.

What are the common forms of text used in classrooms? Figure 8 offers a view which we will explore in more detail. The hierarchy of 'difficulty' implied by the diagram – that is, that the lower order is easier or more accessible than the higher elements – holds in certain circumstances and from certain standpoints. Continuous text generally requires more language, more concentration and more developed reading or listening skills to be accessed than any of the other text types given in the diagram. The middle stratum contains text types which involve language to a greater or lesser extent, but which can be more easily accessed as they require mostly single phrase/sentence or single word processing. Tables, diagrams and flowcharts can (depending on their construction) also imply an additional element of an opportunity for 'language-free' thinking and learning skills such as analysis, synthesis and evaluation. They often rest on a visual reading of material or processes. The

Figure 8: A suggested hierarchy of text types

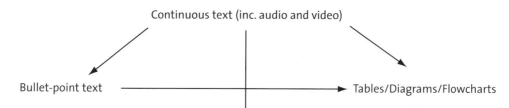

lowest level (artefacts/visuals) represents the most language-free examples of texts and should therefore be valuable for starting points in CLIL classrooms.

Before we explore other potential readings of this text hierarchy, it is worth emphasizing the rationale behind the arrows on the connecting lines. If a teacher is searching for material for a CLIL unit she or he may find a source which contains a range of connected texts from different points on the diagram. In this fortunate situation, the teacher needs to decide the *order* of use of these elements and *how* they can be used. An internet page which contains a connected text, some bullet points, a table of useful statistics and a couple of illustrations would allow for a carefully structured set of input materials and tasks. These tasks would be designed to elicit and supply ideas and language, to engage both individual thinking and dialogue about the subject and to capture the extent of understanding of the material in the process. A more detailed text could possibly also be used for private study as a follow-up. Figure 8 focuses the teacher on how to utilize that range of material. In a less fortunate (and more usual) circumstance, the teacher might find one or two of these elements rather than a full set and would then begin to consider whether it might be necessary to adapt the texts. So a connected text might be turned into a set of bullet points which retains original language and all the specialist vocabulary, but which loses redundancy or unnecessary detail for that point in the unit. With other texts, a table of information or diagram of a process might be constructed. Similarly, a photo from one source might be very useful as a way of offering access to another type of text found at another site. Thus the teacher modifies (rather than needs to construct) texts which are appropriate for their planned CLIL class. Moreover, if we see the arrows as double-headed, the diagram can also be used to provide a process for allowing more able students to adapt texts to more difficult outputs in the later stages of topics (so, for example, to convert bullet-point text to continuous text).

Clearly there could be other interpretations of the text-type hierarchy from the one shown here. For example, it could be argued that before photographic material or artefacts can be used, they need to be described and explained, and questions about them need to be formulated. In these cases, language is required either to be heard or spoken (in rarer cases to be read or written). The language involved would need thoughtful scaffolding as the open-ended nature of language-free items could generate a desire in the learners to use even more complex structures than might be contained within connected text. For this reason, an example of progressive questioning around a visual source is supplied in a later section of this chapter.

Processing input

While language is always needed for this process, the more purely visual the phenomenon is, the less the middle phase (the processing stage) is mediated through language directly. We saw earlier the processes involved in setting up accessible input material, and a simple follow-on example here would be a comparison of one learner reading a continuous text which presents statistics, while another learner looks at a simple table with the same information. In the first case, the understanding of what the input material offers is only possible if the learner has the vocabulary, syntactical understanding and reading skills to construct the meaning of the text before engaging in a task which uses it. In the second example, the learner will need to recognize the words used to set out the table (title and column/row headers) and have the skills to process tables. In both cases, the thinking demanded by a task may not use language to the same extent and in the same way, but language will be required if a response/output is expected by the task (and this will be considered in the next section). The two learners may arrive at a similar response, although the time taken and the mental effort involved could be radically different. The first learner may have formed the view while processing the input material that the task was difficult and that CLIL is difficult, time-consuming and demanding in terms of concentration. The second learner may have decided that the task was manageable and that CLIL is manageable too. Clearly the view must also be considered that the first learner may have gained more through that concentration and may actually know the content material better. However, the affective consequences need to be carefully monitored even if the approach is one based on 'no gain without pain', as the implications for the learner's motivation to learn could be significant.

Task design: Stimulating output?

The designing of materials and of tasks often go hand in hand, but the processes are separate. It is possible to take a text and structure a range of tasks which will be of differing degrees of difficulty. A learner could meet input without a task being involved. Indeed, the example given above of a continuous text set against a table of statistics demonstrates that mentally the learner may create a task for themselves (in this case, of comparing statistics) as a processing response to the input text. But we turn now to the processing and output stages which depend on the precise terms of the task as designed by the teacher.

As mentioned in Section 5.1, a central element of task design is the respective roles, engagement and activity of teachers and learners. Tied into this is both the issue of 'teachers doing too much', leading to learner boredom, surface-level learning and the potential for anxiety generated when teachers demand too much too quickly. In either case, motivation levels will fall. Musumeci (1996) wrote on teacher–learner negotiation in content-based instruction and highlighted what she called 'communication at cross-purposes'. The issues were:

- Teachers speak most of the time.
- They initiate the majority of the exchanges by asking display questions.
- In addition, teachers modify their own speech in response to students' signals of non-understanding.
- Students prefer to verbally request help only in small-group or one-to-one interactions with the teacher.
- Sustained negotiation – in which teachers and students verbally resolve incomplete or inaccurate messages – occurs rarely or not at all in these classrooms.

Clearly, task design needs to cater for scaffolded activity which engages and stimulates thinking in the learners, but which also offers opportunities for specific help to be available when needed from teachers, peers or support material. This leads to a focus on how to manage the important elements of inquiry and problem-solving tasks. The three types of language (*of, for* and ***through***) introduced in Chapters 3 and 4 are a helpful way to classify thinking about an issue highlighted by Jarrett, who reviewed Kessler, Quinn and Fathman (1992):

- In problem solving and inquiry, students need to know how to ask for repetition and meaning; to tell others what and how to do something; to verify and compare information; to participate in discussions and provide feedback; to report findings or a result; to express their opinion and explain their reasoning; and to summarize or draw conclusions.
- To facilitate this, teachers and English-proficient students can model these language skills as well as those for expressing agreement and disagreement.

(Jarrett, 1999: 11)

So, inextricably linked to our choice of material is the question of how we use it, and our introductory questions are:

- What sort of tasks most motivate our learners?
- How much do we wish to use individual reading/writing tasks; paired tasks; group work? What should stimulate these tasks?
- How much do we wish to use research tasks?
- How much do we wish to use presentation tasks?

Following this we need to be clear about:

- the nature of the information required by the task (e.g. does the task ask for summary of facts, analysis, comparison, synthesis, evaluation of information – interpretation/inference?)

- whether the tasks allow learners to show they have understood the concepts
- whether the task output formats are appropriate (e.g. are they visual, tabular, multi-choice, demanding simple language?)
- whether the language requirements of completing the task are appropriate, or whether they represent a barrier to learners in their expression of understanding (e.g. is the syntax/grammar needed too demanding? do the students know the task vocabulary as well as the content vocabulary?)
- whether the tasks are collaborative (e.g. do they involve discussion? do the learners have the language of this discussion?)
- whether the outputs produced allow the learners to revisit the learning or explain it to someone else
- how much thinking is needed.

Using Bloom's taxonomy (1956) – introduced in Chapter 3 – we can illustrate through a few sample task types how the cognitive demand of tasks might progress from the simpler to the higher levels of processing (Figure 9).

Figure 9: Hierarchy of task types

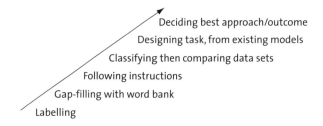

Considering the language levels required we could also construct a hierarchy on the basis of word/sentence/text levels, as follows:

WORD LEVEL
Recognition and use of new vocabulary in order to understand a new concept.
Example: Creating a labelled flowchart to a presentation.

SENTENCE LEVEL
Recognition/use of key concept phrases and/or attention to linguistic accuracy.
Example: Ordering sentences to show a process with or without correction of minor inaccuracies.

TEXT LEVEL
Showing overall gist understanding of an aspect of a topic.
Example: Making simple decisions – using knowledge of the characteristics of two environments (for example, physical data such as land size, relief, features, or economic

data about populations or habitats) to classify information. This offers many opportunities for repetition/consolidation of key vocabulary as part of the process.

Alternatives to the word/sentence/text hierarchy, which also show progression across a unit of work, might be:

- structuring consolidation of concepts and language through classification / comparison / gap-fill tasks / using writing frames of various sorts
- structuring consolidation of concepts and language through games / jigsaw activities / discussion and debating tasks
- structuring consolidation of concepts and language through grid/table filling in order to allow further production work in speech or in writing.

5.3 Creating materials

Teachers will sometimes need to create rather than evaluate or assemble materials and the tasks which use these materials. We must remember that the content subject will demand that any material has accurate and relevant information, and that therefore in most cases the teacher will still be referring to an external source of some kind when creating new materials. This source may be a simple visual (as we will see in an example shortly), which may mean that the teacher's creative focus is more on the task design than on materials writing. But sometimes the stimulus 'text' may need so much modification that, in effect, the teacher is writing a new piece of material for the class. The checklists from section 5.2 of this chapter are still vitally important in such cases.

A poster created by a CLIL secondary-school technology teacher is presented in **Example 1** on page 102. The teacher was working with students who had been learning English for four years but who were new to CLIL. This resource has been designed to give all the absolutely essential vocabulary and definitions of key aspects of the major mechanical systems for transferring motion and forces with clear visuals. No redundant complex vocabulary is involved and the poster serves as a reference tool as well as a stimulus for a task related to an ongoing design project: *Choose a gear/pulley system for the mechanical toy you are designing and say why it is the best option.*

Example 2 (page 103) is of a text completely created by a CLIL teacher who set out to scaffold a continuous text in two major ways: by inserting prompt questions and by highlighting key words. This text contains many key specialist terms for the topic and is also written in learner-friendly sentence structure, where, very importantly, the thinking is logical and supported throughout. The tasks which follow immediately ask CLIL learners to look at modern advertisements which use mythical images and to respond to questions which draw from both the content and the language of this text. The advantage of teacher-created text and teacher decisions about presentation, as this example shows, is that there is complete control over a vital stage in the CLIL learning process: the input and explanation phase.

Example 1

Mechanical systems transfer motion and force

Types of motion

 **Linear motion**    **Rotary motion**   **Oscillating motion**

 **Gears**
These are toothed wheels which interlock. The driver gear transfers *rotary motion* (clockwise) to the driven gear (anticlockwise).

 **Chain gears**
The transmission between gears is by/through a chain.

 **Belt gears**
The transmission between gears is by/through a belt.

 **Worm gears**
One of the gears is an endless screw, so it has a *rotary* and *linear/oscillating motion*. The mechanism is used to obtain great reductions in speed in machines.

 **Gears with rack**
One of the gears is a rack, so it has *linear* and *oscillating motion*.

 **Crank rod**
This mechanism is made up of a crank which connects to a bar called a rod. The bar travels in an *oscillating motion*, dragged by the crank, which has a *rotary motion*.

(Adapted from Quer Ravés, 2008)

Example 2

Myth and Mythology

What is a myth?

A myth is a **story** about **gods** and other **super-natural beings** and how they made or shaped the world and humanity. The events told in these stories happened in a very **remote past**. Myths are a part of **religion**, and they give an explanation of the world from a **moral point of view**; there is an **ideology** under every myth. Myths are also **metaphorical**; they do not try to explain the world in a logical or scientific way, but through imagination. However, we can still use myths to understand and explore culture: its **viewpoints**, **activities** and **beliefs**.

Who made up myths?

Myths are very **old** stories. They are so old, that we do not know who made them up: they are **anonymous**. People told these stories over the years and this is why we have many versions of them. Sometimes these stories – or parts of them – were written down and now we can enjoy them.

Where does the word 'myth' come from?

The word '**myth**' comes from the Greek word μύθος "mythos". It means *word*, *story* and it reveals the oral origin of these stories.

What is mythology?

'**Mythology**', from the Greek words μύθος "mythos" *story* and λόγος "logos" *collection* or *study* means both ***collection of stories/myths*** and ***study of the myths***.

Why classical mythology?

Every civilization has its myths. We call **classical mythology** the **body of myths** of ancient **Greece** and **Rome**. We are going to study them because of their importance and influence on European culture: art, literature, music . . . even on everyday products and advertising!

(Torres Carmona, 2008)

Example 3

(Photograph by Emmeliza 'Miles' Labella)

The role of task setting has been shown to be as important as text selection through-out the chapter and we now consider how a visual text (a photograph) might be used with younger learners who need more extensive scaffolding within a geography CLIL context (**Example 3**). This task demonstrates the first and second quadrants of the CLIL Matrix (see Chapters 3 and 4 and Figures 4 and 6). The end-task being aimed for is the meaningful description of the photograph.

The teacher has 4Cs objectives for a lesson containing this task, which is intended as a starter activity with a resulting homework writing task:

CONTENT
- To enhance understanding of **the effects of flooding**.
- To gain knowledge of **rainfall patterns** in different locations and the reasons behind higher or lower levels of rainfall and flooding. (Note: this is not illustrated by the task outlined here, but is planned for a subsequent task.)
- To practise the skill of 'reading' a photograph (a skill which the learners as 'trainee geographers' will be required to put to use frequently in the subject. Whilst this is a transferable skill – that is, they will also be able to apply it in other subjects – the teacher considers it a core skill for geography and has therefore included it as a content objective).

COGNITION

- To develop thinking skills by using **layers of questioning**.
- To use **comparison** of geographical (rainfall) data between different locations. (Note: again, this is not illustrated by the task outlined here, but is planned for a subsequent task.)

COMMUNICATION

- To enhance the ability to describe a visual by developing **breadth of vocabulary** and **sentence structure** using simple connectives (language *of* learning).
- To model and elicit ways of **justifying** an opinion using 'because' (language *through* learning).

CULTURE

- To develop learners' ability to **empathize**.

The teacher knows that the class will be unable to describe the photograph immediately with any depth or understanding of the context, but wants to use it as a starter which will engage learners and which will be useful to start developing both thinking skills and vocabulary. The photograph will also supply the focus for a homework writing task which will draw in the material from this and subsequent work from the lesson. The teacher therefore decides to keep the title a secret and to work towards a surprise final impact in the questioning sequence. The teacher also wishes to engage as many learners as possible in the task preparation stage and so begins with very simple brainstorming:

1 How many people can you see?
2 Who are these people?
3 Are they in a swimming pool?
4 How do you know this?

The fourth question raises the thinking level a little and invites reasoning and speculation rather than mere observation. The next set of questions 5–7 deliberately requires more thinking and is also open-ended in that there is no immediate correct answer.

5 When was the photograph taken (winter/summer/daytime/weekend)?
6 What are the children doing?
7 How do the children feel?

By this stage some scaffolding will be needed. Each of the above questions can be given to pairs and groups and a form of frame offered, for example:

FRAME FOR QUESTION 5

Give vocabulary headers to be expanded by the pairs/groups before they decide on a response to this question:

Weather: Sunlight, temperature, cloud . . .
Light: Dawn, midday sunlight, evening twilight . . .

Clothing: Swimming costumes, shoes, shorts, T-shirts . . .
Landscape: Warm water, cold water, trees with leaves, trees without leaves . . .

FRAME FOR QUESTION 6

Offer sentence starters – sometimes a response is limited not by language constraints, but by the lack of ideas. Again, groups can agree on a range of responses to this question.

They are sitting . . .
They are lying . . .
They are playing . . .
They are telling stories about . . .

FRAME FOR QUESTION 7

Offer spider diagrams to enable more specific and exact language to be used in simple sentence formats, for example: *They are . . . / They are not . . .* This enables further dictionary work to get a richer response to the question.

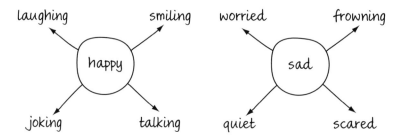

The next stage takes the understanding and speculation further still and leads into the final question which enables the groups to synthesize their previous discussions and should lead to a wide range of suggestions for the title of the photo.

Why do they feel . . . ?
What is the title of the picture?

The learners can now be given the follow-up written task for homework: *Describe the picture to a friend who hasn't seen it.* At this point the teacher may decide to add some scaffolding such as a substitution table for the less able who may still need further support. It is important in CLIL contexts always to make substitution tables a stimulus for thinking and not just for random selection of language to help expression. There should always be some correct and some incorrect combinations of words from a content perspective. This means students think and make decisions as they use the frame:

I think that	they are	happy	because they are	frowning	and they look as if they are	enjoying themselves
	some of the children are	not happy		thinking		having fun
	the boys are			smiling		embarrassed
	the girls are	worried		laughing		scared
				splashing		cold

The title of the photo, which can now be revealed, is: *Children swimming in floodwater.*

Clearly, the learners can now make a very full description which takes into account visual, factual and affective elements of the photograph, and which taps into geographical content which is relevant to this context. This task, if given 'cold' to the learners, would not be as manageable, as fulfilling or as deep in terms of learning potential as it is with the scaffolded preparation, which has involved skilled progressive questioning and valuable peer interaction. Learner roles should have been activated effectively and anxiety reduced through this peer support process. The surprise impact of holding back the title should also have increased motivation for the homework task and for the topic of rainfall and flooding which this activity has introduced.

A subsequent in-lesson activity will now bring in geographical data about rainfall in different regions and how this makes flooding a greater danger in certain parts of the world. This will lead to material being added to the substitution table in the form of further 'because' options, this time specifically to account for the unhappy expressions shown by some of the children which give an indication of the sad circumstances in which the photograph was taken. These 'because' additions are brainstormed within the class and in effect count as 'language *through*'. These will be concerned with danger from flood, loss of home/possessions, loss of family members or pets or other animals. Teachers can offer frames but encourage multiple parallel suggestions to fix language forms whilst allowing creativity and cognition to emerge and be satisfied.

A more advanced model of progressive questions with scaffolding in a business studies context is offered by Rosa Domingo (2008). Her worksheets contain a series of prompts, such as those in **Example 4a** (page 108).

Example 4a

Justify your choice:
- Why? Identify the opportunities.
- How? Explain the process necessary to make your product or to offer your service.
- Where? Describe the location of your business.
- Target market: describe the customers your product or service is targeting.

Use the following writing frame:

The product or service	Our product/service is . . . with these features . . . It is . . .
How?	The process of manufacturing has the following stages: First: . . . Second: . . .
Where?	We are going to sell through the Internet or through a location, or both. It is located in a (central, peripheral), and well/badly connected, main/side street.
Target market	Our product or service is designed for people (customers, consumers) who are: (age, income, sex, studies, hobbies . . .).

After completing a range of questions and equivalent support frames, the learners are given the task in **Example 4b**.

Example 4b

1. Revise your notes.
2. Explain your idea to the rest of the class. You can use a PowerPoint presentation; it must last only 10 minutes and be no more than 15 slides. *Go to the supplementary material to find out how to make an effective presentation.*
3. The class has to evaluate the viability of the idea.
4. Each group must have two representatives. One to explain the ideas, and the other to discuss the viability.

Use this grid to justify your arguments:

ARGUMENTS FOR LAUNCHING THE NEW BUSINESS	ARGUMENTS FOR NOT LAUNCHING THE NEW BUSINESS
Example: cost, experience, competitors, location, economic situation . . .	

Again, this is teacher-created material which has taken into account the content needs (based on learners' existing knowledge) and language needs of the specific group of learners (who have had four years of English but are new to CLIL). The mixture of scaffolding provided by support frames, together with the less structured mechanism of peer support, as pairs work through the material and make decisions together, enables the learners to output their ideas in more sophisticated terms than they would have been able to had the task been given earlier in the unit (this task is included in the plan for the third of eight lessons).

This chapter has explored several aspects of materials and task design. The factors which hold paramount importance for CLIL programmes relate to a series of different issues: how students meet the course content; how they are asked to process this input (both in terms of the ways their thinking is structured and the ways they are asked to express their understanding); the need to keep in mind not just second-language-acquisition research, but also more recent developments in brain research; and the need to acknowledge the influence of affective aspects of learning such as motivation. Transmission teaching is not often effective in CLIL classrooms, but student-centred learning needs to be very carefully structured. We have shown that holding an intention to think through methods of scaffolding is vital throughout. This must be activated in the initial choice of materials, in organizing the sequencing of texts, in any modification of texts we carry out, in our questioning which accompanies our chosen texts and in our design of output frames. We have shown too that we can achieve higher-level thinking in learners by progressing through lower levels and then opening out a more challenging task through a metacognitive review process. This process, involving learning and language use which has been activated by the scaffolded task, is able to be recombined into an output which has more sophisticated thinking and more complex linguistic expression – in other words, where the whole will be more than the sum of the parts.

References

Blackwell, L. S., Trzesniewski, K. H. and Dweck, C. S. (2007) 'Implicit theories of intelligence predict achievement across an adolescent transition: A longitudinal study and an intervention', *Child Development*, **78**, 1, 246–63.

Bloom, B. S. (ed.) (1956) *Taxonomy of Educational Objectives, Handbook I: Cognitive Domain*, New York: Longman.

Domingo, R. (2008) *Starting a Business: Writing a Business Plan. Student's Worksheets* [Online]. Available at: http://www.xtec.cat/cirel/pla_le/nottingham/rosa_domingo/ studentworksheet.pdf [Accessed 29 May 2009].

Dörnyei, Z. (2001a) *Motivational Strategies in the Language Classroom*, Cambridge: Cambridge University Press.

Dörnyei, Z. (2001b) *Teaching and Researching Motivation*, Harlow: Pearson Education.

Dörnyei, Z. and Csizér, K. (2002) 'Some dynamics of language attitudes and motivation: Results of a longitudinal nationwide survey', *Applied Linguistics*, **23**, 421–62.

Encarta Online Encyclopaedia (2009) *Roman Conquest of Britain* [Online]. Available at: http://uk.encarta.msn.com/text_781531758____5/Britain_Roman_Conquest_of.html [Accessed 29 May 2009].

Farabee, M. J. (1992, 1994, 1997–2001, 2007) *Biology Book* [Online]. Available at: http://www. emc.maricopa.edu/faculty/farabee/BIOBK/BioBookTOC.html [Accessed 29 May 2009].

Grant, H. and Dweck, C. S. (2003) 'Clarifying achievement goals and their impact', *Journal of Personality and Social Psychology*, **85**, 3, 541–53.

Hood, P. (2006) Unpublished data from CLIL research interviews with students at Tile Hill Wood Language College, Coventry, UK.

Horwitz, E. K. (2001) 'Language anxiety and achievement', *Annual Review of Applied Linguistics*, **21**, 112–26.

Hulstijn, J. H. (1990) 'A comparison between the information-processing and the analysis/control approaches to language learning', *Applied Linguistics*, **11**, 1, 30–45.

Jarrett, D. (1999) *Teaching Mathematics and Science to English Language Learners*, Portland, OR: Northwest Regional Education Laboratory.

Kessler, C., Quinn, M. E. and Fathman, A. K. (1992) 'Science and cooperative learning for LEP students', in Kessler, C. (ed.) (1992) *Cooperative Language Learning: A Teacher's Resource Book*, Englewood Cliffs: Prentice Hall, pp65–83.

Krashen, S. (1981) *Second Language Acquisition and Second Language Learning*, [Online]. Available at: http://www.sdkrashen.com/SL_Acquisition_and_Learning/index.html [Accessed 24 April 2009].

MacIntyre, P. D. and Gardner, R. C. (1994) 'The subtle effects of language anxiety on cognitive processing in the second language', *Language Learning*, **44**, 283–305.

McGrath, I. (2002) *Materials Evaluation and Design for Language Teaching*, Edinburgh: Edinburgh University Press.

McLaughlin, B. (1987) *Theories of Second Language Learning*, London: Edward Arnold.

McLaughlin, B., Rossman, T. and McLeod, B. (1983) 'Second language learning: An information-processing perspective', *Language Learning*, **33**, 135–58.

Mitchell, T. M. (1997) *Machine Learning*, New York: McGraw Hill.

Musumeci, D. (1996) 'Teacher–learner negotiation in content-based instruction: Communication at cross-purposes?', *Applied Linguistics*, **17**, 3, 286–325.

Onwuegbuzie, A. J., Bailey, P. and Daley, C. E. (2000) 'The validation of three scales measuring anxiety at different stages of the foreign language learning process: The input anxiety scale, the processing anxiety scale and the output anxiety scale', *Language Learning*, **50**, 1, 87–117.

Oxford, R. L. (1999) 'Anxiety and the language learner: New insights', in Arnold, J. (ed.) *Affect in Language Learning*, Cambridge: Cambridge University Press.

Quer Ravés, M. (2008) *Mechanical Systems Transfer Motion and Force* [Online PDF]. Available at: http://www.xtec.cat/cirel/pla_le/nottingham/magda-quer/P1-mechanical%20systems.pdf [Accessed 05 June 2009].

Richards J. (2001) *Curriculum Development*, Cambridge: Cambridge University Press.

Schwartz, M. (2006) 'For whom do we write the curriculum?', *Journal of Curriculum Studies*, **38**, 4, 449–57.

Shkedi, A. (1998) 'Can the curriculum guide both emancipate and educate teachers?', *Curriculum Inquiry*, **28**, 2, 209–29.

Swain, M. (1996). 'Integrating language and content in immersion classrooms: Research perspectives', *The Canadian Modern Language Review*, **52**, 4, 529–48.

Tomlinson, B. (2003) *Materials Development In Language Teaching*, Cambridge: Cambridge University Press.

Torres Carmona, P. (2008) *Classical Mythology: The Olympian Gods Student Worksheets* [Online]. Available at: http://www.xtec.cat/cirel/pla_le/nottingham/pilar_torres/student_worksheets.pdf [Accessed 29 May 2009].

Watson, D. E. (2009) *Photosynthesis* [Online]. Available at: http://www.ftexploring.com/photosyn/photosynth.html [Accessed 29 May 2009].

Westhoff, G. (2004) 'The art of playing a pinball machine: Characteristics of effective SLA-tasks', *Babylonia*, **3/2004**, 58–62.

6 **Assessment issues in CLIL**

The theme of assessment is a difficult and sometimes contentious area amongst CLIL teachers. In some respects it lies at the heart of the question of how to define the level of content–language integration, because, ultimately, no matter what is taught and how it is taught, the mode of assessment determines how the learners perceive the teacher's intention and, of course, also shapes performance data. In this chapter, we are dealing with classroom assessment as opposed to programme evaluation (which is addressed in Chapter 7). Programme evaluation involves looking at a complete CLIL course or an aspect of it and making a judgment regarding its effectiveness, for example through collection of data on learners' performance or attitudes. The distinction between assessment and evaluation is important, as each serves a different purpose. However, there is a potential overlap which is relevant to the question of whether we are assessing content, language or both. Programme evaluation might centre on learners' language attainment (many research reports do so) and this might be an appropriate place and method to carry out discrete language assessment as well.

Assessment processes can be broadly divided into *summative* and *formative* and this division forms a major distinction. Summative assessment makes a judgment on the capability of the learner at that point in time and, apart from offering that judgment back to the learner, it often leads to some form of information-giving to another party, for example the school management or the learner's parents. It is therefore associated with testing in a more formal setting or an end-of-unit, 'final' result, even if this is not obtained through an examination. Across the world there are many variations on final course and module testing processes, with a whole range of criteria in use for both content and language outcomes. CLIL units will need to mirror such systems in order to retain credibility as mainstream educational programmes. This point will be addressed again later in the chapter.

Formative assessment is more complex, as its intention is to be directly diagnostic with a view to immediately impacting on the learner's next steps. It is also formative for the teacher, because it can alter planning and practice mid-unit (or even mid-lesson) and not just after all the work is complete, as a summative test might do. Formative assessment was advocated first by Scriven (1967) and Bloom (1968). In common with these writers, Ames and Ames (1984) suggested moving away from a norm-referencing approach; they advocated a task-mastery approach using a learner's performance to structure goals for future improvement on an individual, rather than competitive, basis. This focus then began to develop in both research and practice. It included writers on motivation – for example

Dweck (1986), who argued that summative assessment demotivated learners – and assessment researchers, such as Sadler (1989), who argued for learners to be given authentic evaluative experience, so that they could identify work of high quality and evaluate their own progress towards it. Cohen (1994) brought a language-learning perspective to the issue by recommending formative activity alongside classroom tasks, so that the teacher could better understand students' skills and competences.

Clarke (2001) likens summative assessment to the simple measurement of a plant, and formative assessment to the feeding process which leads to growth. In the UK, as a result of research into assessment (including an important study by Black and Wiliam, 1998), the term 'Assessment for Learning' (AfL) (in Scotland, 'Assessment is for Learning') was coined to describe processes thought to be desirable across the curriculum. In 2002, the Assessment Reform Group in England produced a document of ten principles for AfL, which makes clear that both teachers and learners will benefit from the processes described and that formative assessment should be central to classroom practice. Some of the key features in this document are:

- the sharing of learning intentions (meaning that teachers tell students at the beginning of the lessons what they will learn)
- the use of success criteria (meaning that students will be told what the task will involve and what the outcome will contain)
- the involvement of learners in self- and peer-assessment
- the importance of feedback, which should be sensitive to learners' self-esteem and which should thereby positively impact on motivation.

Zangl, also advocating a formative approach, includes in her article three major conclusions about language assessment (but in a way that could be applied equally well to content assessment). She states that teachers should try to:

- assess the learner's proficiency within a multi-component framework, comprising not only domain-/structure-specific items, but also the use of language within the social context of the classroom;
- capture both the learner's individual profile and the performance level of the class as a whole; and
- trace the learner *along* his or her developmental path where time and experience act as constructive factors.

(Zangl, 2000: 257)

This chapter will focus on such formative assessment approaches, as it seems to us there is a strong case for formative assessment to be used on a regular basis and summative assessment to be used systematically but rarely. The strength of formative assessment processes, according to the researchers discussed above, is that they enhance learning to an extent where they actively support better summative outcomes. The pressure on CLIL courses to match first-language test results is immense and it is through this regular occurrence of focused classroom practice that CLIL teachers and learners can work towards achieving such parity. We will next consider what the specific assessment issues are for a CLIL programme, and then explore how we might address them. We will use examples from practice of different modes of assessment and rationalize them in terms of the broader aims of CLIL as demonstrated by the theorization and Tool Kit offered in Chapters 3 and 4. Finally, we will summarize by giving some exemplars of good CLIL practice in assessment which reflect the principles of this chapter.

6.1 What are the main issues for assessment in CLIL?

Assessment is often a major area of teacher uncertainty in CLIL contexts and, as with other issues relating to CLIL, must be considered with the CLIL practitioners' specific situation in mind. One group of teachers and trainers in Catalonia met in 2007 to collect together and try to address the major questions regarding CLIL assessment. From amongst these teachers one group suggested the following:

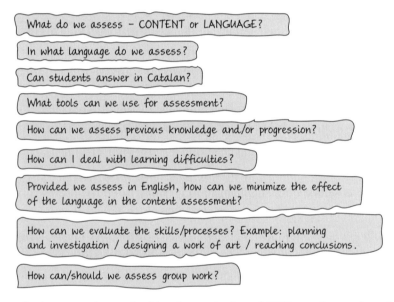

These are the key questions asked by the majority of CLIL teachers when they meet to discuss practice. The starting point usually centres on three basic issues: *Do we assess content, or language, or both? Which is more important? How do we do this?* We can divide this set of questions into a series of more generic questions which probe the needs and demands of a specific CLIL context. For example:

- What do we mean by assessment in CLIL?
- Do we assess language or content first?
- Do we sometimes assess one and not the other? If so, which and when (and, more crucially, why and how)?
- What about cognition and culture?
- Who assesses?

- When do we assess?
- How do we assess?
- What is the role of standard examination systems?
- Is there a role for the Common European Framework (2001)?

The next section of this chapter begins to confront these questions by looking at whether to assess language or content, followed by the issues involved in assessing each of these.

Language or content?

This central dilemma was summarized early in an article by Short (1993), in which she explored alternatives to standard testing in CLIL. Short also raised the two essential questions which lie behind teacher uncertainty about assessment, both the *what* question and especially the *how* question:

> The many varieties of alternative assessment include performance-based tests, portfolios, journals, projects, and observation checklists. Although these measures allow better demonstration of student knowledge, they can nonetheless confound teachers of language minority students. Complications arise first because teachers must determine whether the language or the content is being assessed in these alternative measures. Then teachers must distinguish between the language and content knowledge of the students and decide if one is interfering with the demonstration of the other.
>
> (Short, 1993: 633)

Here we see that the two questions are linked: firstly – as mentioned as a key question in the previous section – should we assess *language* or *content*? Secondly, what methods can we use which will give us *reliable* assessment information – that is, will one element (content or language) impede the other?

The *how* is the bigger question and will rightly occupy a larger proportion of the chapter, but we will address the first immediately. CLIL units will all contain clear objectives, possibly fashioned around the 4Cs. Even if a different approach is taken by the CLIL planners, they will still at some point have had to construct statements regarding the content (concepts, knowledge and possibly skills) which is to be covered by the unit and one or more statements regarding language. The language objectives may relate simply to communicating the content effectively, or they may include notions (such as specialist vocabulary from the unit) or functions (such as the ability to discuss effectively) or even be form-focused (for example, concerning effective use of the past tense). The teacher designing the unit will know what she or he wishes to teach and what the overall purpose of the CLIL module is. Therefore, the answer to the 'language or content' question is determined by the relative priority within those objectives. It is important to have a clear head about that priority; we have taken a position in this book that the content should always be the dominant element in terms of objectives, even though we intend that language will be learned securely alongside the content's concepts and skills. With this perspective in mind, we will turn now to the second question, assuming that it is content first and foremost that is being assessed. However, as we discuss later on in the chapter, many of the principles involved in assessing content can also be applied to the assessment of language, so even practitioners with different priorities should find the information useful.

Assessing content

Assessing content is potentially very challenging. Genesee and Upshur are clear:

> Generally speaking, the same content objectives should be used to assess the achievement of second language and native speakers alike – lower standards of achievement should not be established for second language speakers.
>
> (Genesee and Upshur, 1996: 47)

However, this is not necessarily easy to achieve – content may be understood by a learner, but she or he may not be able to express it sufficiently clearly if the language forms needed are not known, or if anxiety prevents it. Pinker summarizes:

> Any particular thought in our head embraces a vast amount of information. But when it comes to communicating a thought to someone else, attention spans are short and mouths are slow.
>
> (Pinker, 1994: 81)

A practical example would be if a learner were offered two parallel tables of statistics about two different countries being compared in a geography module. Inside the student's head, comparisons would be made instantly and a concept formed relating to this comparison/contrast. The essential knowledge intended to be gained would be gained. The learner's language competence would next determine whether this understanding could be communicated back to the teacher. If the student 'failed' to communicate understanding during the assessment process, then the teacher would not be sure whether this was due to limited language competence, or whether the student had really not understood.

We also need to define which aspect of the content we are assessing. We could be interested in any of the following:

- factual recall (detail)
- general understanding (major points)
- ability to manipulate the content, using higher-level thinking skills such as interpretation, analysis, synthesis or application. This will also reflect objectives regarding cognition (refer to Chapter 4 for some concrete examples), which are best assessed through content assessment, as without it they become simply abstract skills
- ability to research more independently and extend the topic knowledge beyond what has been presented by the teacher.

How should we assess?

While assessing simple detail may be uncomplicated, the other aspects in the list above are more complex for both teachers and learners. For this reason, when designing the means of assessment, teachers should choose – whether assessing learners individually or in pairs/groups – the most direct method which uses the least language. Examples of this are that the learners should complete grids, draw diagrams or pictures, decide if bulleted statements are true or false, correct facts which are wrong, make simple presentations linked to visuals or answer content-based questions with a simple yes/no response. This point will be developed later in the chapter.

But the *how* of assessment also raises other issues. With the current strong focus on concrete objectives and purposeful learning activities which involve students in thinking and problem solving – sometimes in pairs or groups – come regular assessment opportunities, as long as alternative formats are accepted. Creating a specific 'test' may not be necessary if the activities themselves deserve monitoring and can provide concrete evidence of learning. So an ongoing approach to assessment in each lesson can become the norm, as Short's (1993) article suggests. As well as observing learners at work on the tasks set by the teacher, if a three-part lesson structure is implemented (with a starter, main activities and a **plenary**) then the whole-class plenary can double as an opportunity to both monitor understanding and to re-teach the material for those who need to hear it (content or language) again. If the notion of assessment is truly formative, then the teacher wants to monitor the understanding at all the different levels – not to make a judgment on individuals, but to inform her or his own actions and future planning. So it is not a matter of 'catching people out', but of repairing misconceptions and filling gaps.

> The **plenary** is the section of a lesson where the teacher and learners together summarize the learning up to that point in order to move on. This is often towards the end of the lesson.

Alongside this, and in accordance with the principles of AfL or its equivalent, is an understanding that assessment should not always be of individuals, but will sometimes be of groups of learners. Although it may be difficult to decide who has contributed what and who knows what, this is seen as less important, given that there are other gains to be made through collaborative work. The final output may be more than the sum of all the parts with more sophisticated use of language after group negotiation and editing. Research, divided between members of a group and then shared, can also contribute to this refinement. In addition, such tasks potentially raise different areas for assessment, such as teamwork, project management and capacity for self-assessment.

Who should assess?

The possibility of expanding assessment beyond the teacher looking solely at individual learners links partially to the question of *who* assesses. Clearly, teachers wish to retain the major role in this, but we can consider the following factors in establishing the possible range of teacher, self- and peer-assessment methods available:

- Clear success criteria enable learners to peer-assess or self-assess in certain kinds of tasks.

- Assessment can be collaborative within the whole-class setting if the teacher shows anonymous extracts from work and invites constructive amendments.
- Presentations can be assessed for a range of factors; for example, the communication of certain items of content, use of media, use of effects to scaffold understanding and contribution of members of a group.
- Self- and peer-assessment can be used as a platform to elicit comments about the learning process by asking why the judgments are as they are. This, when well established, can lead to insights into cognition, which is the most difficult C to assess.
- Cultural content can be something which learners feel adds interest and which can be peer-assessed through a more subjective system such as, for younger learners *three stars and a wish*, or an equivalent age-appropriate mechanism (this involves the assessor finding three aspects to praise and one to suggest for development).
- Peer-assessment can lead to better self-assessment. If a learner has formulated ideas about a piece of work sufficiently well to communicate and justify those judgments to another learner, she or he will be more able to look at her or his own work in the same objective manner.

The points above all demonstrate that relying on teacher assessment alone could impoverish a CLIL classroom. We will state again that a teacher will still be the main assessor, but there are numerous possibilities to vary this in appropriate circumstances. In considering how and where to add this variety, it is also necessary to weigh up how well learners can assess from a linguistic perspective: is their language capability sufficient to make valid judgments? Will a teacher need to re-assess everything? Collaborative assessment in a whole-class context managed by the teacher will always give an indication as to student capacity for the process.

Assessing content in the first language

We have so far avoided the notion of content assessment carried out in learners' (or the school's) first language. Some CLIL courses have built in the practice of addressing the second-language 'language barrier' issue by monitoring comprehension through a test given in the first language. We should note immediately that this becomes difficult or even impossible in classrooms with a wide variety of first languages and may actually disadvantage some learners if the majority language is assumed to be every learner's first language. But even in classrooms where all students share a first language, it can be problematic for both practical and pedagogical reasons. It can fail on a practical level when the specialist vocabulary needed for the content area is simply not known in the first language, because the topic has been taught through the CLIL language. This is yet more pronounced if the full subject is CLIL-taught for a year or more, as the first-language specialist terminology will be less related to current topics. On a philosophical and pedagogical level it can fail, because the intention of the CLIL programme is to build capacity to cope fully in an additional language, which includes finding strategies to communicate and developing thinking as far as possible in that language. The proponents of this system will argue, of course, that the use of the first language still allows a deeper understanding to be communicated and that the practical problems can be overcome. The issue needs careful thought by those developing the programmes.

This issue does, however, become very difficult when we bring any nationally set testing into play. One of the pioneering schools which developed CLIL approaches in the UK stopped their programme a year away from national examinations, because the vehicular language was not accepted for testing. As the students were less confident with the subject matter in English, they had to carry out a revision programme in English in the lead up to the assessments so as to be able to reach their potential grades. A detailed report by Serra (2007) addresses many of the above issues, focusing carefully on what she calls 'language alternation' (also called 'translanguaging', mentioned in Chapter 2), specifically because of the need to manage first- and second-language capability in the content area (in this case, mathematics).

Assessing language

We have already mentioned the need for CLIL courses to seek parity with first-language programmes by using recognized local testing frameworks. There is clearly a case in language assessment for summative attainment at the end of courses to be stated in terms of levels in an internationally recognized system such as the Common European Framework of Reference for Languages (2001). The self-assessment level descriptors from B1 upwards (ibid.: 26–7) refer to elements of content which could encompass CLIL material. But in common with the rest of this chapter we want to look more at the earlier stages before programme assessment and to answer the question: *How do we assess language on an everyday basis?* To begin with, just as with content, we need to be sure which aspect of language competence we are assessing. It could be the ability to:

- recall subject-specific vocabulary
- operate functionally, using appropriate language structures and forms to discuss and disagree, ask effective questions, report in appropriate language structures, and so on
- listen or read for meaning
- present or discuss effectively
- demonstrate thinking/reasoning in the CLIL language
- show awareness of grammatical features of the language.

Teachers need to be clear both *why* they are assessing language as opposed to content and *how* they wish to do this. If we speak firstly about formative assessment of language, then we could mean ongoing correction in the classroom as well as assessment of written language in workbooks, or of the oral language of presentations after they have been completed. It could be argued that such language correction and assessment should be used specifically to improve the communication of content. If a student is told, as part of 'live correction', that changing the language in a certain way would make the content clearer, then there is also a clear motive for that language assessment. If it is simply made as a correction of a detail of language accuracy, then it will inevitably halt the flow of content communication and could frustrate learners. It is important to be clear that this does not mean we should ignore all errors and never assess language, but we can create specific opportunities to do this rather than offer continual corrective feedback which undermines content confidence. The 'language clinic' is a potentially useful version of this practice: from time to time, the teacher gathers language errors which need to be addressed as a class and holds a language clinic in a lesson, explaining to learners that this is a necessary step to support better communication of content.

When looking at *how* to assess language, we should note that – as with content – language can be assessed through a variety of approaches. Brown and Hudson present the following as types of assessment:

> ... (a) selected-response (including true-false, matching, and multiple-choice assessments); (b) constructed-response (including fill-in, short-answer, and performance assessments); and (c) personal-response (including at least conference, portfolio, and self- and peer assessments).
>
> (Brown and Hudson, 1998: 658)

This links back to the Short article in which she also lists assessment instruments which offer a better range of opportunities for CLIL students to demonstrate understanding:

> ... skill checklists and reading/writing inventories, anecdotal records and teacher observations, student self-evaluations, portfolios, performance-based tasks, essay writing, oral reports, and interviews.
>
> (Short, 1993: 629)

In this article, Short was setting out a new view of assessment for bilingual teaching in America which did not relate to the existing English as a Second Language schemes. The emphasis on classroom processes which lies behind many of these methods is still not completely accepted across the world, but, as we have maintained so far, such methods are vital tools for teachers to gain a full understanding of student progress. In terms of continuous language assessment, the European Language Portfolio scheme (http://www.coe.int/t/dg4/portfolio/) offers a range of material developed in different countries which teachers may find useful, but at present this is not directly inclusive of a CLIL approach. We will next explore some assessment contexts in order to exemplify some of these tools.

6.2 Assessment in action: Examples of practice

In this section, the intention is to develop the threads opened up in the chapter so far, exploring rationale and methods of assessment, and to select assessment types which exemplify certain issues. This cannot be a full guide to CLIL assessment, as both the scope of different methods and the many different levels on which CLIL courses operate would make that impossible. The points made here, however, should be transferable to related types of assessment and to levels of work and ages other than those directly referred to.

Sharing objectives and success criteria

Sharing the objectives and offering success criteria are important first steps towards effective assessment, as learners begin to find out in this way not just what they are likely to be learning, but also how their work will be assessed, both as they work and when they have completed it. It is important to use concrete statements in framing these intentions, not just because of the potential linguistic constraints contained in a CLIL context, but because this is good assessment practice. The older and more advanced learners are, the more complex this stage can be made, so that it remains cognitively appropriate. For example, the objectives / learning outcomes and the success criteria can be referenced more fully to previous knowledge if the linguistic knowledge can accommodate this. The primary-age structures of WALT (<u>we</u> <u>a</u>re <u>l</u>earning <u>t</u>o) and WILF (<u>w</u>hat <u>I</u>'m <u>l</u>ooking <u>f</u>or), comprising criteria outlining what the finished work will contain, sometimes personified into two cartoon characters, provide direction for making the statements concrete. These basic concepts can be adopted in a less 'primary' form for use with older learners. We may be addressing something as simple as: 'Today we are learning to see the differences between the landscapes of La Réunion and the Isle of Skye, so we can decide which pictures show which place'. Or we may be handling more advanced concepts such as: 'Building on last week's work on zonal soils and how Northwest Europe and a tropical environment such as La Réunion show differences, we are looking more closely at intrazonal soils and a feature called podsol in the tropical region. By the end of this week's work you will have a clear view of the soil characteristics of that area and why they might differ from local soils'. In both cases, students start the lesson knowing what they are going to learn, and in both cases the CLIL teacher will need to use some visual support to ensure that all learners follow the content of those learning intentions. Whether it is pictures of two environments, maps of locations, key vocabulary or diagrams, those statements are better supported by these visual elements than if they were just spoken. Success criteria can also be given for a piece of homework, such as the production of a presentation. The example given on page 122 ('Preparing a presentation') acts on several levels, clarifying content (as in the third bullet point), the presentation conventions and the quality expectations. The subject of this task was *Aspects of the weather systems in the Pacific Ocean*, so the checklist of points included explanation of the thermocline and the features of El Niño / La Niña. The set of bullet points here acts as an overall checklist for students when they have completed the task, making the assessment process more overt:

Example: Preparing a presentation

About the PowerPoint presentation:

- There should be a title summarizing what you are explaining.
- There should be the names of the authors.
- There should be all the points of the outline I have given you.
- The explanations should be concise and clear.
- The drawings and/or diagrams should clarify the explanation.
- The presentation of the PowerPoint should be attractive and well organized.

Source: Roser Nebot (2008)

Link to worksheet [Accessed 27 April 09]: http://www.xtec.cat/cirel/pla_le/nottingham/roser_nebot/students.pdf

The grid in the example 'Drawing and painting a landscape' acts as a checklist for a final task, consolidating a unit. This is a good example of where success criteria refer to a non-linguistic outcome, but contain within them a reference to much of the key vocabulary of the unit, so checking comprehension and even language – if the piece of work matches all criteria, the teacher can be sure that the content and the language of the unit have been established. The language does not need to be produced for this process and therefore a discussion with the student about the finished painting would reveal her or his capacity to use the language effectively, but teachers can decide to what degree receptive and productive competence are desirable or required.

Example: Drawing and painting a landscape

During and after your work, check the following points:

Draw the horizon line and add the vanishing point.	
Set the background and the foreground.	
Objects appear smaller as they get further away and with less detail.	
Overlapping tells us which object is in front, closer.	
Objects get higher on the foreground and closer to the horizon line.	
Warm colours advance and cool colours recede.	
Objects in the distance appear pale.	
Do not forget the way light and shadow create forms with colour and shading techniques.	

Source: Isabel Palomares Cots (2008)

Link to worksheet [Accessed 27 April 09]: http://www.xtec.cat/cirel/pla_le/nottingham/isabel_palomares/student.pdf

Alternative assessment formats

It is important to allow learners to express their responses to tasks in the most direct way possible so that language is not a barrier to demonstrating understanding of content. Simple assessment formats such as recording to a grid have several advantages. The format itself requires little language knowledge to stimulate content recall; it activates and organizes thinking to support maximum demonstration of knowledge, thus forming part of the process of working within a student's 'zone of proximal development' (Vygotsky, 1978), which for any individual learner will also involve dialogic interaction with the teacher and/or more able peers. It is therefore part of the formative structure.

In our first geographical example on page 121 (comparing the islands of La Réunion and Skye), learners might have a grid system with individual columns for each of ten photographs and rows, labelled simply with items which might be visible in the photographs, such as *a volcano, a sparrowhawk, a whiteye, the Cuillin Ridge*. Learners tick any items from the list that they see in each photo in turn. This establishes some specialist vocabulary knowledge demanded by the topic, and is at a basic level of comprehension. Once complete, the grid can be used for a further task involving pair work, in which learners produce a short, oral description of a photograph and then come to a decision about where it has been taken. At the simplest level, this may be between two locations, but a comparison of three environments (perhaps the two islands and the school locality for the younger children) makes it a more complex and more cognitively challenging task. The teacher can eavesdrop during this stage of the work to listen for correct location decisions and to evaluate language use beyond the single-word structure which might result from learners' referring to the grid. The language *for* learning (see Chapters 3 and 4) demands the fuller sentence structure which accompanies a description:

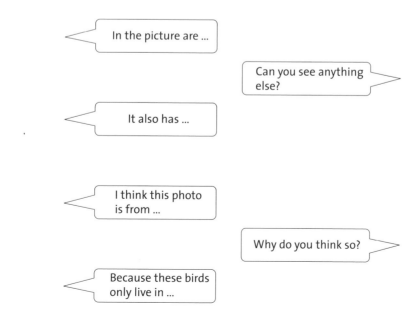

A grid checklist for more advanced work still performs the same function. It allows information, perhaps on a more complex level, to be assembled easily, with thought (rather than language) highlighted at that stage, and then for that assembled information to be used to stimulate language production once the concepts are securely in place.

In the assessment of content comprehension through *receptive* tasks, a major learning tool, and so also a major assessment tool, is reading. Naturally, at primary level, this has to be restricted and carefully planned, and may involve listening rather than reading, especially with the younger ages. But from late primary onwards, visual texts of all types (see Chapter 5) are an integral part of CLIL classrooms. Many task types involve simply reading – for example, matching pictures to vocabulary, 'heads and tails' sentence halves, true/false decision tasks, gap-fill where the missing items are given in a box, decision tasks where two versions are given and the correct one has to be chosen and, in more practical subjects, following instructions to create an outcome. Most writing tasks also begin with reading, as we will see later in this section.

Matching information

The assessment instrument which involves matching information, for example by 'heads and tails' (joining two halves of several definitions or sentences), also serves more than one purpose simultaneously. In this type of learning/assessment task, demonstrating comprehension should always involve real decisions based on concept understanding and not on other elements, such as linguistic forms. In the example 'Identifying coordinates' – a simple task at CLIL beginner level – the 11 target sentences often have the same sentence structure. This means that, when pairing the sentence halves, learners are faced with between two and six possible tail matches for each head, each of which would produce a structurally sound sentence. Only the simplest pair of sentences is open to a straightforward 50/50 choice (they being the first and the fifth sentences). Learners must therefore focus on meaning in order to match the correct tail to each head. The assessment is designed to be carried out in pairs, so offering the teacher another opportunity to listen to dialogue and assess to what extent learners' understanding seems to be based on concept knowledge, as well as whether the learners have internalized the language needed to explain that understanding. Additionally, other elements can be evaluated, such as the pronunciation of key vocabulary. The intention signalled in the task rubric is for the pair work to be followed by a plenary, during which the rationalization of choices can be tested in open class discussion. For those who were less sure either of their choices or of the reason for their choices, this will offer another chance to consolidate learning.

Example: Identifying coordinates

Join the following heads with the correct tails (working in pairs, and later in a plenary):

The horizontal axis is called . . .	. . . positive x and positive y coordinates.
The point (−2,−3) is . . .	. . . 2 units to the left, 3 units up.
The first quadrant contains all the points with . . .	. . . the x-axis.
The fourth quadrant contains all the points with . . .	. . . 2 units to the right, and 3 units up.
The vertical axis is called . . .	. . . the y-axis.
The point (2,3) is . . .	. . . negative x and positive y coordinates.
The point (2,−3) is . . .	. . . 2 units to the left, 3 units down.
The point (−2,3) is . . .	. . . on the x-axis.
The second quadrant contains all the points with . . .	. . . negative x and negative y coordinates.
The point (2,0) is . . .	. . . 2 units to the left, 3 units down.
The point (0,2) is . . .	. . . on the y-axis.

Source: M. Luz Esteve (2007)

Link to worksheet [Accessed 27 April 09]: http://www.xtec.cat/cirel/pla_le/nottingham/mluz_esteve/worksheet1.pdf

Productive assessment tasks

Those productive tasks which elicit content from students either orally or in written format are clearly the more difficult assessment instruments to structure, because they require not just recognition of key language, but also accurate memory for it. Students need not only to understand the topic, but to be able to use language in a way which communicates that understanding, and this will rarely be in single-word form (except in a simple labelling task). Often the material for labelling is given either in an accompanying text or in a box (and so it is another example of the reading-based tasks described in the previous section), but there will be times when the teacher will wish to establish whether the class has properly internalized the key vocabulary and the associated concepts. In this case, the teacher will use an open labelling task for this purpose, such as that shown in the example 'Labelling a diagram' on page 126.

Beyond such simple labelling, students' use of speaking/writing to express understanding needs to be scaffolded. With primary-age children, learners early in a secondary-level CLIL unit, or CLIL beginners in secondary education, this scaffolding is best achieved

Example: Labelling a diagram

Label the diagram with the joints:

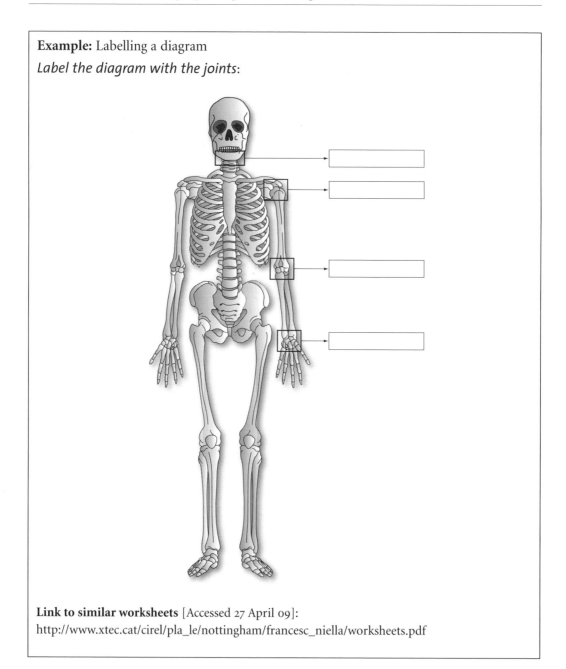

Link to similar worksheets [Accessed 27 April 09]:
http://www.xtec.cat/cirel/pla_le/nottingham/francesc_niella/worksheets.pdf

by using a modelling approach. Diagrammatic structures are still the most useful ways of starting a writing process, as they require key vocabulary and an understanding of processes, but do not necessarily need connected text. A branched or statement key which uses yes/no questions to lead the reader to the correct definition of, for example, an animal, is an example of a real-purpose comprehension task which can also be used as a model for the construction of a different key. A similar way of eliciting key vocabulary is to use a Venn diagram for classification with visuals as a source. By locating the items into separate or joint sections of the Venn diagram (which could consist of between two and five circles with a range of overlap possibilities), learners are demonstrating a conceptual understanding, but without the more complex language which a branched key requires. In this way, the essential descriptive or definitive terms can be tested along with the understanding of how they link and differ, without the need for other language which might divert attention. This works especially well as a group task, because it involves an initial brainstorming of relevant ideas, which should inevitably produce a more comprehensive outcome if shared by a number of students. This will then lead to a group reasoning process in order for decisions to be made about the placement of the assembled ideas onto the diagram. The need to state the reasons for the decisions 'out loud' supports the deeper concept comprehension of individuals and of the group collectively. However, for the production of longer, connected texts, a simple task brief which begins with instructions to *describe*, *explain* or – at a higher level – *justify* is rarely sufficient to elicit a response which will truly represent as full an understanding as learners may actually possess (except with more linguistically advanced students). Using a heard text as the model (such as a short clip of a documentary) is a more demanding bridging task which will ultimately allow learners to produce a fuller, richer text. This is because the task requires the information to be captured as it is spoken and in context rather than through multiple readings carried out at the student's own speed. 'Watching a documentary' gives an example of a heard-text bridging task.

Example: Watching a documentary

Watch the video and list the sources of CO_2 emissions that appear in it.

While listening, read the transcription of the video and complete the gaps.

Energy-dependent . . . . appliances are part of our modern way of life. Most of the energy they use comes from burning gas, ..., which emit carbon dioxide, CO_2, into the atmosphere, ... the planet's climate . . .

Source: J. Miquel Montesinos (2008)

Link to worksheet [Accessed 27 April 09]: http://www.xtec.cat/cirel/pla_le/nile/ miquel_montesinos/students_worksheets.pdf

---

Another variant on this is a task which requires learners to take notes or fill in a diagram or grid, whilst listening to the teacher give a presentation which consolidates and synthesizes previously learned material from the unit. Shorter writing or speaking tasks are appropriate once the modelling is partially or wholly removed. The example task 'Thinking about a problem' scaffolds the language of conclusion but not the actual mathematical reasoning – this needs to come from the students, either individually or in groups.

Example: Thinking about a problem

It's impossible to fold a piece of paper more than eight times!
Sounds odd, doesn't it? What is the reason for that?

Try it yourself and try to answer. Think about the thickness of the paper, the
number of layers and the mathematical rule.

| I think that the reason for this is that . . . |
| I think it is impossible because . . . |
| This is due to . . . |

Source: Imma Romero (2007)

Link to worksheet [Accessed 27 April 09]: http://www.xtec.cat/cirel/pla_le/nottingham/
imma_romero/student.pdf

Science investigations offer opportunities for short pieces of writing or speaking from notes. Once the language of report has been established, the scaffolding can be at least partly withdrawn. This is a good example of the integration of teaching, learning and assessment, as there will be a series of stages involved in the whole process.

1   First of all, modelling or instruction-giving will set out the objectives and will establish the success criteria (not for the investigation, but for the reporting of it).

2   During this process, scaffolding will take place as the teacher circulates and encourages pairs or groups to discuss what they are doing. At this stage, the teacher will sample individuals' and groups' understanding of the concepts behind the investigative work, as well as their ability to see *what* is happening and *why* as the investigation proceeds.

3   The teacher will also become aware during the modelling stage of any really specific language needs which might prevent accurate and full reporting of the investigation.

4   As an assessment opportunity, the reporting stage will be divided into two sections. Firstly, the pairs/groups will create the report using peer scaffolding. Individuals will write this formally or make notes for an oral report. The teacher will then either see the written reports and assess them or will listen to oral reports and offer feedback. In either case, the assessment will still be formative and so form part of the ongoing teaching and learning process.

6.3 **Peer- and self-assessment**

We should lastly explore the subject of peer- and self-assessment, which has been alluded to throughout the chapter. It was noted earlier that there needs to be a close link to success criteria for this to be effective, and that quality and accuracy of expression will not be included in these judgments, except for the most advanced and able learners (although clarity can certainly feature in them). There are numerous reasons for using peer- and self-assessment in the CLIL classroom. From a long-term perspective, we can assert that learners who understand what they are learning, as well as how to demonstrate high-quality understanding, will make greater progress than they might otherwise do if 'kept in the dark'. Black and Wiliam make these two comments:

> [S]elf-assessment by pupils, far from being a luxury, is in fact an essential component of formative assessment. When anyone is trying to learn, feedback about the effort has three elements: recognition of the desired goal, evidence about present position, and some understanding of a way to close the gap between the two.
>
> (Black and Wiliam, 1998: 4)

Peer-assessment which refers to specific criteria and is carried out in discussion between two partners in a class is valuable, because it centres on a process where each student puts into words – and therefore also rehearses – their individual understanding of the topic material. Negotiation takes place and a finer understanding of that material by both parties is possible as a result. This can also be modelled before being completely handed over to students. Language or content 'clinics', as suggested earlier, provide an opportunity for whole-class discussion of issues concerning aspects of the CLIL programme, in which the use of success criteria can be properly explained and demonstrated, and also a model for positive and constructive statements can be given. Self-assessment and self-evaluation are both likely to be better informed if they follow peer-assessment, meaning that target-setting will subsequently also be more relevant. Peer-assessment can also be a larger-scale exercise, including the whole class listening to presentations by other groups and 'marking' them all with reference to a set of criteria. We include on page 130 an example of criteria included in a peer-assessment grid used to assess a PowerPoint presentation (Figure 10).

6.4 Summary of assessment principles

This chapter has attempted to provide a discussion of issues in and potential approaches to the difficult question of assessment in CLIL. It cannot of course do justice to the enormous range of possible differences between contexts, but it has taken a philosophical line which we hope is coherent. We conclude with a set of summary principles which we feel have underpinned the discussion throughout, and which, echoing Short's (1993) plea, advocate alternative assessment methods:

- Clear learning objectives are needed before an assessment focus can be chosen. Learning objectives/outcomes should use a format which acknowledges the different areas of learning in the classroom (such as the 4Cs approach) – this will usually include content/skills first, then language in some form. In a CLIL classroom there are likely to be more possible angles of assessment at any one point because of the integrative nature of content and language. Therefore, even more than in first-language lessons, we cannot always assess everything.

Figure 10: A grid for peer-assessment

PowerPoint	Beginning 1	Developing 2	Accomplished 3	Excellent 4
General aspects of slides	Disorganized and difficult to follow	Organized but difficult to follow	Disorganized but easy to follow	Organized and easy to follow
Pictures and graphics	Small and impossible to understand	Big but difficult to understand	Small but easy to understand	Big and easy to understand
Texts	Small and impossible to understand	Big but difficult to understand	Small but easy to understand	Big and easy to understand
Content	Does not cover all appropriate topics	Covers some of the appropriate topics	Covers most of the appropriate topics	All topics covered. Also interesting facts
Speech	Beginning 1	Developing 2	Accomplished 3	Excellent 4
Matching between speech and images	Speech has nothing to do with slides	Speech is substantially different from slides	Only a few items of the speech are not reflected in the slides	Speech and slides match perfectly
Language	Many pronunciation and grammatical errors	A few errors	Only one or two errors	Pronunciation and grammar are perfect
Communication	The speech is read all the time	The speech is read most of the time	The speech is read sometimes	The speech is not read
Timing between team members	Only one member speaks	One member speaks most of the time	One member speaks more than the other	The two members share speech equally

(Adapted from Alberich, 2007)

- We should use a mixture of formal and informal assessment which is both task-based and assignment-based, and a mix of specific test times and classwork sampling.
- We should familiarize the learners with the assessment measures and success criteria, expressed in a student-friendly format.
- Content knowledge should be assessed using the simplest form of language which is appropriate for that purpose.

- Language should be assessed for a real purpose in a real context – sometimes this will be for form/accuracy, sometimes for communicative competence and/or fluency.
- If the assessment is orally based, 'wait time' is crucial, as in CLIL contexts we should be asking students to think, and thinking takes time and the expression of that thinking takes longer.
- Scaffolding is not 'cheating' – we need to assess what students can do with support before we assess what they can do without it.
- Students need to be able to take some responsibility for their own assessment, both in terms of self- and peer-assessment. This will enhance their longer-term learning potential.

References

Alberich, J. (2007) *English through Science* [Online lesson plans and worksheets]. Available at: http://www.xtec.cat/cirel/pla_le/nottingham/joan_alberich/index.htm [Accessed 29 April 09].

Ames, C. and Ames, R. (1984) 'Systems of student and teacher motivation: Toward a qualitative definition', *Journal of Educational Psychology*, **76**, 4, 535–56.

Assessment Reform Group (2002) *Assessment for Learning: 10 Principles. Research-based principles to guide classroom practice* [Online]. Available at: http://www.qca.org.uk/libraryAssets/media/4031_afl_principles.pdf [Accessed 27 April 2009].

Black, P. and Wiliam, D. (1998) 'Inside the black box: Raising standards through classroom assessment', *Phi Delta Kappa*, [Online] **80**, 2. Available at: http://www.pdkintl.org/kappan/kbla9810.htm [Accessed 28 April 2009].

Bloom, B. S. (1968) *Learning for Mastery. The Evaluation Comment*, Los Angeles: University of California.

Brown, J. D. and Hudson, T. (1998) 'The Alternatives in Language Assessment', *TESOL Quarterly*, **32**, 4, 653–75.

Clarke, S. (2001) *Unlocking Formative Assessment: Practical Strategies for Enhancing Pupils' Learning in the Primary Classroom*, London: Hodder and Stoughton.

Cohen, A. (1994) *Assessing Language Ability in the Classroom* (Second edition), Boston: Newbury House/Heinle and Heinle.

Common European Framework of Reference for Languages: Learning, Teaching, Assessment (2001) Cambridge: Cambridge University Press.

Dweck, C. S. (1986) 'Motivational processes affecting learning', *American Psychologist*, **41**, 1040–8.

Genesee, F. and Upshur, J. A. (1996) *Classroom-Based Evaluation in Second Language Education*, Cambridge: Cambridge University Press.

Pinker, S. (1994) *The Language Instinct: How the Mind Creates Language*, New York: Harper Collins.

Sadler, D. R. (1989) 'Formative assessment and the design of instructional systems', *Instructional Science*, **18**, 119–44.

Scriven, M. (1967) 'The methodology of evaluation', in Stake, R. E. (ed.) (1967) *Curriculum Evaluation* (American Educational Research Association Monograph Series on Evaluation, 1), Chicago: Rand McNally.

Serra, C. (2007) 'Assessing CLIL at primary school: A longitudinal study', *International Journal of Bilingual Education and Bilingualism*, **10**, 5, 582–602.

Short, D. (1993) 'Assessing integrated language and content instruction', *TESOL Quarterly*, **27**, 4, 627–56.

Vygotsky, L. (1978) *Mind in Society*, Cambridge, MA: Harvard University Press.

Zangl, R. (2000) 'Monitoring language skills in Austrian primary (elementary) schools: A case study', *Language Testing*, **17**, 250–60.

7 Evaluating the impact of CLIL programmes

This chapter explores the types of evidence that should be produced during an evaluation of the impact of a CLIL programme. It firstly reviews the scope of earlier evaluations of bilingual immersion programmes, which have focused mainly on programmes' effect on learners' linguistic rather than content progression. It then offers an initial template for future evaluations in order to ensure a sufficient evidence-base to make secure judgments. This template synthesizes potential approaches which might relate to performance or attitudes, which might involve students and teachers as research subjects and which might use quantitative or qualitative data. The template sections are then used as a basis for a review of more recent investigations into CLIL programmes. The intention is to make the template more meaningful through illustrations of how such evaluations have supplied the types of data it suggests and to review potential gaps which might be filled in future investigations. The chapter concludes with a summary and some next steps.

7.1 The research background: How far is immersion research applicable to CLIL?

Within the very rich vein of research into immersion education stemming from Canada are the key summaries by Lambert and Tucker (1972), Swain and Lapkin (1982, 1986), Cummins and Swain (1986), Genesee (1987) and Lapkin, Hart and Swain (1991). Such reviews suggested that early **total immersion** programmes through French enabled a similar level of language performance in mathematics and science lessons as did English-only instruction amongst English-speaking learners. Clearly, learners of different abilities always achieve different levels of content competence, but the range was similar across the bilingual and first-language groups. Cummins' (1981) work on BICS (Basic Interpersonal Communication Skills) and CALP (Cognitive Academic Language Proficiency) showed that this took a comparatively long time (at least five years) and that form-focused language lessons were still needed for linguistic accuracy as opposed to fluency. **Partial immersion** programmes were not as successful, but **late immersion** variants achieved comparable levels as long as there had been instruction in French for a number of years before immersion began, possibly due to the need for language (competence) threshold levels to be attained (Johnson, Shek and Law, 1993). Later reports (for example, Swain, 1996; Tisdell, 1999; Hagino, 2002; Thompson et al., 2002; MacSwan and Pray, 2005) still focused strongly on the effect of bilingual programmes on the second-language development of learners.

In **total immersion** education, the whole curriculum is taught in the second language from the beginning of formal education.

In **partial immersion**, certain aspects of the curriculum are taught through the second language.

In **late immersion**, the curriculum is taught through the second language from a later start point, for example from the age of 11.

This attention to language competence tends to suggest (even if it is not the case) that the content subject is being used as a mere vehicle for language enhancement, as is advocated by writers on English for Specific Purposes (for example, Dudley-Evans and St John, 1998). A similar perspective is found in initiatives such as the ESL Standards (referred to by Short, 2000), which includes a goal of being able to use English to achieve academically in content areas, but nevertheless focuses on essentially language-related targets. Fortune-Tara and Tedick (2003) reviewed the evidence on immersion programmes and also consistently avoided a focus on content-subject knowledge, skills and understanding, considering almost entirely linguistic skills development in the first and second language. They did acknowledge in a single sentence (by citing evidence from Cloud, Genesee and Hamayan, 2000) that studies have consistently shown that learners achieve as well as non-bilingual learners on standard mathematical tests. Hofstetter (2004) and de Jong (2002) reported on the language and mathematics attainment of learners, but the overwhelming thrust of the conclusion was centred around the language element. Housen (2002), who writes in the European context, alluded to successful learning outcomes in content-subject areas through the European baccalaureate programme, but conceded that the evidence was not as detailed or comprehensive as that available for Canadian French immersion programmes and presented evidence which was mainly linguistic.

A few researchers have studied the effect of a bilingual programme on some aspects of content knowledge (for example, de Jabrun, 1997; Turnbull, Lapkin and Hart, 2001; Kirk Senesac, 2002; Yang-Yu et al., 2005; Lindholm-Leary and Borsato, 2005). But of these, only de Jabrun and Kirk Senesac evaluated the effects on more than simply language and mathematics. De Jabrun (op. cit.), writing in Australia, found that after a year, immersion maths students outperformed mainstream students, and immersion science students performed as well as their mainstream counterparts. He concluded that this showed that immersion students were the more efficient learners. Kirk Senesac (op. cit.), evaluating a US two-way bilingual programme, found that students experiencing partial immersion through English achieved higher scores in language, maths, science and social science and that the English-speaking students achieved a high mastery in Spanish at the same time. Within an exploration of the role of cognition and creativity in bilingualism and multilingual classrooms, Baetens Beardsmore (2008) offers a very useful summary of some key research by Gajo and Serra (2002) and Cavalli (2005). This research showed that, in some cases, while factual material was learned better in first-language environments, skills-based learning was superior in bilingual contexts. This could be due to the enhanced interactivity often present in good CLIL classrooms. In another departure from the language focus in immersion research, de Jong (2006) examined the additive benefits in a *social* sense of an integrated programme, and evaluated this programme through qualitative teacher evidence. This focus on affective elements is a welcome and necessary element of evaluation in the light of current evidence from psychological studies of the integration of the cognitive, motivational and emotional aspects of learning (Dai and Sternberg, 2004, and see Chapter 5 of this volume).

This book has shown through the earlier chapters how important the content element of a CLIL programme is – indeed, content and cognition objectives are often set as advance parameters, and communication objectives supply the means of meeting these parameters (Coyle, 2005). Clearly then, if a CLIL programme is to teach geography, science, art or mathematics through a second or foreign language, we need rigorous assessments of the outcomes of that subject, both in terms of conceptual knowledge and understanding (through statistics drawn from tests parallel in design to those which would be taken in the first language) and through the comparison of work produced by CLIL learners with that of students operating in the first language.

When a CLIL programme emerges gradually and the staff leading it add content or range when appropriate, and in response to evaluations of specific aspects of the programme, the evidence available tends to be piecemeal and less coherent as a package. But such an 'organic' evaluation can also be useful in helping us to determine the parameters we should establish as we seek a more rigorous methodology. This chapter now presents a template for evaluation and subsequently uses a body of such evidence (taken from published research reports and one unpublished, more *ad hoc* case study) to exemplify how the measures recommended can contribute to a secure and global understanding of the success (or otherwise) of a CLIL initiative.

7.2 A template for evaluations

There is a clear need now for more rigorous and regular monitoring through a range of measures chosen to bring together a broader range of perspectives on CLIL programmes. We need to gain more depth of analysis and understanding of the processes and outcomes of these courses. This is mirrored in a recent article by Kiely on the evaluation of language learning programmes, in which he summarizes:

> Any programme can be effective in promoting language learning. The key issues are how it has been made to work, and which factors and events have shaped success . . . Evaluation then becomes a set of strategies to document and understand the programme.
>
> (Kiely, 2009: 114)

We now suggest and subsequently discuss a portfolio of evaluation measures, summarized in Table 3 on page 136.

Table 3: Portfolio of evaluation measures

Evaluation element	Subjects	Nature of data	Method of analysis
Performance evidence	Learners	• Testing which is commensurate with national methods and expectations	Statistical, comparative
		• Informal assessment within teaching programmes	Criterion-referenced
		• Portfolios of work	Criterion-referenced, comparative with work in L1
		• Summary, predictive and value-added data	Statistical, comparative
Affective evidence	Learners (and potentially also their families)	• Questionnaires	Statistical and qualitative for open-ended questions
		• Interviews (group and individual)	Qualitative
		• Motivational evidence (take-up)	Statistical
	Teachers	• Questionnaires	Statistical and qualitative for open-ended questions
		• Interviews (individual)	Qualitative
Process evidence	Learners	• Transcripts of verbal reports arising from individual think-aloud or paired/group tasks	Qualitative / coded interaction / discourse analysis
Materials and task evidence	Materials and tasks	• Materials analysis • Task analysis	Qualitative / coded by theoretically underpinned criteria / discourse analysis

Performance evidence (that is, how well the learners perform in the CLIL subject) is clearly vital and, as we show in this chapter, can be compiled in several different ways. In education systems which are heavily dependent on centralized set measures, CLIL programmes need to show they stand up to the scrutiny that all subjects are required to undergo. This might include comparative test results as well as predictive and value-added data in countries such as the UK, where established expectations exist about progression between testing points (for example, learners are expected to make two national curriculum levels' progress in English, maths and science between the ages of seven and 11 and again by the age of 14 – if they make more progress than this expected amount, then this indicates that the school is 'adding value'). Elsewhere, more informal teacher- or school-centred measures will be acceptable. A very good way of evaluating CLIL outcomes which avoids statistical measures (which will not always translate between contexts, especially internationally) is by simple portfolios of work. As long as the context and some evidence of the processes which produced them is also provided, they have a real power to speak to other professionals in the field. Indeed, teachers often find concrete visible learner outcomes (rather than statistics) to be the most interesting and most significant evidence of a programme's success. Such portfolios can usefully be comparative within the context (between first- and second-language outcomes) so as to demonstrate the ability of CLIL to teach content effectively.

But the *affective* evidence (regarding motivation, anxiety and so on) is also very important. We need testimony from both learners and teachers, and from different points in the learning process – from CLIL beginners to those with complete experience of a programme. Larger scale questionnaire evidence is essential to ensure that focus-group interviews are not biased by the selection of subjects (participants). Nevertheless, targeted focus-group work adds much to the baseline data, as it provides opportunities for exploring the reasons for both positive and negative attitudes in greater depth.

Taking performance and affective evidence together, we can aim for a fuller cross-referenced portfolio using a range of students across the ability range. The portfolio can include statistical performance data with examples of outcomes, and student testimony in the form of questionnaire data and interview transcripts. Such a combination would demonstrate to an external evaluator that individuals are achieving, and that they feel positive about both the process of CLIL and its outcomes. Any positive changes in views about CLIL across the year groups (which appears to be normal judging by the focus-school evidence) should offer, internally, opportunities for more experienced students to mentor those beginning the programme. Student testimony will always carry more weight than teacher testimony in this respect.

The above two elements constitute the large majority of current available evidence on CLIL or bilingual programmes. But as the portfolio of evaluation measures shows, we will also benefit from a collection and analysis of data around *learning processes* and *materials/tasks*. This is more complex both from a logistical standpoint, with regard to data collection or analysis, and as regards the establishment of appropriate analysis tools. The analysis of learning processes is fundamental as we attempt to locate the basis of both content and language acquisition in a best-practice CLIL programme. Westhoff (2004) suggests that successful learning occurs through a process of natural repetition and juxtaposition when a range of stimulus types accompanied by a task stimulate and strengthen a whole set of neural connections. If this is indeed the case, then we need to find ways to see this in action more clearly. In time, the neurosciences will probably be able to give further insight into what happens in the brain when a person learns through first and additional languages. In the here and now, we can already utilize collaborative think-aloud protocols, centred on carefully constructed tasks which generate a visible/audible problem-solving process. If this is then recorded as evidence of knowledge construction as it happens, we will gain better insights into the dynamic of content learning which also causes real language learning to occur as part of an integrated process.

Alongside this knowledge about learning processes, we should be able to develop insights into the nature of tasks and the combination of input stimuli which cause more and better learning to occur. This will generate a set of criteria against which new materials and tasks can be evaluated, and this in turn gives us a fourth area of CLIL programme evaluation – one which new programmes can apply at the design stage and then revisit. This last element is new but not completely untried, and should certainly form part of a future agenda.

Beyond this introduction of greater detail and rigour in the evaluative systems adopted, it may also be important to review the CLIL provision and to attempt to ascertain whether the current level of this is appropriate and effective. For example, if learners currently have progressive contact with a single content subject, is this more beneficial than a change between years from one content subject to another? Should the programme even be expanded to two content subjects for all, thus moving closer to partial immersion? Where a secondary school with a CLIL programme has very close links with local primary schools, it is also in a position to review the nature of provision in the pre-secondary sector and this could enable an earlier start to CLIL programmes where appropriate.

Performance evidence

Performance evidence is a vital component of any evaluation, as those who doubt the efficacy of CLIL programmes often suspect that learners' content knowledge will suffer when compared with their attainment via first-language programmes. The older evaluations of bilingual education focused heavily on language outcomes, as was shown in the short review earlier in this chapter, and this did little to allay such suspicions. All CLIL evaluations should therefore build in assessment of outcomes in the content subject. There are at least three possible ways to achieve this (outlined in this paragraph), but it is important to bear in mind that understanding a concept is a different capability from expressing that understanding to someone else, and an awareness of this issue should inform how such assessments are made. Stages of understanding are involved irrespective of the vehicular language, for example Tzur's (2007) distinction between participatory and anticipatory understanding in mathematics, where the former needs a prompt to be activated, while the latter is independently held. In addition to this, the CLIL language may be a limiting factor unless the appropriate format for the expression of that understanding is offered by the teacher. Chapter 6 explored this issue in more detail, but we will reiterate the important points here. Tests in the CLIL vehicular language which are simply a translation of a test set in the first language may not provide reliable comparative data if, for example, they demand responses in continuous text which might be beyond the additional language competence of the learner. Material may be understood, and this understanding can be demonstrated through means other than linear writing – for example, through visuals, tabular writing or supported oral presentations. A second method might be to assess understanding through a first-language test, but the draw-back of this approach is that specialist language for the topic may only have been learned in the CLIL language. A third and better method might be to gather a portfolio of work on the topic which shows in various formats the understanding of elements of the topic; a comparison between the output of a first-language group and a CLIL group can be made by professionals working in the content subject area and this would offer a more reliable and fuller evaluation of the success of the unit.

Recent evaluations of performance in CLIL programmes still tend to focus mainly on the language outcomes. These include those by Admiraal, Westhoff and de Bot (2006), Lasagabaster (2008), Campo, Grisaleña and Alonso (2007) – also published in a shorter version as Alonso et al. (2008) – and de Zarobe (2008). An unpublished case study (Woodfield and Neofitou, 2006) also looks at content outcomes in geography. Some of these studies present comparative data drawn from CLIL classes and non-CLIL control groups. Such investigations clearly need to address the methodologies of data-gathering very carefully, as direct comparisons need to be fully justified through sample matching and parallel testing. So far, standardised instruments have been adopted so that validity does not have to be separately demonstrated. Various approaches are possible. For example, in the Basque region of Spain, Lasagabaster (2008 – see page 140) set up a series of four hypotheses to test, whereas the studies by Admiraal, Westhoff and de Bot (2006) in the Netherlands, and Campo, Grisaleña and Alonso (2007), also in the Basque Country, made simple direct comparisons between bilingual and non-bilingual groups using standard measures of English language proficiency. The language measures were Cambridge ESOL tests (Campo, Grisaleña and Alonso, ibid.) and established tests in vocabulary, reading comprehension and oral proficiency (Admiraal, Westhoff and de Bot, op. cit.). As generalized measures, they were of course not related to the teaching and learning which had actually taken place in the CLIL programme.

There is a dilemma here which will need to be considered in future evaluations which focus on language: should the language gains be measured in more global terms, using an acknowledged standard instrument, or should the actual gains of the CLIL programme be measured? Moreover, should a language skill such as reading comprehension or oral competence be evaluated, and, if so, how can any differences in performance between groups be ascribed to the CLIL and non-CLIL programmes without very close sample matching? What about the role of different teachers? Would an ideal scenario involve a single teacher teaching different matched groups in both the first language and a CLIL language?

Admiraal, Westhoff and de Bot's (2006) findings that the bilingual group achieved significantly better in some respects – including final English examination performance – but no differently in others, were partially conclusive but not wholly so, ('ambiguous' in the authors' own words):

> The bilingual school programme had strong positive effects on students' reading comprehension and oral proficiency in English, but did not appear to affect the growth curve in the receptive word knowledge of students.
>
> (Admiraal, Westhoff and de Bot, 2006: 91)

As the authors identify in the article, the control and experimental groups were not directly comparable at the start of the programme, and the bilingual groups began with higher levels of competence in the measures used. Differences in the later teaching programmes also made the final results difficult to compare. Such an evaluation makes a valuable contribution to our understanding of the potential effects of CLIL programmes, partly because of what it does show and partly through its own acknowledged limitations, which point the way to future amendments to evaluation practice.

Two of Lasagabaster's (2008) four hypotheses related to a CLIL/non-CLIL comparison, but he also investigated performance within CLIL groups according to gender and sociocultural status measures. The results of his evaluation show unequivocal gains made by CLIL learners over non-CLIL learners, measured by a mixture of objectively marked receptive-skill tests and a profiling technique (which inevitably has a subjective element) for productive skills. The groups which were compared were not matched except on their English learning histories, and although the CLIL sample sizes were comparatively large, the non-CLIL group was a single class. The work by Campo, Grisaleña and Alonso (2007) – which was a longitudinal study on a broad basis involving a range of types of data – sought to address the issue of matching by selecting a control group of ten for each of their experimental groups which was as carefully matched as was possible on the basis of existing academic performance. However, the authors note that the initial testing showed the experimental groups were higher achieving than the control groups. Lasagabaster also acknowledges a factor which could potentially skew the results of his own study in the Basque Country:

> In the case of this study it is possible that the CLIL students could be more gifted and motivated to learn English as a foreign language than their non-CLIL counterparts, and this is obviously a question to be considered.
>
> (Lasagabaster, 2008: 38)

Lasagabaster defends his position by quoting Collins et al. (1999), who justify the ecological validity of findings of evaluations in existing educational contexts where variables cannot always be controlled. In fact the data show a significant gain through CLIL, with a CLIL group surpassing a non-CLIL group, even though the CLIL learners were a year younger. Moreover, there were no significant differences within the CLIL groups by gender or sociocultural status, suggesting that CLIL offers potential gains to all students. Also in the Basque region of Spain, de Zarobe (2008), focusing on the narrower field of speech production, established a superiority of CLIL over non-CLIL groups. Again, although the groups were not matched, the evaluation was rigorous, the testing was criterion-referenced, and the inclusion of **type/token ratio** (which is objective) added to the measures taken. This showed higher scores by the bilingual programme students. The analysis was statistically based and measures of significance were produced as evidence. The language benefits of CLIL programmes are clearly demonstrated by these evaluations and each gives a clear methodology and uses appropriate rigour in drawing its conclusions. Future work on language competence should build on these examples, perhaps focusing more now on defining what the CLIL learners are achieving rather than comparing them with non-CLIL learners, so taking away the issue of 'control' and 'experimental' group matching and ensuring that the results of the CLIL programme itself are measured, rather than using a standardized test which does not reflect at all the teaching and learning which has taken place.

> **Type/token ratio** refers to the ratio of the number of different words (*types*), to the total number of words (*tokens*). The richness of a text can be measured by calculating this ratio – shorter texts tend to have higher scores.

The unpublished evaluation mentioned previously (Woodfield and Neofitou, 2006), conducted in a UK secondary context, had some individual strengths, although it emerged in a more *ad hoc* fashion as the programme developed, and was therefore not as scientifically rigorous as the other studies cited here. Interestingly, however, the study showed definite gains from the CLIL programme for less able learners. Using standard UK predictive measures based on national tests in literacy and mathematics at 11 years old, the authors showed the least able in a cohort of approximately 200 girls reaching targets for foreign language attainment earlier than expected, and making at least expected progress with the content subject (geography). The measures, which related to work produced which matched English National Curriculum attainment target descriptors, inevitably have an element of subjectivity, but this was a clear attempt to look at both language and content. (As with the majority of research into the effectiveness of immersion programmes, the previous studies cited in this section gave little or no detailed attention to content achievement; if achievement had been made in this area, it had clearly not been as rigorously evaluated.) The teachers involved felt that the increased focus demanded of the less able may have contributed to this enhanced performance. One teacher stated:

> 93 per cent of the students involved in two immersion classes have decided to opt for immersion geography in Year 8. These are from a wide range of abilities. Many of these students know that it is more difficult but are prepared to rise to the challenge.

Clearly it is vital to evaluate the success in terms of learning outcomes when deciding if a programme is appropriate, and to measure this accurately for the whole ability range. Apart from collecting some statistical evidence over three years, the focus school also began to create a collection of work, as they realized the limitations of simply statistically comparing different groups which were not easily strictly matched, and which were taught by different teachers through two different languages – one through the majority first language and one through a common second language.

Affective evidence

High motivation, which helps to enable deeper concentration, is especially important to success in learning through an additional language, and it follows therefore that monitoring participants' attitudes towards CLIL and their motivational level should be a key element in an evaluation process. Within this broad area of research are many different approaches to establishing data and many different questions to address, as we will see in the review below. It is vital that the data-gathering and analysis processes are seen as rigorous in this area, especially if qualitative approaches are used. Some will doubt that data on affect (such as learner motivation) have as much significance as those on performance; some will doubt that smaller group interviews will have as much significance as broad-scale questionnaires; some will prefer data to be statistically rather than interpretively analysed. But the social and emotional dimensions of learning have established importance (Dai and Sternberg, 2004) and teachers' knowledge of the affective side of their learners is vital in their own understanding of how to determine both the task styles and outcomes which will inspire learners and also the degree of scaffolding needed to support their learning.

Interviews with CLIL learners (Hood, 2006) demonstrate that, in the early stages of a CLIL programme, enjoyment, motivation and self-esteem can be at risk as students come to terms with the initial challenges of adapting to a CLIL methodology. The interviews also establish that CLIL is more demanding, but is geared to greater achievement. Compare these two sets of extracts from the same focus-group interview with a group of 11-year-old girls (Year 7 in the English/Welsh system), three weeks into a CLIL programme at the school which was evaluated in Woodfield and Neofitou's unpublished data (2006). *R* is the researcher and *P1–P4* are the learners:

Extract 1 (first year of CLIL):
>   **R**   What do you think so far of doing geography in French?
>   **P1**   This is crazy.
>   **P2**   No!
>   **P3**   I was expecting that she [the teacher] was going to translate but she didn't.
>   **P4**   I didn't know what to think – we wanted her to speak English, not French.

Extract 2 (first year of CLIL):
>   **R**   So is it different from French lessons – do you learn more or less in geography?
>   **P4**   You do pick up words.
>   **P1**   I did know what she meant if she points at things.
>   **P2**   French lessons are different – they're, like, the basics.
>   **P4**   You learn a lot more than just the basics. French geography is something different. You do pick up on things – it's more interesting. It's not just, like, one, two, three – you're learning a proper subject.
>   **P1**   When you say to other people – 'I've learned geography in French', then they think 'Wow!'.

(Hood, 2006)

The Year 8 group (aged 12–13 years), just beginning their second year of geography in French, had a stronger view on CLIL. Extracts from their interview transcript are as follows:

Extract 3 (second year of CLIL):

> **P5** When we started it in Year 7 we felt we didn't understand it at all, but now it's not as bad.

Extract 4 (second year of CLIL):

> **P6** In French, you just learn about animals and stuff like that, but in geography you have to learn about the world. Because we're doing geography in French, our levels are higher.

Extract 5 (second year of CLIL):

> **P7** Each subject is helping the other subject. It's easier to understand the French lessons, because you're doing geography.

Extract 6 (second year of CLIL):

> **P6** You have to take more notice in French geography. In French you don't really need to concentrate.

(Hood, 2006)

The major instruments for investigating the affective dimension are questionnaires and interviews, with the former useful in gauging the opinions of large cohorts and the latter the more detailed views of individuals. The data presented above clearly indicate the benefits of interviewing learners. A questionnaire might very well have elicited the comments in Extract 1 from the first-year CLIL learners, which were based on a more superficial and highly anxious initial response to geography in French. The comments in Extract 2 from later in the 20-minute interview, however, demonstrate a more thoughtful response. CLIL evaluations need both types of instruments to ensure breadth and depth in the affective data we gain. The members of that group were nominated by the teacher, who deliberately included people whose views might have been less positive. Many interview groups emerge through a volunteering process and could be said to be unrepresentative for that reason, and so following established focus-group formation (see, for example, Greenbaum, 1998) is an important element of rigour. The questions which prompted those responses were open and tried to avoid leading the interviewees. It is very important to report the questions as well as the responses if an evaluation is to be transparent and authoritative.

In recent research, Woodfield and Neofitou (2006), Campo, Grisaleña and Alonso (2007), Marsh, Zajac and Gozdawa-Gołębiowska (2008), Alonso, Grisaleña and Campo (2008), Dalton-Puffer et al. (2009), Lasagabaster and Sierra (2009) and Yassin et al. (2009), have all investigated the affective dimension as part of their evaluations. Both the advantages and disadvantages identified by learners in the Polish Profile Report (Marsh, Zajac and Gozdawa-Gołębiowska, 2008) show evidence of integrative as well as instrumental motivation – for example, that CLIL allowed them to participate in foreign exchanges (integrative) and bilingual education broadened learners' horizons (instrumental – see Chapter 5 of this volume for an outline of motivation theory). Given the scope of the evaluation (19 schools were involved), this offers a reliable view that CLIL programmes, just as any other educational provision, will be perceived in radically different ways by their participants, who will of course have differing priorities. Detailed analysis is not given, but the very varied profile of perceived advantages and disadvantages seems to vindicate the use of a questionnaire approach to a large number of participants to secure a full overview of the important factors. Campo, Grisaleña and Alonso (2007) highlight the role of gender in learners' affective responses to CLIL, demonstrating in their analysis of a questionnaire that female students have a more positive view of CLIL programmes than males. They are also less likely to believe that content results will be worse and that it will need more time and effort. However, the authors also show that, in both populations, a majority believe their achievement in the content subject will be as good as it would be with non-CLIL instruction, while acknowledging that this achievement takes more effort. In both reports of the same programme (Campo, Grisaleña and Alonso, 2007, and Alonso, Grisaleña and Campo, 2008) the affective evidence is again not as detailed as the performance evidence, but the research team usefully also talked to the families of learners, the vast majority of whom believed the programme had real value. The younger the learners, the more important is parental knowledge about and support for the programme, especially given the acknowledged need for deeper concentration on the part of the learners.

Dalton-Puffer et al. (2009) investigate specifically vocational CLIL with a large-scale questionnaire of former students, including a small proportion who had experienced a CLIL programme, and a set of 20 interviews with current CLIL students in the 17–19 age range. The questionnaire findings point to a mixed response with strong but certainly not unequivocal support for a CLIL route, especially with regard to the question asked about the potential loss of content depth when working in a foreign language. However, the former CLIL students rated their own foreign language competence more highly than did those who had not followed a CLIL route. Interestingly, the notion emerged from the interviews that, if the content teacher's capability in the CLIL language was less than perfect, this could involve students in more independent work, giving them in the end more self-assurance. The views of teachers themselves, parallel to those of learners in any evaluation, is another important dimension and will be explored later in this section.

Lasagabaster and Sierra (2009) carried out a study with slightly younger secondary-age CLIL learners and specifically investigated through a large-scale questionnaire their attitudes towards English and towards the two other languages which formed part of their education – Basque and Spanish. This was achieved by a measure which collected their views on a range of antonyms applied to each language. They also addressed a question on whether there might be differences in these attitudes by gender. Their findings are clear that CLIL experience enhances attitudes towards other languages and that this is more prevalent amongst female learners. They found a strong instrumental motivation, although this is harder to extrapolate reliably as it depends so much on the choice of adjectives for the antonyms set. But again, this raises an important issue – what really motivates CLIL learners to work harder (as all seem to say they do)? Is it principally an intrinsic or extrinsic motivation? Yassin et al. (2009), writing in a Malaysian context, raise the issue of less able learners' right to a CLIL programme, but one which takes their attitudes and learning needs properly into account. The authors' sampling of attitudes gave a clear indication that lower

English proficiency students had a more negative view of CLIL, because it did not cater for them directly. This finding also underpins the need for the process and materials research suggested in the next two sections.

From Woodfield and Neofitou (2006) comes an attempt to use an alternative measure of affect, that of 'classroom climate'. This was a measure adapted specifically for geography, based on a general instrument devised by Hay McBer (2000). The figures from two years' use of this instrument – albeit with slightly different descriptors for the choice of agreement – are not unequivocally in favour of CLIL. At this point the significant differences between geography taught through English or French seemed to be between different teachers rather than between the different media of instruction, and so the measure proved inconclusive. But such instruments, piloted and then used as part of a rigorous external evaluation, could provide a very useful scale against which to measure CLIL and non-CLIL programmes where the same teacher or the same class is involved. Along with the classroom climate questionnaire, students were asked the question: *What prevents you from learning in geography?* The results reflected a range of elements, the majority of which concerned behaviour/concentration issues in the classroom. Only six per cent of responses directly concerned the language of delivery of the subject (which was French).

Another potential type of affective evidence is the actual number who opt for a CLIL course. Woodfield and Neofitou (2006) found that, after two years of running a CLIL programme, in September 2005, 50 per cent of learners chose to continue CLIL geography into a second year, while in September 2006, 93 per cent chose to do so. In addition to this, in 2006, 72 per cent opted to maintain their personal, social and health education (PSHE) programme in French into a second year, although this could have been because the tutor delivering the programme moved with them. These figures demonstrate well, although in a very simple way, the developing success of a programme which is clearly attracting greater motivation as it 'beds in' and is seen as both 'normal' and achieving.

The CLIL teacher should not be forgotten as we seek evidence of the affective dimension. CLIL courses, especially when new and developing, ask much of those teachers, who may either have language or content expertise, but often do not have both. Campo et al. (2007) sought the opinions of teachers about their confidence in their ability to teach the programme and their teaching strategies. They found a high level of confidence, but this occupies a very limited space in their report and was not investigated in any detail. An MA dissertation by Moate (2008) explored in more depth Finnish CLIL teachers' anxieties, including their views on whether their own practice was amended (voluntarily or unwillingly) by the CLIL programme. Here there were mixed views. Teachers were able to see the benefits of CLIL for learners, but this might be at the expense of their own comfort as teachers. Hard questions need to be posed to teachers out of respect for their crucial role in the process; their commitment may be greater or less depending on how they are allowed to manage the programme and to voice concerns where they feel them. All evaluations should therefore include a teacher dimension.

The two major types of study – seeking performance and affective data – account for the majority of work accomplished so far and will continue to feature strongly in future evaluations, but there is also some work going on in two further areas: the learning process and materials/task evaluation. These areas should not be neglected as they offer a different level of insight into CLIL learning and teaching, although it is not so easy to generalize from them, as it is more likely that they will reflect a single setting in a single context. In addition to the data gathering and analysis, there is even more of a need in these less researched areas also to evaluate the instruments used. Some reports mentioned below have done this and demonstrate an additional strand to be considered.

Process evidence

Until now, far fewer researchers have investigated the learning process in CLIL classrooms. This is clearly a very fruitful area for research as one strong data-type for learning is evidence of it in action. CLIL is often associated with social-constructivist classroom settings involving active learning in groups. Transcripts of dialogue from such group tasks can powerfully demonstrate evidence of higher-level thinking and the inter-action between content and language. For those not yet experienced in CLIL, the question 'What does a CLIL classroom really look like?' can best be answered by examining detailed, accurate transcripts of learners engaged in the process. As we have indicated before, there is a need for analysis of such transcripts from a content-subject perspective, so teachers considering engagement with CLIL can judge how far the depth and cognitive challenge really are delivered by CLIL programmes. Moreover, a newer approach to practice-based evidence for effective CLIL introduced in Chapter 4 – the LOCIT process (Coyle, 2005) – not only involves CLIL teachers in articulating their own theories of prac-tice based on the evidence they collect in their classrooms, it also engages the learners in discussing their CLIL learning.

The focus of the analysis so far in the few studies undertaken which investigate the learning process in the CLIL classroom has tended to be on aspects of *language* learning; for example, Dalton-Puffer and Nikula (2006). Airey (2009) has also investigated a con-tent-based outcome linked to a performance measure. In his study, Airey used statistical measures from applied linguistics to measure CLIL learners' speech rate and length of utterances when they worked in a science content area. But he also sought to establish the level of scientific literacy in the CLIL language through a more subjective analysis of the *content* of their talk. Findings were mixed, and seemed to show simply that individuals could be more or less successful, depending on a number of factors connected with both content and language. The report both analyses the data obtained and discusses the valid-ity of such measures for the CLIL context, which is a very useful added benefit for other researchers who wish to develop the direction. Dalton-Puffer and Nikula (2006) made a very detailed analysis of language data showing both teacher and student statements and questions from instructional and regulatory (that is, classroom management) discourse. The rigorous approach, using a large sample of lessons from the two contexts (Austria and Finland), explored the nature of CLIL classroom discourse and demonstrated that it was more limited in certain respects than some might expect, as, after all, it is still set firmly in a classroom with its own contextual expectations of the subject and style of dialogue. The purpose of the investigation was to qualify how important awareness of discourse might be in determining the best structure for CLIL lessons:

> We want to argue, awareness of the specific conditions of language use in classrooms should serve as a starting point for considering which pedagogical action would best ensure students' access to a maximally rich linguistic learning environment within the constraints of the institutional context in question.
>
> (Dalton-Puffer and Nikula, 2006: 264)

This is a clear example of the type of evaluation which focuses on a very specific aspect of CLIL classrooms in a very detailed manner. There is much scope for this approach, but we will need very many such investigations to build up a complete and generalizable picture.

Evaluations of language use in classrooms can take a broad variety of forms. Some will focus entirely on linguistic questions and analyse how learners are using language from a perspective of how much and what kinds of language they use (this itself is varied and could include notions, functions, or syntactical or grammatical competence). Others will focus on the way use of language shows understanding, or how language is used to explain concepts. Further types of analysis might centre on specific aspects of learner dialogues, showing how meaning of texts is constructed or how understanding is negotiated within a group.

Materials and task evidence

Research is also needed into the nature of effective CLIL materials, from both a design and a task perspective. In a time of rapidly emerging new technologies and the subsequent multimodal learning opportunities, the nature of good CLIL input for both teacher-directed and student-centred learning is very much open to scrutiny and development. Similarly, task styles and the learning dialogues or individual outputs they generate may be uncovered by process research, as explored in the previous section. Scaffolding has such an important role within CLIL courses, especially in contexts where the language is not intensively developed beforehand. We noted in the section about research into affect the comments from learners in the earliest stages about the seeming impossibility of the content/language combination. The balance between challenge and a level of demand which makes learning difficult or unlikely is a fine one (Chapters 3, 4 and 5 all explore this issue).

Westhoff (2004) and de Graaff et al. (2007) have focused on this area from a standpoint centred on **connectionism**, and in so doing have opened the door to a much wider perspective on research into learning in CLIL classrooms. Their work, centred in the Netherlands, is still oriented more towards language development than content-subject learning. Indeed, de Graaff et al. (ibid.) overtly tested an observation tool designed to measure how much the CLIL lessons resemble good language teaching. This built on Westhoff's earlier work, in which he explored task types which might be beneficial for CLIL and referenced them to connectionist theories about processing and learning. The notion that concepts have a range of features (some linguistic, some not), and that activating a range of features strengthens neural networks and thereby supports learning, resonates with a CLIL approach. In CLIL, content and language are integrated and careful repetition of language and multi-modal input can supply the 'range of features', as shown below:

> It seems to be logical to hypothesise that retention and ease of activation is improved by mental activities involving:
>
> - many features
> - from many different categories
> - in current [that is, recently used] combinations
> - in great frequency
> - simultaneously.

(Westhoff, 2004: 60–1)

He linked these features to tasks related to language learning such as webquests (see Chapter 5) and suggested that CLIL might benefit from such a focus. Ongoing work by the research team in Utrecht is designed to focus more closely on the effects of differing task types on the ability to produce better output.

> The major use of the term **connectionism** is to describe the activity around neural networks in the human brain. Babies are born with these networks which are activated by cognitive (as well as other forms of) stimulation. Connections are strengthened or decay from frequency or lack of activation and this is linked to learning and memory.

Developing frameworks for analysis such as this is a really useful activity, both because it can be used to investigate classrooms in a structured way and because, once presented, it can be challenged, developed, refined or refuted by research teams in other contexts. This area of research, linked to classroom processes, will provide a very positive alternative to the ongoing performance and affective evaluations.

This chapter has reported on a very broad set of research, and has shown that already there is an existing set of approaches which range across paradigms, subjects and foci. Some use quantitative/statistical data, some analyse qualitatively; some look at performance, some at affective elements; and some focus on people (learners, families, teachers) and some on materials or processes. By presenting the template, we do not advocate a division into radically different strands, nor do we suggest that all evaluations should contain everything. It is clear that all four sections are interlocking: for example, affect and performance are often intricately linked (a vigorous on-going motivation of teachers and learners is key to the success of CLIL programmes to an even greater extent than it is to conventional language-learning programmes); investigating classroom language in use can explain performance data; discovering in detail attitudes towards task types can contribute to a more meaningful materials-design process. This awareness that there are different approaches can support the design of more rigorous, more targeted and more sophisticated combinations of data. We should remember that student testimony is vital and forms part of the 'performance' data, as the student view of the value of a programme is ultimately dependent as much on the perception of its outcomes as it is on the nature of the lessons. Similarly, data on student attitudes offer a lens on the very important affective elements of learning where the motivational, emotional and cognitive dimensions interact. In other words, the combination of these approaches and types of data are vital to any evaluation of a CLIL programme. We have advocated that a focus on the content subject is essential in both the statistical evidence presented and the teacher and student testimony, because all client groups (students, teachers, parents, senior managers and inspectors) rightly ask firstly about that. As we saw earlier, there is a tendency in the literature to dwell on language outcomes, but if the CLIL programme is the sole means of contact with the content subject, then it is right that language learning should be examined after it has been established whether content-subject learning is intact.

The process and task-design strands are of value in their own right, but also as means to open up the performance and attitudes data to closer scrutiny and, indeed, to explain the findings revealed by more statistical approaches. What is certain is that, despite the recent surge in evaluative reports, there is much, much more still to investigate. Chapter 8 develops this theme and makes suggestions for directions which this research could take.

References

Admiraal, W., Westhoff, G. and de Bot, K. (2006) 'Evaluation of bilingual secondary education in the Netherlands: Students' language proficiency in English', *Educational Research and Evaluation*, **12**, 1, 75–93.

Airey, J. (2009) 'Estimating undergraduate bilingual scientific literacy in Sweden', *International CLIL Research Journal*, **1**, 2.

Alonso, E., Grisaleña, J. and Campo, A. (2008) 'Plurilingual education in secondary schools: Analysis of results', *International CLIL Research Journal*, [Online] **1**, 1. Available at: http://www.icrj.eu/index.php?page=742 [Accessed 08 May 2009].

Baetens Beardsmore, H. (2008) 'Multilingualism, cognition and creativity', *International CLIL Research Journal*, **1**, 1.

Campo, A., Grisaleña, J. and Alonso, E. (2007) *Trilingual Students in Secondary School: A New Reality*, Bilbao: Basque Institute of Educational Evaluation and Research.

Cavalli, M. (2005) *Education bilingue et plurilinguisme – Le cas du Val d'Aoste*, Paris: LAL, Didier.

Cloud, N., Genesee, F. and Hamayan, E. (2000) *Dual Language Instruction: A Handbook for Enriched Education*, Boston, MA: Heinle and Heinle.

Collins, L., Halter, R., Lightbown, P. M. and Spada, N. (1999) 'Time and the distribution of time in L2 learning', *TESOL Quarterly*, **33**, 4, 655–80.

Coyle, D. (2005) *Developing CLIL: Towards a Theory of Practice*, APAC Monograph 6, Barcelona: APAC.

Cummins, J. (1981) 'The role of primary language development in promoting educational success for language minority students', in California State Department of Education (1981) *Schooling and Language Minority Students: A Theoretical Framework*, Evaluation, Dissemination and Assessment Center, California State University.

Cummins, J. and Swain, M. (1986) *Bilingualism in Education: Aspects of Theory, Research and Practice*, London: Longman.

Dai, D. Y. and Sternberg, R. J. (2004) 'Beyond cognitivism: Toward an integrated understanding of intellectual functioning and development', in Dai, D. Y. and Sternberg, R. J. (eds.) (2004) *Motivation, Emotion and Cognition: Integrative Perspectives on Intellectual Functioning and Development*, Mahwah, NJ: Lawrence Erlbaum Associates, pp3–39.

Dalton-Puffer, C. and Nikula, T. (2006) 'Pragmatics of content-based instruction: Teacher and student directives in Finnish and Austrian classrooms', *Applied Linguistics*, **27**, 2, 241–67.

Dalton-Puffer, C., Hüttner, J., Schindelegger, V. and Smit, U. (2009) 'Technology-geeks speak out: What students think about vocational CLIL', *International CLIL Research Journal*, [Online] **1**, 2. Available at: http://www.icrj.eu/index.php?vol=12&page=741 [Accessed 11 May 2009].

de Graaff, R., Koopman, G. J., Anikina, Y. and Westhoff, G. (2007) 'An observation tool for effective L2 pedagogy in Content and Language Integrated Learning (CLIL)', *The International Journal of Bilingual Education and Bilingualism*, **10**, 5, 603–24.

de Jabrun, P. (1997) 'Academic achievement in late partial immersion French', *Babel*, **32**, 2, 20–3.

de Jong, E. J. (2002) 'Effective bilingual education: From theory to academic achievement in a two-way bilingual program', *Bilingual Research Journal*, [Online] **26**, 1, 1–20. Available at: http://brj.asu.edu/content/vol26_no1/abstracts.html [Accessed 11 May 2009].

de Jong, E. J. (2006) 'Integrated bilingual education: An alternative approach', *Bilingual Research Journal*, [Online] **30**, 1, 23–44. Available at: http://brj.asu.edu/vol30_no1/art2.pdf [Accessed 11 May 2009].

de Zarobe, Y. R. (2008) 'CLIL and foreign language learning: A longitudinal study in the Basque Country', *International CLIL Research Journal*, [Online] **1**, 1. Available at: http://www.icrj.eu/index.php?page=744 [Accessed 08 May 2009].

Dudley-Evans, T. and St John, M. J. (1998) *Developments in English for Specific Purposes*, Cambridge: Cambridge University Press.

Fortune-Tara, W. and Tedick, D. (2003) *What Parents Want To Know about Foreign Language Immersion Programs* (ERIC Digest ED482493), Washington, DC: ERIC Clearinghouse on Languages and Linguistics.

Gajo, L. and Serra, C. (2002) 'Bilingual teaching: Connecting language and concepts in mathematics', in So, D. and Jones, G. M. (eds.) (2002) *Education and Society in Plurilingual Contexts*, Brussels: Brussels University Press, pp75–95.

Genesee, F. (1987) *Learning Through Two Languages: Studies of Immersion and Bilingual Education*, Rowley, MA: Newbury House.

Greenbaum, T. L. (1998) *The Handbook of Focus Group Research*, London: Sage Publications.

Hagino, S. (2002) *Young Children's L2 Oral Production in Japanese Immersion Classrooms* (Unpublished thesis), Monash University, Clayton Victoria.

Hay McBer (2000) *Research into Teacher Effectiveness: A Model of Teacher Effectiveness. Research Report 216*, London: Department for Education and Employment.

Hofstetter, C. (2004) 'Effects of a transitional bilingual education program: Findings, issues and next steps', *Bilingual Research Journal*, [Online] **28**, 3, 355–77. Available at: http://brj.asu.edu/content/vol28_no3/art3.pdf [Accessed 11 May 2009].

Hood, P. (2006) Unpublished data from CLIL research interviews with students at Tile Hill Wood Language College, Coventry, UK.

Housen, A. (2002) 'Processes and outcomes in the European schools' model of multilingual education', *Bilingual Research Journal* [Online] **26**, 1, 1–20. Available at: http://brj.asu.edu/content/vol26_no1/pdf/ar4.pdf [Accessed 11 May 2009].

Johnson, R. K., Shek, C. K. W. and Law, E. H. F. (1993) *Using English as the Medium of Instruction in Hong Kong Schools,* Hong Kong: Longman.

Kiely, R. (2009) 'Small answers to the big question: Learning from language programme evaluation', *Language Teaching Research*, **13**, 1, 99–116.

Kirk Senesac, B. V. (2002) 'Two-way bilingual immersion: A portrait of quality schooling', *Bilingual Research Journal*, [Online] **26**, 1, 1–17. Available at: http://brj.asu.edu/content/vol26_no1/pdf/ar6.pdf [Accessed 11 May 2009].

Lambert, W. E. and Tucker, G. R. (1972) *Bilingual Education of Children: The St Lambert Experiment*, Rowley, MA: Newbury House.

Lapkin, S., Hart, D. and Swain, M. (1991) 'Early and middle French immersion programs: French language outcomes', *Canadian Modern Language Review*, **48**, 11–40.

Lasagabaster, D. (2008) 'Foreign language competence in content and language integrated courses', *The Open Applied Linguistics Journal*, **1**, 31–42.

Lasagabaster, D. and Sierra, J. M. (2009) 'Language attitudes in CLIL and traditional EFL classes', *International CLIL Research Journal*, [Online] **1**, 2. Available at: http://www.icrj.eu/index.php?vol=12&page=73 [Accessed 11 May 2009].

Lindholm-Leary, K. and Borsato, G. (2005) 'Hispanic highschoolers and mathematics: Follow-up of students who had participated in two-way bilingual elementary programs', *Bilingual Research Journal*, [Online] **29**, 3, 641–52. Available at: http://brj.asu.edu/content/vol29_no3/art8.pdf [Accessed 11 May 2009].

MacSwan, J. and Pray, L. (2005) 'Learning English bilingually: Age of onset of exposure and rate of acquisition among learners in a bilingual education program', *Bilingual Research Journal*, [Online] **29**, 3, 653–78. Available at: http://brj.asu.edu/content/vol29_no3/art9.pdf [Accessed 11 May 2009].

Marsh, D., Zając, M. and Gozdawa-Gołębiowska, H. (2008) *Profile Report Bilingual Education (English) in Poland*, Warsaw: CODN.

Moate, J. (2008) *The Impact of Foreign-Language Mediated Teaching on Teachers' Sense of Professional Integrity in the CLIL Classroom*, MA dissertation, University of Nottingham (Unpublished).

Short, D. (2000) *The ESL Standards: Bridging the Academic Gap for English Language Learners* (ERIC Digest ED447728), Washington, DC: ERIC Clearinghouse on Languages and Linguistics.

Swain, M. (1996) 'Discovering successful second language teaching strategies and practices: From programme evaluation to classroom experimentation', *Journal of Multilingual and Multicultural Development*, **17**, 2–4, 89–104.

Swain, M. and Lapkin, S. (1982) *Evaluating Bilingual Education: A Canadian Case-Study*, Clevedon: Multilingual Matters.

Swain, M. and Lapkin, S. (1986) 'Immersion French in secondary schools: 'The Goods' and 'the Bads'', *Contact*, **5**, 2–9.

Thompson, M. S., Di Cerbo, K. E., Mahoney, K. and MacSwan, J. (2002) 'Exito en California? A critique of language program evaluations', *Education Policy Analysis Archives*, **10**, 7.

Tisdell, M. (1999) 'German language production in young learners taught science and social science through partial immersion German', *Babel*, **34**, 2, 26–30.

Turnbull, M., Lapkin, S. and Hart, D. (2001) 'Grade 3 immersion students' performance in literacy and mathematics: Province-wide results from Ontario (1998–99)', *Canadian Modern Language Review*, **58**, 1, 9–26.

Tzur, R. (2007) 'Fine grain assessment of students' mathematical understanding: Participatory and anticipatory stages in learning a new mathematical conception', *Educational Studies in Mathematics*, **66**, 273–91.

Westhoff, G. (2004) 'The art of playing a pinball machine: Characteristics of effective SLA-tasks', *Babylonia*, **3/2004**, 58–62.

Woodfield, J. and Neofitou, A. (2006) *Immersion Project Research Findings* (Unpublished data).

Yang-Yu, N., Li-Yuan, H., Tompkins, L. J. and Modarresi, S. (2005) 'Using the multiple-matched-sample and statistical controls to examine the effects of magnet school programs on the reading and mathematics performance of students', Paper presented at the *Annual Meeting of the American Educational Research Association* (Montreal, Canada, April 2005).

Yassin, S. M., Marsh, D., Ong, E. T. and Lai, Y. Y. (2009) 'Learners' perceptions towards the teaching of science through English in Malaysia: A quantitative analysis', *International CLIL Research Journal*, [Online] **1**, 2. Available at: http://www.icrj.eu/index.php?vol=12&page=75 [Accessed 11 May 2009].

8 Future directions

In writing this book, we have explored the development of CLIL from both theoretical and pedagogic perspectives. We have considered how CLIL classrooms might operate effectively in a range of contexts, using fundamental principles which permeate a vision for preparing a future workforce, as well as the situated practicalities of classroom learning. In the 19th century, John Dewey (1897) famously wrote: 'Education is a social process. Education is growth. Education is not a preparation for life; education is life itself.' And now, in the second decade of the 21st century, life is changing at an unprecedented rate and it is within this rapid process of globalization that we have positioned our thinking 'with at least one certainty: that the world in which the next generation will grow up, learn, work and play will be very different from the one we know' (Nuffield Languages Inquiry, 2000: 12).

The shifting dynamic of concepts associated with globalization, change processes and the 'Knowledge Age' are embedded in educational discourse with little shared understanding. As the rift widens between informal and formal learning, the OECD (2000) *Knowledge Management in the Learning Society* raises concerns about contrasts between the kind of knowledge with which young people are engaging in school, and the kind of knowledge which they will need in their working lives. The centrality of knowledge to social and economic prosperity has far-reaching implications for learning and teaching in general, and for the role of language using for knowledge creation and sharing in particular. The shift from knowledge transmission to knowledge creation (evaluation, organization and management) in multilingual settings requires learners to be skilled in not only assimilating and understanding new knowledge in their first language, but also in using other languages to construct meaning. Moreover, according to Hargreaves, if we are to realize 'life-shaping' potential, then it seems imperative that schooling goes beyond merely transmitting knowledge and towards:

> developing the values . . . of young people's character; emphasising emotional as well as cognitive learning; building commitments to group life . . . not just short-term teamwork; cultivating a cosmopolitan identity which shows tolerance of race and gender differences, genuine curiosity towards and willingness to learn from other cultures, and responsibility towards excluded groups.
>
> (Hargreaves, 2003: xix)

CLIL has a significant contribution to make not only to providing learners of all ages with motivating experiences which are appropriate for knowledge creation and sharing, but also, fundamentally, to cultivating the 'cosmopolitan identity' advocated by

Hargreaves – where learning and using languages for different purposes generates tolerance, curiosity and responsibility as global citizens. If CLIL is to work towards the high demands set out by Hargreaves, it has to be a dynamic and highly complex global movement.

This final chapter therefore draws together our thinking in terms of future directions for CLIL. These directions are neither straightforward nor without far-reaching consequences. As we have emphasized throughout the book, CLIL cannot be separated from the contexts in which it develops. In rapidly changing times, CLIL is adapting to the growing need for nations to invest in human capital. According to the OECD, the growth of human capital to ensure economic success requires the development of 'the knowledge, skills, competences and attributes that allow people to contribute to their personal and social well-being and that of their countries' (2007: 5). As we have pointed out, multilingual settings common in today's world make linguistic capital an important component of human capital. Therefore, whilst it may seem that discussions involving human capital are far removed from CLIL and its future developments, nothing could be further from reality. Countries across the globe are responding at a national level to the need to increase or sustain their linguistic capital through a range of language policies, some of which are highly controversial (for example, the Malaysian government's introduction of the English language policy for science and mathematics in 2002, which was eventually amended in 2009). At regional and local levels, many schools are facing challenges in dealing increasingly with a mobile multilingual population, and within the classroom, more teachers are now being required to operate using more than one language or a language which is not their first language, often without specialized training. As CLIL develops and expands, it is inextricably linked to the educational evolution which is accompanying these changes, bringing with it both opportunities and 'threats' to practices which have been used to date.

We shall explore in this chapter some of the factors which we believe will impact on the future of CLIL, including globalization and change, sustainability, connecting languages and literacies across the curriculum, and the growth of a robust evidence base to justify and guide further developments of CLIL across global settings.

8.1 **Globalization and change**

International convergence and national priorities

In recent years, there appears to have been a high degree of international convergence resulting from globalization, which has affected educational policies across different countries and regions, typified by the PISA process (see Chapter 1). However, for governments, the relationship between local, regional, national and international languages is highly complex with regard to priorities and societal needs and is closely tied to their social and cultural contexts. There may be significant differences even within the same country in relation to curriculum design and implementation and the policies and laws which determine issues relating to language and language education (such as the medium of instruction or the languages to be learned).

These attributes are often subject to major political decision-making processes. If we take two examples: in the autonomous region of the Basque Country in Spain, some children are educated through at least three languages (Basque, Spanish and English); in Qatar, whilst children are educated through Arabic, a programme is now in place for English to be used for both mathematics and science. In neither place is English usually spoken at home, but in terms of human capital, English is considered necessary for future work and social cohesion. Language choice for instruction brings into question what Spolsky calls Q-value, that being: 'a language's worth' and 'the position of a language within the world's language system' (2004: 90). Putting a 'value' on different languages gives rise to strong feelings, as people often feel their cultural identities are being threatened. Changing the language of instruction in some areas across the globe has been met with open hostility, not least from parents who wish their children to develop a cultural identity through their 'own' language. Such parental concerns are increased if children are not being exposed to the highest quality learning experiences in the new language of instruction due to problematic teacher supply and little or no teacher development.

Language changes involving the medium of instruction are often based on long-term gains and on future needs, such as increasing competitiveness and economic prosperity. However, in the short or medium term, such policies can have deep-seated effects on the linguistic capital under cultivation (Ain and Chan, 2003). These changes can lead to disquiet about cultural identity, concern about differentiated levels of linguistic competence across several languages, and feelings of exclusion and decreasing self-confidence. Policy changes at national or regional level are sometimes volatile, sometimes evolutionary, and sometimes absent. For the teachers and learners involved in CLIL, who turn policies into reality, the challenges are high. CLIL is not a phenomenon which can be isolated from the wider context, and it therefore brings with it big situational questions which lie outside individual classrooms and schools. In other words, conceptualizing CLIL beyond the classroom level is as fundamental as planning lessons. As more countries are addressing issues concerning human capital through language policies, this situation is likely to become increasingly complex.

In Anglophone countries in Europe, many governments acknowledge that 'English is not enough' (Commission of the European Communities, 2003: 449) to achieve a 'cosmopolitan identity', yet there is little inclination to insist on language policies which challenge the status quo and fundamentally change schools, unless these are tied to socio-economic or political gains. For example, heads of state or governments of the European Union have signed agreements concerning the learning of at least two foreign languages from an early age, in addition to the first language, to further the long-term objective that each European citizen should have practical skills in at least MT+2 (mother tongue and two additional languages). In England, however, many citizens are unaware of European agreements, and educational policies do little to promote the learning of two or more languages: human capital does not extend to linguistic priorities in these contexts despite warnings about 'being left behind' (Nuffield Languages Inquiry, 2000: 14).

There is also growing concern that CLIL is becoming increasingly associated with the promotion of English (including the newer World Englishes). However, as can be seen in the Eurydice report (2006: 17), there are already a number of vehicular languages used for CLIL provision within Europe. Moreover, given what Graddol (2006) calls the transitional stage in global development, the future for CLIL is likely to see a surge in interest in using a much wider range of vehicular languages. Economic growth is not solely (or even primarily) dependent on English. There are vast areas across the world where languages such as Spanish, Arabic, Mandarin and Swahili are shared across national and regional borders and are often used as a lingua franca. As Graddol points out, 'In each of the world regions, English already finds itself in a different mix – nowhere does it enjoy complete hegemony' (2006: 113). Increasingly, there are examples of CLIL practice across the globe which use vehicular 'languages other than English' (LOTE) – not only in predominantly Anglophone countries, but also in areas which are aiming to preserve minority or heritage languages, cultural identities and to prepare for global economic trends. As technology enables disparate groups to connect and flourish, teacher groups associated with LOTE are becoming more active, building on a 'collective voice', and are bringing to the fore a wide range of pedagogic issues, such as learner motivation and linguistic gains. In the meantime, CLIL contexts which promote LOTE have a crucial role to play in the future of our complex global linguistic evolution. For social, cultural and economic reasons, it is essential that our profession continues to encourage, support and disseminate such diverse practice.

The place of CLIL in particular countries and regions thus depends largely on the global and regional priorities of the policy makers and how CLIL is implemented. Poor implementation or inappropriate decisions (in terms of the language for instruction chosen, for example, or the time given to a CLIL programme) can lead to disquiet amongst parents, learners and teachers. Moreover, although empowering teachers to articulate their own theories of practice and to engage in professional debate is especially important if CLIL is to be effective, this crucial stage is usually absent from policy documents. Both top-down and bottom-up perspectives are essential for the success and sustainability of CLIL: top-down support, realistic timeframes and appropriate training opportunities accounted for by policy makers and governments, and bottom-up active participation in professional learning, curriculum development and classroom inquiry by teachers for teachers.

Competence-based education

In line with socio-economic priorities, there has also been a recent trend towards competence-based education. This has been long established in some countries, but the need to develop a 21st-century workforce has further stressed the importance of perceiving competence as an amalgamation of knowledge and skills. Indeed, the 4Cs principles actively promote both knowledge and skills development and are therefore suited to differentiated learning outcomes across a range of contexts. In terms of language competence, it is interesting to note, for example, that the framework for key competences for *Lifelong Learning in Europe* (Commission of the European Communities, 2006) lists communication in languages (including the first language) alongside mathematics, science and technology, digital applications, learning approaches, interpersonal, intercultural and social competences, entrepreneurship, and cultural adaptability. If communication in languages is identified as a key skill for lifelong learning, this has clear implications for a more integrated language approach where first and other languages are concept-ualized *together* as being complementary and contributory conduits for developing communication skills for lifelong learning. These ideas will be further developed in section 8.2.

Building on the potential of developing and supporting a learner's first and other language skills has led to current developments in and the expansion of individual linguistic profiles. Success in effective communication skills, for example, is no longer seen in terms of attaining near-native competence in several languages, but in developing different, appropriate skill levels in different languages according to need. High-level writing skills across three languages may be inappropriate for some learners, whereas high-level oracy in three languages with well-developed writing and reading skills in two languages may be life skills for others. In other words, in plurilingual settings it is neither essential nor feasible to have identical skill sets in different languages, but instead learners need to develop a range of linguistic skills according to their specific needs. Curriculum design which takes account of defined differentiated outcomes from within a broad skill set for a range of languages, including the first language, is a desirable way forwards, rather than relying on an abstract ideal of 'a future multilingual workforce'. There are moves towards personalized linguistic profiling such as found in the Europass Language Passport (a link to Europass is given in the list of references at the end of this chapter), an evolving tool which documents individ-ual skills in different languages as they develop, not only in formal educational settings, but throughout life. The idea of dynamic linguistic competence and language skills as an asset in lifelong learning is gathering momentum. In the CLIL context, differentiated targeted skill sets for learners have implications for the future design of the curriculum and assess-ment if such personalized and diverse outcomes are to be achieved and celebrated.

Plurilingual citizens in multilingual societies

The Council of Europe defines multilingualism as 'the presence of several languages in a given space, independently of those who use them' (2007: 17), and plurilingualism refers to 'the capacity of individuals to use more than one language in social communica-tion whatever their command of those languages' (Beacco, 2005: 19). Both of these defini-tions reflect the diversity increasingly found in 21st-century communities, some of which are traditionally and 'confidently' multilingual, whereas others are facing rapid change, adaptation or linguistic isolation. Globalization invites language shift, especially in terms of human mobility and migration, which leads to dynamic multilingual societies. Because of the impact of multilingualism and plurilingualism on societies, educational systems are under pressure to adapt quickly and accordingly. This adaptation, however, is not solely dependent on language policy, but is often a reaction to the presence of a mobile workforce and the children and families involved.

In the early stages of the development of CLIL, the vehicular language tended to be a language which was not commonly used in a given community or society, such as English-medium classes in Finland or Indonesian-medium classes in Australia. However, in the last decade, linguistic diversity has increased with mobility, meaning that the CLIL vehicular language may be the first language of some learners, a language which has already been acquired by other learners, a new language which is also being acquired at the same time as the main language of instruction, a new language which is neither the learners' first language nor the language used in local or national settings, and so on – the linguistic boundaries associated with the medium of instruction are becoming increasingly 'fuzzy'.

Attempts to celebrate diversity are exemplified in *Multilingualism: An Asset for Europe and a Shared Commitment* (Commission of the European Communities, 2008), where a successful multilingual policy is described as having the potential to:

> . . . strengthen life chances of citizens: it may increase their employability, facilitate access to services and rights and contribute to solidarity through enhanced intercultural dialogue and social cohesion. Approached in this spirit, linguistic diversity can become a precious asset, increasingly so in today's globalised world.
>
> (Commission of the European Communities, 2008: 3)

It is an approach to 'intercultural dialogue' that we have tried to address in this book, since without appropriate and effective communication – and its practice and development in pedagogic contexts – language policies will not translate into lived realities. However, understanding and profiting from the value and opportunities of 'linguistic diversity' are still in their infancy with regard to formal education. As the complexities of plurilingual contexts increase, we predict that the fourth *C* – intercultural understanding – will become increasingly important. In many urban classrooms, several linguistic scenarios regularly occur or overlap: some 'newly arrived' learners may be extracted for additional language support in the main language used in the community, other groups of students who share and use a different language at home may be using that shared language for informal talk, all students may be learning a new language and some may be attending a class where they learn science through a language such as English or Mandarin. Scenarios such as these can be an asset for both learners and teachers, provided that the linguistic and intercultural potential and demands are addressed.

To realize this potential, there has to be a shift from perceiving CLIL as a means of teaching some content through an alternative language, to considering 'language' as a multilingual and multicultural phenomenon. It must be recognized that individual learners bring with them rich linguistic and cultural resources that can change a classroom from a place which promotes mainstream monolingualism, to a dynamic intercultural and multilingual environment in which to learn. However, profiting from the multilingual classroom means that new demands are being put on CLIL and on the curriculum as a whole. Throughout this book we have explored how content and language can be successfully integrated. Integration, as we have suggested, becomes even more challenging when several languages and cultures are used. The way is open here for further research and inquiry work, so that learning environments which nurture intercultural meaning-making and deep thinking in more than one language and across languages can embrace the complexities of multilingual potential. This idea is developed further in the next section.

8.2 **Integrating language across the curriculum**

As linguistic diversity increases and has to be factored into regular classroom learning, teachers coming from different professional backgrounds with different specialisms are being brought together. We have explored how CLIL teachers and language teachers must work together to engage in curriculum planning, in order to bring about a fundamental shift in conceptualizing teaching and learning. In the future, this collaboration will need to be more clearly defined. Curriculum design needs to involve language teachers and subject specialists, or class teachers with dual roles, in an understanding of the different contributions they make to more holistic CLIL experiences. Currently, collaborative planning and cross-disciplinary delivery of the curriculum, especially in secondary schools, is often left to chance or is dependent on the 'goodwill' of head teachers or senior management teams.

Collaboration between content-subject and CLIL language specialists has been debated for some time, but now a newer connection is emerging in English-medium schools, where the CLIL language is not English. In these schools, subject specialists and CLIL language teachers collaborate with each other and with EAL (English as an Additional Language) teachers who are dealing with learners whose first language is not English. These teachers all have in common that they work with learners whose level in the language used for learning is likely to be lower than their individual cognitive levels. It is now becoming clear that there is commonality of teaching approaches, strategies and tasks which emphasize scaffolded learning and in particular language as a *learning tool* across first, second, new and other language contexts. Work by second-language specialists such as Gibbons (2002 – *Scaffolding Language, Scaffolding Learning*) and Hall (2001 – *Bilingual benefits*) not only targets EAL learners and teachers, but also includes first-language specialists to provide 'joined up' approaches to literacy and language-rich learning environments. Linking first-language and additional-language approaches has significant implications for CLIL practice. As Mohan (2007) reminds us, education is 'the language socialization of learners into social practices of communities'. We have to look beyond languages as separate linguistic systems and instead:

> . . . consider language as a medium of learning, the coordination of language learning and content learning, language socialization as the learning of language and culture, the relation between the learners' languages and cultures, . . . and discourse in the context of social practice.
>
> (Mohan, 2007: 303)

This perspective suggests that a learner's languages – first language, second language, foreign language, heritage language and so on – all connect and can all be exploited as tools for learning. It also introduces salient points regarding the interrelationship between a learner's different languages – for example:

- the relationship between first-language literacy and the development of oracy in other languages
- the effects of code-switching between languages in CLIL settings as a positive pedagogic strategy, rather than a default position to address breakdowns in comprehension

- the notion of the development of 'academic expertise' (Cummins, 2000) across languages, including the learner's first language
- the transferability of linguistic and intercultural skills across the curriculum
- the role of discourse across different languages to support and promote deep learning in CLIL and non-CLIL classrooms.

Such a shift in thinking about language and learning shares some similarities with the 1970s' *Language across the Curriculum* movement in the UK, which attempted to change the way that teachers of all subjects used the first language to support learning (where in many cases, teacher and learners either shared the first language or ignored any differences). Forty years later, as we have discussed in this chapter, whilst the linguistic context of education has significantly changed and will continue to do so, some of the theoretical underpinnings remain constant, such as the importance of classroom discourse to mediate, support and advance learning.

The next decade will see a renewal of interest in language as a learning tool which embraces the whole curriculum and wider social context of the learners. Indeed, there is evidence that this move is already advancing (Anderson, 2008; Cummins, 2008; Dillon, 2008; Merisuo-Storm, 2007; Hornberger, 2003). This could contribute to the evolving concept of literacy and literacies which unites languages and explores how learners can be supported and thrive in multilingual learning environments. This is as pertinent in contexts where there is a dominance of one language as it is in those where there are many. The United Nations Educational, Scientific and Cultural Organization (UNESCO) defines literacy as:

> ... the ability to identify, understand, interpret, create, communicate, compute and use printed and written materials associated with varying contexts. Literacy involves a continuum of learning to enable an individual to achieve his or her goals, to develop his or her knowledge and potential, and to participate fully in the wider society.
>
> (UNESCO, 2004)

It is clear from this broad definition that literacies which span languages and cultures are an essential part of learning. By enabling more learners to become pluriliterate, CLIL is accessing potential which often remains untapped. If, however, we consider further the notion of enabling 'an individual to achieve goals and develop knowledge and potential', then issues of equity and inclusion are brought into the frame. For example, van Kraayenoord, Elkins, Palmer and Rickards refer to inclusive education as 'the practice of providing for students with a wide range of abilities, backgrounds and aspirations in regular school settings' (2000: 9). Definitions such as these acknowledge the growing and dynamic diversity of students and their individual developmental, cultural and personal differences, as well as the requirement of schools to ensure that students' needs, which are a consequence of these differences, are met. Supporting diversity might mean actively acknowledging that there are individuals who have physical and intellectual additional needs, but equally it might mean considering additional needs related to linguistic and cultural difference. This brings us back to the argument that equity in education must transparently address linguistic and cultural inclusion. Inclusive practice relates to Cummins' (2005) 'transformative pedagogies', where students are enabled through collaborative critical inquiry to analyse and understand issues of social relevance and power structures in society at different levels. However, for some students, additional linguistic and cultural support will be essential in order to express, understand and engage with these inclusive processes. Inclusive practice has tended to focus principally on physical and cognitive disabilities; we are now suggesting that inclusive practice could more overtly capture linguistic and cultural inclusion, and be extended to a more holistic approach to learning through different languages and cultures. Holistic and inclusive approaches to languages and literacies embrace a learner's first language, the language or languages used as a medium for learning, new languages learned in formal settings and languages used in the community. In the next decade, we foresee a focus on inclusive literacies, where CLIL principles for effective practice are shared and merged with a range of other approaches to encourage coherent and personalized learning for many more learners. Indeed, this focus may point the way towards CLIL experiences becoming an entitlement for all learners – a pathway open to debate.

8.3 **Sustainability and teacher education**

In the 1990s, strategies for dissemination of CLIL dominated agendas. There is now a shift in emphasis. If CLIL is to continue to develop, to be adopted by governments and welcomed rather than rejected by teachers, parents and learners, and if CLIL is to be linked to the dynamics of change in terms of social, economic and technological evolution, then it must be sustainable.

CLIL changes the *status quo*. Mehisto (2008) talks of 'disjuncture', or the tension between current practice and an alternative approach. He focuses on the need to promote and acknowledge the value of CLIL in education, teacher training, stakeholder responsibilities and professional learning communities, so that CLIL becomes embedded in different educational systems. For example, there are certain stakeholders involved with educational processes who act as gatekeepers. Examination boards and curriculum administrators are key examples in education. Implementation of an approach as innovative as CLIL requires assessment approaches and curricular alignment which are not only recognized, but also facilitated. However, bringing about change in educational systems is notoriously difficult and slow. The added value of CLIL rests with enabling short-term changes to take root which may be profound for education as a whole.

We would argue that teacher supply and the quality of CLIL practice lead to the systemic growth of CLIL through integration in different ways in different educational systems, and that the key to future capacity building and sustainability is teacher education. Without serious attention being paid to implementing strategies for training the professional workforce, which include longer-term plans for skilling multilingual teachers, then quality CLIL is not sustainable. Indeed, it could be said that poor-quality CLIL could contribute to a 'lost generation' of young people's learning. Thus, for teacher education in CLIL to be fit for purpose, there must be urgent and significant changes.

Teacher education in CLIL at both pre- and in-service levels needs to involve a range of programmes which address a wide range of CLIL training needs. More recently, there has been an expansion in teacher education courses for CLIL, but without quality assurance measures in place, it is unlikely that some of the programmes will even address the complexities which we have been discussing. There is a need, for example, for programmes which:

- are research-led, international and collaborative, to crucially allow for the dynamic global picture to be interpreted at the local level
- are online as well as face-to-face, to enable CLIL teachers to interact and to share ideas and practice
- conceptualize the integration of content and language in a holistic way using principled approaches such as those suggested in this book
- bring together content teachers, language teachers, language support teachers and literacy specialists, at all levels of education
- address the needs of learners in different phases of their education
- encourage participants to become skilled in terms of language competence and content knowledge
- empower teachers to create their own resources and share these using digital repositories
- enable practitioners to work in interactive classrooms where learners and teachers engage in effective discourse and communication for learning
- are both inclusive and holistic in terms of languages and literacies, including the appropriate use of more than one language for learning
- make different aspects of high-quality CLIL experiences more transparent to all those involved.

There is growing evidence (such as Lucietto, 2008; Elorza and Muñoa, 2008; de Graaff, Koopman, Anikina and Westhoff, 2007; Socrates-Comenius 2.1, 2006; CLILCOM) that approaches to CLIL teacher education are starting to change, to move away from traditionally defined language courses (such as TESOL/TEFL, in cases where the vehicular language is English), which pay lip service to CLIL, to courses which are conceptualized specifically for CLIL teachers and are delivered by those who work in the CLIL field. Such training courses need to go far beyond language development and progression, as the list above suggests. CLIL science teachers, for example, should be exposed not only to the role of language as a medium for learning, but also to how this impacts on learning science. Especially crucial is the need to involve both content-subject and language teachers. Factors such as these require teachers to move out of a traditional 'comfort zone' and enter into a more complex and less secure space, which has implications for teacher confidence and can lead to teachers feeling anxious in their new role. CLIL teacher-education programmes will have to address these more opaque affective elements of CLIL in order to equip CLIL teachers to work confidently and to encourage innovative practice – this involves breaking into new territory.

Moreover, as the number of CLIL training courses is set to rise, quality assurance measures have become evermore necessary. Countries such as the Netherlands (see the reference to European Platform at the end of this chapter) have developed accreditation models where the national language agency monitors the quality of CLIL through school visits and certification. Inspection teams comprising national CLIL experts, teacher educators, researchers and experts in the field of internationalization use national Dutch CLIL standards for quality-assurance purposes. Schools are accredited with national recognition and status if they satisfy these standards, which include measures of teacher and learner linguistic competence. Such an example provides a useful model for further development in other contexts. It is clear that quality measures will need to address fundamental issues, such as the language competence of teachers and the planning, monitoring and evaluation of units of work which address learner progression over time, rather than external visits which focus on individual lessons. It may be that institutions across regions and nations collaborate to share high-quality training, using different technologies such as online communities, video-linked networks and digital repositories for shared materials. In the transition period between the current teaching workforce and those who will enter the profession having had CLIL learning experiences themselves, increasing the number of relevant and appropriate teacher education programmes is a priority.

However, it would be naive to assume that such demands on teacher education can be met without financial support. Some countries have invested heavily in teacher education, whereas in others, teachers are left to cope with changes of policy and direction, sometimes leading to self-help groups which cut across national boundaries. The balance between macro-level initiatives and micro-level development is open to wide interpretation and thus, in terms of sustainability and quality measures in CLIL teacher education, the future remains very challenging.

8.4 Growth of teacher-led learning communities

As more schools take on the challenge of CLIL in its different forms, effective classroom practice and the theories which inform it take on greater significance. Sharing successes and problems depends on groups of schools, teachers, learners and researchers collaborating and working together locally, nationally and internationally. As we suggested in Chapters 3 and 4, approaches to professional learning such as the LOCIT process make CLIL a focus for classroom inquiry and empower CLIL practitioners to engage in meaningful collaboration to share successes and challenges, and to play a role in future directions. This professional dialogue is of central importance if research into CLIL is to inform practice and be 'owned' by those involved in CLIL classrooms, and indeed if the research agenda is to respond to the needs of CLIL teachers and learners.

Also in Chapters 3 and 4, we suggested that CLIL teachers could support each other by reflecting on and sharing their theories of practice. According to Kumaravadivelu (2001), theories of practice are a conduit for developing what he calls post-method pedagogy – that is, an inclusive approach to learning, which is not reliant on prescriptive strategies, but which unites learners, teachers and teacher educators as 'co-explorers', and which 'facilitates the advancement of context sensitive education based on a true understanding of local linguistic, socio-cultural and political particularities' (ibid.: 537). This collaborative approach certainly responds to Alexander's (2005) case for transparent pedagogic repertoires, since a prescriptive model for CLIL is neither desirable nor achievable. What Canadian and European investigations have shown us is that different kinds of bilingual education use different models which develop skills for learning in more than one language in very different ways. This highlights again the importance of balancing contextual demands and realizations for CLIL with robust pedagogic principles which permeate all models.

A more recent development in supporting CLIL professional learning communities is linked to the digital explosion of social networking and Web 2.0 technologies. Wikis, blogs and interactive web spaces for CLIL practitioners are rapidly growing, as teachers and professional organizations set up their own sites and invite CLIL practitioners across the globe to join the community. As knowledge sharing is being realized through digital networking, teachers are becoming empowered to set up digital resource banks where they can share materials and resources, solve problems in a collegial way and increase the accessibility of the CLIL knowledge base around the world. In terms of professional development, these networks encourage participants to engage together in exploring theories of practice which are rooted in *what* they do and *why*. Participants are also guided by knowledgeable others, who signpost relevant practice already being used to encourage participants to engage in critique, cooperation, collaboration and partnerships for learning. The networks involve content-subject and language teachers working together, content-subject and language teacher trainers sharing ideas, networks of CLIL teachers supporting each other in classroom inquiry, and learners working on joint curricular projects. There is a shared belief that, for CLIL theories to guide practitioners, they must be 'owned' by the community, developed through classroom exploration and understood *in situ* – theories of practice developed *for* practice *through* practice.

Hargreaves (2003) promotes professional communities, since he believes that one of the most powerful resources that people in any organization have for learning, improving and sustaining innovative ideas is each other. Knowledge economies depend on collective intelligence and social capital, both of which involve sharing and creating knowledge amongst professionals.

> Sharing ideas and expertise, providing moral support when dealing with new and difficult challenges, discussing complex individual cases together – this is the essence of strong collegiality and the basis for professional communities.
>
> (Hargreaves, 2003: 84)

A few years ago, these networked communities would not have existed; now they present themselves as powerful inclusive spaces where CLIL teachers can work together to form a collective 'voice'. The advantage of these websites is that they cost little to access, provided of course that the technology is available. Whilst these networks are practitioner-oriented, perhaps they also hold the key to bridging the gap between class-based inquiry and scientific, large-scale empirical research carried out by academics. In effect, professional learning communities are poised to provide practice-based evidence which informs and is informed by evidence-based practice.

8.5 **Expanding evidence-based research**

In 2007, Coyle argued that future research agendas should map the evolving CLIL terrain and respond to rapid societal change, thereby both 'connecting' and 'being connected' within a range of research communities. This connecting of research includes both academic research and classroom inquiry using different approaches. In particular, CLIL invites investigation which draws on a much wider field of research than is associated with language learning *per se*, including learning theories, language-learning theories, cognitive science and neuroscience, and intercultural and social processes, in order to provide a range of perspectives for interpreting integrated learning. In the previous section, we explored ways in which the 'practitioner voice' can contribute to the research agenda. This section considers the implications of the rapidly growing CLIL research base.

Whilst a large body of research on forms of integrated learning – particularly bilingual education and immersion – has been built up over the last 30 years, we are still exploring not only multilingualism, but also the impact of approaches such as CLIL on broader student achievements. As discussed in Chapter 7, whilst some early CLIL research data tended to focus on the development of mainly linguistic competence in CLIL, more recent research is linking CLIL with more general learning gains relating to levels of understanding and cognitive skills using higher-order thinking, problem solving and creativity.

However, there are problems to be grappled with within the research agenda. For example, it is difficult to claim conclusive and generalizable evidence from CLIL research due to the complexities of investigating learning in the contexts in which it occurs, and of then relating findings to other unique contexts. However, as our collective understanding of CLIL develops, a wide range of research themes is now emerging: content-subject competence (see, for example, Gajo, 2007); intercultural competence, content-subject methodologies and discourse genres (Llinares, Dafouz and Whittaker, 2007); literacies, cognitive processing, language mixing and code-switching (Serra, 2007); motivation, cognition and neuroscience (Van de Craen, Mondt, Allain and Gao, 2007); deep-level concept formation and information processing (Ting, 2007 and 2009); discourse as a learning tool (Dalton-Puffer, 2007) and so on. The potential research agenda is vast, especially if one considers CLIL from a more holistic perspective, since this will draw on existing research in fields such as bilingual education, LEP (Limited English Proficiency) and EAL, second languages in plurilingual settings, additional support needs, subject teaching, cross-curricular initiatives, technology-enhanced learning and transformative pedagogies.

One area of research already making headway involves the neurosciences in examining multilingualism and the brain and highlighting implications for education. It had been widely assumed that cognitive gain from second-language learning would not be enabled until the individual reached a certain level of language mastery (Cummins, 1977); but evidence is emerging that gains may be activated even with relatively low levels of language competence. This is significant for those CLIL contexts where learners have low levels of vehicular language competence. Researchers such as Eviatar and Ibrahim claim that 'even low levels of ability in the second language are related to metalinguistic advantages' (2000: 462). Since metalinguistic skills relate to awareness of language as a tool for thinking, the development of these skills provides potential for enriched information processing. This has direct implications for CLIL-type provision and learner achievement and may account for some of the successes which have been reported in very different contexts over the years (see, for example, Mehisto, 2008 or Ricciardelli, 1992).

As CLIL research gains momentum and as it gains recognition in research associations through SIGs (Special Interest Groups) and the expansion of thematic conferences, as well as dedicated academic journals, CLIL is coming of age and asserting itself as a field of research in its own right. The growing CLIL research base enables all stakeholders to take account of relevant and related research findings, apply these critically and appropriately to CLIL contexts and go beyond the current boundaries so that new research questions evolve and existing ones are addressed.

CLIL has come a long way in the past two decades. Unprecedented developments in technology and global communication have radically altered the way people learn and behave. CLIL is deeply implicated in social, cultural and economic developments across the globe as it becomes inextricably linked – directly and indirectly – with a range of national and international policy implementations. However, whilst we believe that CLIL teachers need to be aware of the 'big picture' (including global thinking, transnational innovation and networking opportunities), we have tried throughout the book to focus on what really matters – teachers and learners, classrooms and schools, and especially the principles and practice which have the potential to provide more learners with high-quality, accessible, motivating and challenging plurilingual and pluricultural learning experiences. Therein lies our collective challenge – practitioners, teacher educators, researchers and policy makers: to transform this potential into classroom practice over the coming decades and beyond.

References

Ain, N. A. and Chan, S. H. (2003) 'Gaining linguistic capital through a bilingual language policy innovation', *South Asian Language Review*, **XIII**, 1/2, 100–12.

Alexander, R. J. (2005) *Towards Dialogic Teaching: Rethinking Classroom Talk*, York: Dialogos.

Anderson, J. (2008) 'Towards integrated second language teaching pedagogy for foreign and community/heritage languages in multilingual Britain', *Language Learning Journal*, **36**, 1, 79–89.

Beacco, J-C. (2005) *Languages and Language Repertoires: Plurilingualism as a Way of Life*, Strasbourg: Council of Europe.

CLILCOM Virtual Learning Environment [Online]. Available at: http://clilcom.stadia.fi/ [Accessed 15 April 2009].

Commission of the European Communities (2003) *Promoting Language Learning and Linguistic Diversity: An Action Plan 2004–2006. Report 449*, Brussels.

Commission of the European Communities (2006) 'Recommendation of the European Parliament and of the Council of 18 December 2006 on key competences for lifelong learning', *Official Journal of the European Union*, **L 394/10**.

Commission of the European Communities (2008) *Multilingualism: An Asset for Europe and a Shared Commitment*, Brussels, [Online]. Available at: ec.europa.eu/education/languages/pdf/com/2008_0566_en.pdf [Accessed 16 February 2009].

Council of Europe (2007) *From Linguistic Diversity to Plurilingual Education: Guide for the Development of Language Education Policies in Europe* [Online]. Available at: http://www.coe.int/t/dg4/linguistic/Guide_niveau2_EN.asp [Accessed 29 June 2009].

Coyle, D. (2007) 'Content and Language Integrated Learning: Towards a connected research base', *International Journal of Bilingual Education and Bilingualism*, **10**, 5, 543–62.

Cummins, J. (1977) 'Cognitive factors associated with the attainment of intermediate levels of bilingual skills', *Modern Language Journal*, **61**, 3–12.

Cummins, J. (2000) 'Academic language learning, transformative pedagogy and information technology: Towards a critical balance', *TESOL Quarterly*, **34**, 3, 37–48.

Cummins, J. (2005) 'Using information technology to create a zone of proximal development for academic language learning: A critical perspective on trends and possibilities', in Davison, C. (ed.) (2005) *Information Technology and Innovation in Language Education*, Hong Kong: Hong Kong University Press, pp105–26.

Cummins, J. (2008) *Diverse Futures: Immigration, Education and Identity in Changing Times*, Seamus Heaney Lecture, St. Patrick's College Drumcondra, 17 November 2008.

Dalton-Puffer, C. (2007) *Discourse in Content and Language Integrated Learning (CLIL) Classrooms*, Amsterdam: John Benjamins.

de Graaff, R., Koopman, G. J., Anikina, Y. and Westhoff, G. (2007) 'An observation tool for effective L2 pedagogy in Content and Language Integrated Learning (CLIL)', *Bilingual Education and Bilingualism*, **10**, 5, 603–24.

Dewey, J. (1897) 'What education is', *The School Journal*, **LIV**, 3, 77–80. Also available in the informal education archives: http://www.infed.org/archives/e-texts/e-dew-pc.htm [Accessed 13 July 2009].

Dillon, A. M. (2008) 'The CLIL approach in Irish primary schools: A multilingual perspective', *CLIL Practice: Perspectives from the Field*, [Online]. Available at: http://www.icpj.eu/?id=2 [Accessed 29 June 2009].

Elorza, I. and Muñoa, I. (2008) 'Promoting the minority language through integrated plurilingual language planning: The case of the Ikastolas', *Language, Culture and Curriculum*, **21**, 1, 85–101.

Europass. Available at: http://europass.cedefop.europa.eu/europass/home/hornav/Introduction.csp [Accessed 29 June 2009].

European Platform. Available at: http://www.netwerktto.europeesplatform.nl/ep.php?taal=Engels#4 [Accessed 13 July 2009].

Eurydice (2006) *Content and Language Integrated Learning (CLIL) at School in Europe*, Brussels: Eurydice.

Eviatar, Z. and Ibrahim, R. (2000) 'Bilingual is as bilingual does: Metalinguistic abilities of Arabic-speaking children', *Applied Psycholinguistics (Psychological Studies of Language Processes)*, **21**, 4, 451–71.

Gajo, L. (2007) 'Linguistic knowledge and subject knowledge: How does bilingualism contribute to subject development?', *Bilingual Education and Bilingualism,* **10**, 5, 563–81.

Gibbons, P. (2002) *Scaffolding Language, Scaffolding Learning: Teaching Second Language Learners in the Mainstream Classroom,* Sydney: Heinemann.

Graddol, D. (2006) *English Next,* London: British Council.

Hall, D. (2001) 'Bilingual benefits', *Literacy Today,* **27**. Also available at: http://www.literacytrust.org.uk/Pubs/strong2.html [Accessed 13 July 2009].

Hargreaves, A. (2003) *Teaching in the Knowledge Society,* Maidenhead: Open University Press.

Hornberger, N. (2003) 'Continua of biliteracy', in Hornberger, N. (ed.) (2003) *Continua of Biliteracy: An Ecological Framework for Educational Policy, Research, and Practice in Multilingual Settings,* Clevedon: Multilingual Matters, pp3–34.

Kumaravadivelu, B. (2001) 'Toward a post-method pedagogy', *TESOL Quarterly,* **35**, 4, 537–60.

Llinares, A., Dafouz, E. and Whittaker, R. (2007) 'A linguistic analysis of compositions written by Spanish learners of social sciences in CLIL contexts', in Marsh, D. and Wolff, D. (eds.) (2007) *Diverse Contexts – Converging Goals,* Frankfurt am Main: Peter Lang, pp227–36.

Lucietto, S. (2008) 'A model for quality CLIL provision', *International CLIL Research Journal,* [Online] **1**, 1. Available at: http://www.icrj.eu/index.php?vol=11&page=746 [Accessed 29 June 2009].

Mehisto, P. (2008) 'CLIL counterweights: Recognising and decreasing disjuncture in CLIL', *International CLIL Research Journal,* [Online] **1**, 1. Available at: http://www.icrj.eu/index.php?vol=11&page=75 [Accessed 29 June 2009].

Merisuo-Storm, T. (2007) 'Pupils' attitudes towards foreign language learning and the development of literacy skills in bilingual education', *Teaching and Teacher Education,* **23**, 2, 226–35.

Mohan, B. A. (2007) 'Knowledge Structures in Social Practices', in Cummins, J. and Davison, C. (eds.) (2007) *International Handbook of English Language Teaching. Vol. II,* Norwell, MA: Springer, pp303–16.

Nuffield Languages Inquiry (2000) *Languages: The Next Generation,* London: The Nuffield Foundation.

OECD (2000) *Knowledge Management in the Learning Society,* Paris: OECD. Available at: http://www.mszs.si/eurydice/pub/oecd/lnowledge.pdf [Accessed 16 June 2009].

OECD (2007) *Human Capital: How What You Know Shapes Your Life,* Paris: OECD. Available at: http://wdn.ipublishcentral.net/oecd/viewinside/3087342988182 [Accessed 16 June 2009].

Ricciardelli, L. (1992) 'Creativity and bilingualism', *Journal of Creative Behaviour,* **26**, 4, 242–54.

Serra, C. (2007) 'Assessing CLIL at primary school: A longitudinal study', *Bilingual Education and Bilingualism,* **10**, 5, 582–602.

Socrates-Comenius 2.1 (2006) *CLIL across Contexts: A Scaffolding Framework for CLIL Teacher Education.* Available at: http://clil.uni.lu/ [Accessed 29 June 2009].

Spolsky, B. (2004) *Language Policy,* Cambridge: Cambridge University Press.

Ting, T. Y. L. (2007) 'Insights from Italian CLIL-Science classrooms: Refining objectives, constructing knowledge and transforming FL-learners into FL-users', *View[z] Vienna English Working Papers,* **16**, 60–9. Available at: http://www.univie.ac.at/Anglistik/ang_new/online_papers/views/archive.htm [Accessed 29 June 2009].

Ting, T. Y. L. (2009) Personal Communication, 27 June 2009.

UNESCO (2004) *The Plurality of Literacy and its Implications for Policies and Programs: Position Paper,* Paris: UNESCO. Available at: http://unesdoc.unesco.org/images/0013/001362/136246e.pdf [Accessed 17 June 2009].

Van de Craen, P., Mondt, K., Allain, L. and Gao, Y. (2007) 'Why and how CLIL works: An outline for a CLIL theory', *View[z] Vienna English Working Papers*, **16**, 3, 70–8. Available at: http://www.univie.ac.at/Anglistik/ang_new/online_papers/views/archive.htm [Accessed 29 June 2009].

van Kraayenoord, C., Elkins, J., Palmer, C. and Rickards, F. (2000) *Literacy, numeracy and students with disabilities*, Canberra: Department of Education, Training and Youth Affairs.

Index